KU-119-768

OF IRELAND
LIBRARY

Labour Law and Industrial Relations in Poland

by Prof. Maria Matey

WITHDRAWN FROM STOCK

This book was originally published as a monograph in the
International Encyclopaedia for Labour Law and Industrial Relations

1988

Kluwer Law and Taxation Publishers

Deventer · Boston

Kluwer Law and Taxation Publishers
P.O. Box 23   Tel.:   31 5700 47261
7400 GA Deventer Telex: 49295
The Netherlands   Fax: 31 5700 22244

Cover design: B. Betzema

ISBN 90 6544 401 7

© 1988, Kluwer Law and Taxation Publishers, Deventer/Netherlands

All rights reserved. No part of this publication may be reproduced, stored in a retrieval system, or transmitted in any form or by any means, electronic, mechanical, photocopying, recording or otherwise, without the prior written permission of the publisher.

Labour Law and Industrial Relations in Poland

NATIONAL COLLEGE OF IRELAND LIBRARY

WITHDRAWN FROM STOCK

WITHDRAWN FROM STOCK

Barcode No: 3900600446539
Dewey No : 344.1041
Date Input : 01/06/2012
Price : DONATION

Table of Contents

NATIONAL COLLEGE OF IRELAND LIBRARY

WITHDRAWN FROM STOCK

Table of Contents

NATIONAL COLLEGE
OF IRELAND
LIBRARY

Table of Contents

Table of Contents

Part II. Collective Labour Relations 139

Table of Contents

List of Abbreviations

CPR   Central Annual Plan
NSZZ   Independent and Self-Governed Trade Union
OPZZ   All-Poland Trade Unions Alliance
PFAZ   Vocational Activation State Fund
PIP   State Labour Inspection
PRL   Polish People's Republic
PRON   Patriotic Movement for National Revival
PZPR   Polish United Workers' Party
SD   Democratic Party
SL   Peasants' Party
SFZZ   World Federation of Trade Unions
ZUS   Social Security Board

Selected Labour Law Bibliography

(most recent years)

Jończyk Jan	Labour Law, PWN (Polish Scientific Publishing House), Warsaw, 1984, (in Polish), pp 595;
Jackowiak Czesław, Jaśkiewicz Wiktor, Piotrowski Włodzimierz	Outline of Labour Law, PWN (Polish Scientific Publishing House), Warsaw, 1985 (in Polish), pp 543;
Zieliński Tadeusz	Labour Law – Outline of the System, 3 volumes, PWN (Polish Scientific Publishing House), Warsaw, 1986 (in Polish), pp 1015;
Szubert Wacław	Social Security – Outline of the System, PWN (Polish Scientific Publishing House), Warsaw, 1987 (in Polish), pp 335;
Salwa Zbigniew, Matey Maria (editors)	Trends and premises of the Labour Law Reform, 'Ossolineum' Publishing House, Warsaw, 1987 (in Polish), pp 201

Introduction

Chapter I. The General Background

§1. GEOGRAPHY

1. Poland has a population of 37.5 millions (1987). It is situated in the centre of Europe, at the intersection of major East-West and North-South transportation routes. Its area is 312,683 sq. km., making Poland the seventh largest country in Europe, and 62nd in the world. Poland borders the USSR (1,244 km), Czechoslovakia (1,310 km) and the German Democratic Republic (460 km); the length of its Baltic coastline is 524 km. Most of the country is a lowland plain. Compared with Western Europe average temperatures in Poland are much lower and the range of temperatures far greater. Arable land accounts for 61 per cent of the entire territory of the country and forest for 28 per cent. Poland has many natural resources: anthracite (as regards coal mining Poland ranks second in Europe and fourth in the world), brown coal, the world's richest sulphur deposits (second place in Europe), copper deposits (fourth place in Europe) and rich deposits of iron, zinc, lead and rock salt, as well as raw materials for the building industry. Poland has no notable sources of oil, all of which she has to import.

As regards administration, Poland has, since 1975, been divided into 49 provinces (*voivodships*) with 803 cities, and 2,070 rural communes. A two-tier structure of local administration has also existed since 1975: the commune or the town, and the province.

§2. HISTORY

A. The Independent Polish Kingdom (960–1795)

2. Many vestiges of Proto-Slavic and Slavonic culture have survived in Poland from the period preceding our era and from the first millennium of that era. The first Polish tribal state was organised in the ninth and tenth centuries, and in 960 the first monarch known from historic sources, Mieszko I of the Piast dynasty came to power; he introduced Christianity in 966 and soon united under his authority the majority of ethnically Polish territories. Under the rule of later Piasts Poland acquired considerable power and international importance, waging wars with Germany and Russia. In 1138

King Bolesław Wrymouth (Krzywousty) divided the country among his sons, thus initiating a long period of division into regions, struggles between princes over principalities, and further partition of the country as a result of subsequent divisions among heirs. In spite of the weakening of state authority, the twelfth and thirteenth centuries were a period of rapid economic development, the extension of the area of land under cultivation, the development of settlements, the location of new towns, the organisation of a system of municipal administration, and the growth of a class of townspeople. The political situation of Poland, divided into duchies, was worsened by the aggression of the German Brandenburg mergraviate, destructive Tartarian, Prussian, and Lithuanian invasions, and the settlement in the North of the country in 1226 of the Teutonic Order, whose knights were brought in by the Polish Prince Konrad Mazowiecki to fight the Prussians. In spite of the territorial losses incurred, especially to the Teutonic Order, Poland became united again in 1320 and, under the last Piast king, Casimir the Great, regained its political and economic power in a period of flourishing cultural development (the establishment in 1364 of Cracow University, etc.).

3. The conclusion of the Polish-Lithuanian Union in 1385 enabled the elimination of the growing Teutonic threat by the Polish victory at the 1410 Battle of Grunwald by King Jagiełło, the founder of the Jagiellonian dynasty. After the final defeat of the Teutonic Knights and the subordination of Prussia to Poland, the latter became – at the turn of the fifteenth century – one of Europe's most powerful states, and the Jagiellons – one of the most influential families reigning in Europe. From the fifteenth century onwards, the economic situation in Poland began to change, an extension of the estates of the nobility occurred in the sixteenth century and brought about an increase in serfdom and peasant dependence on the gentry; the towns developed into major centres of trade and handicrafts (Cracow, Gdańsk, Lublin, and later Warsaw). A development of Renaissance art, literature and science (Nicolaus Copernicus) also occurred in that century, called 'the Golden Age'. The Reformation developed, and thanks to religious tolerance Poland became a shelter to many refugees of countries where religious wars were waged. Availing itself of its political rank, the nobility acquired privileges from the kings, who reduced the rights of peasants and townspeople. A class of magnates evolved, powerful, influential families accumulating large landholdings.

4. After the extinction of the Jagiellonian dynasty (1572) the system of elective monarchy was introduced in Poland which resulted in an increase of the influence of foreign states. A period of prolonged wars with Russia, Sweden and the Turks attacking from the South began late in the sixteenth century; the situation was aggravated by Cossack uprisings in South-eastern Poland. In spite of forcing back the Swedish invasion (the so-called 'deluge') in 1660, Poland lost a part of her northern territories; moreover, availing itself of the situation, Eastern Prussia freed itself from Polish supremacy. The

Turkish expansion in Europe was stopped by the victories of commander (later king) Jan Sobieski near Chocim (1673) and at Vienna (1683). However, war had ruined the country. The rivalry of magnates' groups, the interference of foreign powers, the abuse by the *Seym* (Parliament) of the principle of unanimity (the use of the *liberum veto* by a deputy terminated debates), deepened the anarchy and chaos. The development of science, culture and the economy ceased. The affluence of both villages and towns decreased. In the first half of the eighteenth century Poland ceased to play any active part in the international arena because of the increased power of her neighbours, namely Prussia, Russia and Austria.

5. In the second half of the eighteenth century, the Age of Enlightment, under King Stanislaus August Poniatowski, efforts were made to stop Poland's decline through the economic and cultural reconstruction of the country. The Commission for National Education was established in 1773 as Europe's first Ministry of Education and Science. The struggle for political and social reforms resulted in the enactment of the 1791 Constitution.

However, the neighbouring powers would not accept the strengthening of the Polish state, and, plotting against it they abolished the 1791 Constitution and invaded the country. The second partition followed. After the failure of the Kościuszko Insurrection of 1794 the third partition of Poland took place in 1795, with the total annexation of the Polish state by Prussia, Russia and Austria. The period of partition lasted from 1795 to 1918.

B. Poland in the Period of Partition (1795–1918)

6. Immediately after the partitions, the Poles started the struggle for independence, both at home and abroad. A major role was played by the political emigration which found shelter in France, expecting assistance from the French revolution and later from Napoleon. On the basis of the Tilsit Treaty (1807) concluded by Napoleon with the Russian Tsar Alexander I, the so-called Duchy of Warsaw was created out of a part of Polish territory, enlarged in 1809 after the victories of Napoleon, aided by Polish troops under the command of Prince Józef Poniatowski. Napoleon's defeat brought about the fall of the Duchy of Warsaw and a new partition of Polish territories by the Congress of Vienna (1815). The policy of the occupying powers of destroying the nation, its economy and culture and – in particular – the violation of consititutional rights and tsarist police oppression on the territory of the Congress Kingdom of Poland, *i.e.* part of that land under the Russian occupation, resulted in the outbreak of the November Insurrection (1830–1831). After its defeat those territories lost the remaining vestiges of Polish statehood and became subject to intensive russification. The patriotic forces which survived the defeat of the November Uprising formed the so-called Great Emigration operating chiefly in France (its members included such figures of Polish national culture as the great poet Adam Mickiewicz, Frederic Chopin, and others), and also in England and Switzerland, preparing –

through their emissaries – further military activity on Polish territory. Such operations took place in the years 1846–1848, but once more proved unsuccessful.

Simultaneously, the Poles played an important part in the European revolutions of that period, especially in Germany, Italy, and Hungary. As a consequence of the nation's oppression and of police activities on the territory of Russian Poland, the January Uprising broke out in Poland (1863–1864), and after its defeat russification was intensified. Under Prussian occupation the Polish people also struggled with ever increasing germanization and economic oppression (colonization, buying out of land by the Germans, etc.). The most economically backward was the territory under Austrian occupation, where poverty in the countryside was more acute than in the other regions, and only the landowners, loyal to Austria, enjoyed considerable prosperity.

By the end of the nineteenth century a workers' movement was organised and began to develop on the Polish territories of all three empires; workers' parties and other political parties were established. The 1905–1907 revolution in Russia had direct repercussions in Poland, especially for that part under Russian occupation. Struggles for independence were reactivated and intensified. The Catholic Church and the patriotic Polish clergy played an important role in supporting Polish patriotism and the national spirit throughout the whole period of occupation. At the outbreak of World War I the will for independence was universal in Poland illustrated by the organisation of Piłsudski's legions, although the existence of various political parties with different programmes hampered this struggle.

C. The Second Republic (1918–1939)

7. The striving for independence, encouraged by the abolition of tsardom in 1917, the acknowledgement of Poland's right to independence by the Soviet Union, the declaration of President Wilson, and the final defeat of the Central Powers in World War I, resulted in the establishment of the Polish state in 1918, after 123 years of enslavement. The process of establishing the Polish frontiers continued until 1923 and was affected by anti-German insurrections in Greater Poland (the region around the city of Poznań) and Silesia and by the Piłsudski-inspired Polish-Soviet war. In 1923 Poland occupied an area of 388,000 square kilometers, with a population of 27 million (about 30 per cent of whom were national minorities). 72 per cent of the population was employed in agriculture, with only ten per cent in industry and mining.

8. The first Polish government came into being in 1918; it proclaimed Poland to be a democratic republic with a parliamentary system of government. The first constitution was enacted in 1919 (the 'Little Constitution'). In the same year land reform was inaugurated with a gradual, mandatory breaking up of the large landed estates, with partial indemnification. In 1921

the *Seym* enacted the so-called March Constitution. The fierce struggles among the political parties, with the predominance of the right, in conditions of economic instability, caused frequent changes of government and enabled Józef Piłsudski to carry out a rightist *coup d'etat* in 1926 (the 'May Coup'). There followed a period of authoritarian rule until his death in 1935, although the forms of parliamentarism continued and the office of President was held from 1926 to 1939 by Professor Ignacy Mościcki. The period inaugurated in 1926, called *sanacja* or cleansing, was in fact a retreat from the democratic achievements of the first years of independence. In 1935 the government enacted the anti-democratic April Constitution which remained in force until the onset of Nazi occupation in 1939.

9. Over the twenty-year period between the two World Wars Poland had to struggle with many economic difficulties. From 1929 to 1939 the country suffered acute economic crisis with high levels of unemployment. The period of crisis caused an intensification of class struggle and the activation of the leftist opposition, the leaders of which were illegally arrested in 1930 (the 'Brzeski' trial). Along with the anti-democratic changes of the regime, political opposition increased, accompanied by demonstrations of farmers and by massive industrial strikes. A certain economic improvement was noted from 1937 to 1939; some of the major attainments of that time worthy of notice were the economic integration of the country, the reform of the financial system, the construction of a modern sea port at Gdynia, and the organisation of the Central Industrial District.

10. As regards relations with foreign countries, Poland in the inter-war period conducted a policy of *rapprochement* with and reliance on Western Europe, France and England in particular, rejecting the possibility of alliance with the USSR in order to resist the increasing threat from Nazi Germany. The Third German Reich demanded the annexation of the Free City of Gdańsk to the Reich and the construction on Polish territory of an extra-territorial transportation route between Germany and East Prussia. Poland refused these demands, and she reacted similarly to the further escalation of the Reich's demands. The aggression of Nazi Germany against Poland began on 1 September 1939, thus initiating World War II.

11. During the five-year occupation by Nazi Germany Poland suffered enormous losses of population, national wealth, and cultural achievements as a result of the efforts of the occupying power, which aimed at a total destruction of the country, the annihilation of the Polish nation by genocide, terror, Nazi concentration camps, and mass resettlement. More than six million Poles lost their lives during World War II, including about three million Polish citizens of Jewish origin. At the same time Poland lost 40 per cent of her total pre-war national wealth, including one-third of her capital goods, fifteen per cent of agricultural equipment, 84 per cent of rolling stock, and 60 per cent of her scientific and educational base. Many Polish towns were destroyed by the Germans. More than 90 per cent of the capital –

Warsaw – was destroyed as a result of systematic razing by the Germans after the defeat of the 1944 Warsaw Uprising.

D. The Polish People's Republic (1944 to the present)

12. The Polish People's Republic was established as a result of the struggle for liberation from Nazi occupation and for social liberation by the re-volutionary seizure of the power by the working people of the cities and of the countryside. The participation of the USSR and her army with the Polish Army in the historic victory over the Nazi invader was of the highest importance for the establishment of People's Poland. Immediately after both armies of liberation entered Polish territory in July 1944, the first people's government was organised, namely the Polish Committee of National Liberation operating under the direction of the National People's Council. Based on workers' political and partisan organisation established during the occupation, this government set up a new, democratic state administration on the liberated territories and started the reconstruction of the country. The basis of the foreign policy of the new government became a close alliance with the USSR and other countries of the anti-Nazi coalition. The conference of the Allied powers at Potsdam (July 1945) finally determined the area and frontiers of the Polish state. A decree on agrarian reform was issued in 1944, expropriating landed estates exceeding 50 hectares on behalf of the peasants, and the 1946 nationalisation laws became the basis for the nationalisation of major enterprises employing more than 50 workers. In 1947 the *Seym* enacted the so-called 'Little Constitution', laying down the legal principles of the new system. A consolidation of Polish society took place at the same time, aimed at the reconstruction of the economy and the development of Northern and Western Poland, the recovered territories. This task was realised with the assistance of the USSR and other neighbouring countries, which in 1949 established the organisation known as the Council for Mutual Economic Assistance (CMEA). The union of the two major Polish political forces took place in 1948; the Communist and Socialist parties merged in the Polish United Workers' Party (PZPR) which has since that time been the leading political party of the Polish People's Republic. The Democratic Party and the United Peasant Party operate in Poland in alliance with the PZPR.

The economy of the country developed in periods of either extensive or intensive growth. The first three-year Plan (1947–1950) was the plan of Economic Reconstruction; the next six-year plan (1950–1955) – a plan of socialist industrialisation and the reconstruction of the social and professional structure of society. The realisation of these plans affected profound socio-economic and cutural changes; the foundations of subsequent socialist transformation were laid down at that time. Many large industrial plants were built between 1950 and 1955, such as Nowa Huta near Cracow, shipyards in Gdańsk and Szczecin, and the Warsaw Automobile Enterprise.

The Constitution of the Polish People's Republic enacted by the *Seym* in 1952 ratified the changes and defined the new character of the state; it also replaced the position of President, held up to that time by Bolesław Bierut, by a collective body – the Council of State.

13. In 1956, following the political changes which took place at the twentieth Congress of the Communist Party of the Soviet Union, the Polish United Workers' Party too laid down anew the principles of socialist democracy and goals consistent with the new era of building socialism in Poland; Władysław Gomułka was elected First Secretary of the Party. As a result of these changes new, improved methods of economic administration were applied and the role of workers' self-government increased. In the first half of the 1960s further economic growth took place; industrial production increased by 50 per cent, new branches of industrial production were organised (sulphur, copper, natural gas, coking coal), and engineering and the chemical industry expanded. Agricultural production, based mainly on individual farms, associated in farmers' circles, increased considerably. In the late 1960s a slow-down in economic growth became apparent, as well as negligence and delays in the raising of living standards and the improvement of social conditions of the working people, which caused social tensions in December 1970. The newly appointed leaders of the PZPR with Edward Gierek at their head took immediate measures to overcome these difficulties.

14. The new socio-economic policy was initiated in 1971, the positive effects of which were characteristic of the first half of the 1970s. Poland then entered a period of a rapid development, excessively based on foreign loans. From 1971 to 1975 national incomes increased by 62 per cent, the average rate of economic growth was ten per cent; outlays for capital goods doubled, real income increased by 40 per cent, pensions and workers' family and sickness benefits were raised; conditions for earlier retirement were created; maternity leave was extended, and the system of national education was modernized. Public outlays for the health service increased by more than 50 per cent, while the principle of free medical care was extended to the rural population; a pensions' scheme for individual farmers was organised, and the process of the gradual introduction of additional days off was started ('free Saturdays'). During that period major new projects were initiated, such as the Katowice Steelworks, the Gdańsk Northern Port, the Low-Capacity Passenger Car Factory at Bielsko-Biała, and many big power plants; and a large-scale, countrywide programme of Vistula river development was planned.

15. However, the pace of economic expansion slowed in the second half of the 1970s. The economic policy conducted by Gierek's political team, based on credits granted by Western countries and characterized by an excessively wide front of investments, resulted in a socio-economic crisis which became noticeable by the late 1970s and was the cause of justified workers' protests in 1980. The recognition by the new political authorities of the country of the justice of these protests permitted the conclusion in the Autumn of 1980 of the Gdańsk, Szczecin, and Jastrzębie (Silesia) Social Agreements and the emergence of a new social movement established as the trade union Solidarity

(Solidarność), of which Lech Wałęsa was appointed chairman. At the same time, in order to master the economic chaos prevailing throughout the country, the cumulative effect of previous economic errors, and the continuous wave of strikes throughout 1981, the post of chairman of the Council of Ministers was assumed in February 1981 by General Wojciech Jaruzelski to whom, in October of the same year, the function of First Secretary of the PZPR was also entrusted. The impossibility of achieving the cooperation of conflicting political forces, especially due to the radicalisation of the Solidarity movement, led to an acute stage of the political crisis, as a result of which martial law was declared late in 1981 over the entire area of Poland. This dramatic decision was treated by the polish authorities as a necessary measure for preventing a major nationwide tragedy. With the introduction of martial law the activity of most social organisations was suspended, including all previously operating trade unions (both Solidarity and the former so-called branch and other unions); all these trade unions were finally dissolved in October 1982.

16. Martial law ended on 22 July 1983. The most acute symptoms of the economic crisis were gradually overcome. Over the 1983–1987 period Poland entered a path of progressive normalisation, including the favourable development of the range and forms of cooperation between the state authorities and the Roman Catholic Church, which has always played a great role in the life of the country. In early 1987 a Consultative Council was appointed to the President of the Council of State, General Jaruzelski. It included representatives of different political orientations including those connected with the political opposition. A wide-ranging economic reform is being introduced, entering its second phase in 1987. By that year the self-management of state enterprises organised on new principles was operating in 90 per cent of work-places. Based on a new law, reborn trade unions emerged; in 1987 they had a membership of 7 million workers or 60 per cent of the labour force. In 1987 the law on social consultation and national referendums was adopted (first such referendum was held in November 1987) and the office of Ombudsman for Civil Rights was established. The political opposition is legitimated. However, the progress of normalization between 1983 and 1988 does not mean that full national consensus has been achieved, based on rational and realistic foundations – considering unrest incidents in May 1988 this goal still requires a long-term policy. In 1988 specific forms of dialogue with political opposition are sought for, aimed at bringing into being a kind of pro-reformatory national coalition or an 'anti-crisis pact'.

17. Important constitutional and codification efforts were undertaken in post-war Poland. The Polish Constitution of 1952 was extensively amended in 1976, with a further series of essential amendments: in 1980 (the subordination of the Supreme Board of Control directly to the *Seym*), in 1982 (the creation of constitutional bases for establishing the Tribunal of State and the Constitutional Tribunal), in 1983 (constitutional determination of the position and role of the Patriotic Movement of National Revival, guarantee of

individual land ownership, authorisation for the Council of State to introduce martial law in the event of external danger, and an emergency law in the event of an elemental disaster) and in 1987 (introduction of the provisions for national referendum). Works have been initiated in 1987 to prepare a substantial amendment to the Constitution or a draft of a new Constitution for 1991.

The Civil Code and the Code of Civil Procedure were enacted in 1964 (with subsequent amendments); the Criminal Code and Code of Criminal Procedure – in 1969 (with subsequent amendments); the Labour Code in 1974 (subsequently amended) and the new Code of Administrative Procedure in 1979. An important measure of both legal and structural consequence was the reform of local administration carried out from 1973 to 1975, amended by the law of 1983 on people's councils (new amendment in preparation in 1988).

Over the past few years several laws of a fundamental significance for the economy have been enacted: the Law of 25 September 1981 on state enterprises, that of the same date on workers' self-management, the Law of 1983 on improvement of the economy of state enterprise and on bankruptcy, the Law of 1987 on anti-monopolistic actions in the national economy. There have also been important laws in the field of Labour Law: the Law of 1982 on trade unions (substantially amended in 1985), the Law of 1986 on the reform of settlement of individual labour disputes, the Law of 1986 on collective agreements. A wide-range amendment to the Labour Code is in preparation.

18. Since World War II the basis of Poland's foreign policy has consisted of an alliance and cooperation with the USSR and other socialist countries, solidarity with and support for countries struggling for national and social liberation, the realisation of the principles of peaceful coexistence between countries of different socio-economic systems, and striving for the strengthening of international security and non-interference in the affairs of other states.

§3. THE CONSTITUTIONAL SYSTEM

A. The political system

19. The Polish People's Republic is a socialist state in which – according to the Constitution of PPR – authority belongs to the working people of cities and villages. The basis of the people's authority in Poland is the alliance of the working class with other social strata, the reflection of which is the Polish party system. This system consists of: the Polish United Workers' Party (Communist Party) – PUWP playing the leading role in the party system; the United Peasant Party, and the Democratic Party (a party uniting representatives of urban small producers' circles). The role of the PUWP is defined thus in the Constitution:

Art. 3, sec. 1:

'The guiding political force for the building of socialist society is the Polish United Workers' Party'.

and

Art. 4, sec. 2:

'The Polish United Workers' Party realises the nationwide strivings of the working class, avails itself of its achievements and activities, expands the share of workers in the solution of problems of the state, the community and the economy, and consolidates the worker-peasant alliance'.

The cooperation of these parties, based on socialist principles, determines political life in Poland and finds its institutional reflection in the Patriotic Movement of National Revival (PRON).

The essence of PRON has been laid down in the Constitution of the PPR:

Art. 3, sec. 3:

'The Political Movement of National Revival is a forum for uniting the community for the benefit of the Polish People's Republic and also for the cooperation of Polish parties, social organisations and associations and of citizens regardless of their world outlook – in matters involving the functioning and strengthening of the socialist state and for the multi-faceted development of the country'.

There has been favourable development in Poland of cooperation between the state authorities and the Roman Catholic Church (a Joint-Committee of the government and the Episcopate for examining the key problems of the country has been appointed). Since the political events of 1980–1981 the objective of the political system has been to achieve National Agreement (consensus) based on the principles of moral redress and pro-reformatory activities; in 1988 specific forms of dialogue with political opposition are sought for, aimed at creating an 'anti-crisis pact' based on national alliance.

20. The political system of the Polish People's Republic is based on the Constitution (of 1952, as amended in 1976, 1980, 1981, 1983 and 1987). The working people execute state authority through representatives elected to the *Seym* (Parliament) and to the people's councils. The state serves to implement the basic goals set down by the Constitution of the PPR. In its domestic policy the PPR realises and develops socialist democracy (Art. 7 of the Constitution), secures and develops the socialist achievements of the working people, their authority and freedom, guarantees the participation of citizens in the government, and supports the development of various forms of self-management, develops the productive forces and the economy of the country through the planned utilisation and expansion of material resources, the rational organisation of work, and the steady progress of science and technology. The Polish People's Republic strengthens social property as the mainstay of the economic power of the country and the welfare of its people, realises the principles of social justice, eliminates the exploitation of man by man, and prevents violation of the rules of community life. It creates the conditions for the steady increase of prosperity and the gradual elimination of differences between cities and villages and between physical and mental labour. Concerned about the development of the nation, the Polish People's Republic protects the family, maternity and the education of young people; provides free medical care, develops and extends education, and ensures the overall development of science and national culture (Art. 5 of the Constitution).

The basis of Poland's foreign policy is the interest of the Polish nation, its sovereignty, independence and security, the aims of peace and cooperation between nations. Poland refers to the glorious traditions of solidarity with the forces of freedom and progress, strengthens friendship and cooperation with the USSR and other socialist countries, and bases her relations with states of different social systems on the principles of peaceful coexistence, non-interference, and cooperation (Art. 6 of the Constitution).

B. Supreme organs of state authority

1. The Seym (Parliament)

21. Poland was one of the world's first countries to develop a parliament (in the fifteenth century). The Polish parliament continues to bear its traditional name, the *Seym*. The *Seym* of the Polish People's Republic is the highest organ of state authority as the supreme representative of the nation. It enacts the laws, passes resolutions outlining the main directions of state authority, and supervises the activity of other state organs and administration. Legislative initiative comes from the Council of State, the government, and the deputies.

The *Seym* enacts national socio-economic plans for periods of several years as well as the annual national budget; it also approves accounts of the implementation of the budget and the national socio-economic plan by the government for the previous year. The *Seym* appoints and removes members of the government. It is composed of 460 deputies elected for four-year terms by general, equal, direct and secret ballot.

22. Seym debates are held in sessions summoned at least twice a year by the Council of State. The *Seym* elects from among its members a president (the 'Marshal') and vice-presidents (the Presidium of the *Seym*), and various committees. The president, or vice-president as his/her deputy, directs debates and supervises the *Seym*'s activity. Among the permanent *Seym* committees are: the Legislative Committee, the Committee for the Administration of Justice and Internal Affairs, the Committee of Labour and Social Affairs, and the Workers' Self-Management Committee (since 1981). Deputies to the *Seym* have the right to question the Prime Minister and individual ministers; interpellations must be answered by them within a fixed period of time. Interventions of deputies, addressed to the heads of ministries and institutions, must be handled without delay and are also of fundamental importance.

2. The Council of State

23. The Council of State is the second-ranking organ of state authority in Poland. Its competence is diversified and includes the traditional functions of the head of state. The Council of State is a collective organ elected by the *Seym* from among its deputies. The Council of State is represented by its president or his/her deputy. The Council of State is permanently in office and may hold its sessions at any time. The term of offices of the Council of State is longer than that of the *Seym* which elects it – it acts until the election of a Council of State by the newly elected *Seym*.

24. The Council of State has many functions as the collective head of state. It nominates and removes diplomatic representatives of the Polish People's Republic abroad and accepts the credentials of foreign diplomats.

It ratifies and renounces international agreements. The Council of State also has many functions in relation to the *Seym* and on behalf of the *Seym* when the latter is in recess; some of these decisions require subsequent approval by the *Seym*. Accordingly, the Council of State:
1. orders elections to the *Seym*;
2. summons its sessions;
3. supervises the conformity of law with the Constitution;
4. sets down the common mandatory interpretation of the law;
5. issues decrees having the force of law (to be ratified later by the *Seym*);
6. appoints various civil and military officers;
7. bestows orders and distinctions;
8. has the right of pardon and reprieve;
9. takes decisions on the granting, change and withdrawal of Polish citizenship.

Prior to 1983, the Constitution of PPR endowed the Council of State with the right to introduce martial law without envisaging the form of emergency law (this is why, in December 1981, the only measure for controlling the situation in the country was martial law). Under the Law of 20 July 1983 amending the Constitution of the PPR, the jurisdictions of the supreme state organs were divided in the following way:
– the *Seym* or, when the *Seym* is not in session, the Council of State, may resolve a decision on the state of war solely in the event of an armed attack

NATIONAL COLL
OF IRELAN
LIBRARY

on the Polish People's Republic or if international agreements provide for the necessity of joint defence against aggression;
- the Council of State may introduce martial law on part, or the whole territory of the PPR, if required by security considerations or external danger to the security of the state;
- the Council of State or in an emergency the Chairman of the Council of State may introduce emergency law for a specified period of time on a part or the whole territory of the PPR if internal security is threatened or in the event of an elemental disaster.

As a supreme organ, the Council of State supervises the people's councils, the territorial organs of state authority. It also supervises the activity of the State Labour Inspectorate.

3. The Constitutional Tribunal

25. The basis for the creation of the Constitutional Tribunal was provided by the amendment of 1982 to the Constitution of the PPR. The Law of 1985[1] determines the competence, the organisation and the procedure at the Constitutional Tribunal which was appointed in 1985 and started operating early in 1986. The Tribunal rules on the conformity of laws with the Constitution and on the conformity with the Constitution and other laws of normative provisions enacted by the Council of State, central state administrative organs and other state bodies. Rulings of the Tribunal on the incompatibility of laws with the Constitution have to be examined by the *Seym* for final decision; rulings of the Tribunal on the incompatibility of other normative provisions with the Constitution or with other laws – are binding. The Tribunal examines the contents of law provisions, as well as the competence of enacting bodies and procedures followed for enactment.

Members of the Constitutional Tribunal are elected by the *Seym* from among persons outstanding for their thorough knowledge of the law.

In 1986–1987 the Tribunal examined 24 cases; in 19 cases non-conformity with the Constitution or with laws was determined, or the government renounced from its provisions before the decision of the Tribunal had been taken (as in the coal allowances' case, discussed in para. 391).

1. See the Law of 29 April 1985 on the Constitutional Tribunal (Journal of Laws No. 22, item 98).

4. The Tribunal of State

26. The Constitutional amendment of 26 March 1982, and the law of the same date on the Tribunal of State created the basis for establishing that Tribunal. The years 1982–1987 were the initial period of activity of that Tribunal. The Tribunal of State rules on the responsibility of persons holding

supreme state position for violating the Constitution and the laws. Responsible to the Tribunal of State can be:
– members of the Council of State,
– members of the Government,
– the Chairman of the Supreme Board of Control, the Chairman of the National Bank of Poland, and the Prosecutor General of the PPR,
– Managers of Central Offices.
The *Seym* alone is authorised to bring the above indicated persons to constitutional accountability. This responsibility embraces actions which do not constitute offences by which these persons have violated in a culpable way – within the scope of their office or in connection with the position held by them – the Constitution or other law. The Tribunal of State may also rule on the penal responsibility of persons brought to constitutional accountability for offences committed in connection with the position held by them.

The Tribunal of State is elected by the *Seym* from among persons who are not deputies for the duration of its term in office. The Chairman of the Tribunal of State is the First President of the Supreme Court. The judges of the Tribunal are independent and subordinate only to the law.

5. The Ombudsman for Civil Rights

27. The office of Ombudsman for Civil Rights was established in 1987.[1] The responsibility of the Ombudsman is to investigate whether or not actions or omissions of state organs violate citizens' rights or the rules of community life and social justice.

The Ombudsman is appointed by the *Seym*, after consultation with the Patriotic Movement of National Revival (PRON) for a period of four years. In his/her activities the Ombudsman is independent and subordinate only to the *Seym*.

The Ombudsman undertakes investigations:
1. on the request of individual citizens;
2. on requests by PRON or social-political or professional organisations;
3. on his own initiative.

1. See the Law of 15 July 1987 on the Ombudsman for Civil Rights (Journal of Laws No. 21, item 123).

6. The Supreme Board of Control

28. The Supreme Board of Control (NIK) is an organ directly subordinate to the *Seym*. It is appointed to supervise the economic, financial, organisational and administrative activity of the state administration and state-run enterprises. This supervision concerns legality, economic management, expedience, and integrity. The Board may also supervise social and cooperative organisation as far as management of public property is concerned. It is also

authorised to supervise private economic units in the sphere of their economic and financial obligations towards the State. The supervisory activities of the Board may be undertaken on the order of the *Seym*, of the Council of State, of the Council of Ministers, and on its own initiative. The President of the Supreme Board of Control is appointed and removed by the *Seym*. He takes part in sessions of the *Seym* and is authorised to participate in sittings of the Council of Ministers. The Supreme Board of Control submits annual reports on its activity to the *Seym*.

7. Central Organs of State Administration

29. The central organ of state administration, *i.e.* the supreme executive and managerial organ is the Council of Ministers, *i.e.* the government of the Polish People's Republic, and its individual members. The Council of Ministers and its members are appointed and removed by the *Seym*. The Council of Ministers is responsible to the *Seym*, and – when the *Seym* is in recess – to the Council of State. The internal organ of the Council of Ministers is the Presidium of the Government, composed of the President of the Council of Ministers as its Chairman, the Vice-presidents of the Council of Ministers, and other members of the government appointed by the Council of Ministers.

As of 1973, the Legislative Council of the President of the Council of Ministers has operated as a consultative organ regarding lawmaking; as of 1982 a special Section for Labour Law and Social Security Affairs started operating within the framework of the Legislative Council, consisting principally of distinguished labour law specialists.

8. Territorial Organs of State Authority and Administration

30. Poland is divided administratively into 49 provinces (*voivodships*), with 810 cities and 2,327 communes as the basic units of territorial division. The territorial organs of state authority and representation are the provincial municipal and communal people's councils. The territorial organs of state administration and, at the same time, the executive and managerial organs of the respective people's councils are: the *voivodes* – in *voivodships*; the mayors – in cities of population exceeding 50,000 and in cities which are seats of *voivodships*; heads of cities – in other towns; and heads of communes – in communes. The people's councils, defined by the Constitution of the Polish People's Republic as

'territorial organs of state authority and the basic organs of social self-government of the working people of cities and villages',

participate in the shaping and implementation of state policy and, along with their other constitutionally determined functions,

31

'direct the entire socio-economic and cultural development, influence all administrative and managerial units on their territories, inspire and coordinate their activities and supervise them. The people's councils combine the needs of the region with the nationwide goals and objectives' (Art. 46 of the Constitution).

Members of people's councils are elected by the people in general elections. The term of office of the people's councils, like that of the *Seym*, is four years. According to the law of 20 July 1983 on the people's councils and territorial self-government system, the people's councils elect from among their members a chairman and vice-chairman who form the council's Presidium – an organ initiating and organising the council's work. The people's council's also appoint permanent committees for the individual spheres of their activity. A new amendment to the law on the people's councils is in preparation in 1988, tending to strengthen the powers of the councils.

31. A *voivode* is, on the territory of his/her *voivodship*, the representative of the government endowed with special functions. *Voivodes* are appointed by the Prime Minister on the advice of the Presidium of the appropriate *voivodship* people's council. Mayors of cities, heads of cities and communes are elected by the appropriate people's councils; the person elected is then appointed to his job by the *voivode*. The *voivodship*, municipal and communal offices are the executive apparatus of *voivodes*, mayors of cities, and heads of cities and communes.

The *voivodes*, mayors and heads of the cities and communes are controlled in two ways. As the territorial organs of state administration, they are subject to the administrative organs of a higher level, *i.e.* the *voivodes* and mayors of the *voivodship* cities – to the Prime Minister, the heads of cities and communes – to the *voivode*. At the same time, as the executive and managerial organs of the people's councils, they are responsible to their respective people's council for implementation of tasks set down by the council. The legal basis of the activity of the two-tier territorial state authority and administration is the Law of 20 July 1983 on the people's councils and territorial self-government system (subsequently amended). The activity of the people's councils is subject to control by the Council of State.

32. Self-government by the inhabitants of cities and villages operates at the lowest level of organisation of society. The representative organs of self-government of the urban population are meetings of residents of residential districts or conferences of delegates of residents' meetings. The executive organs of urban self-government are composed of representatives elected by the meetings of residents or by the conferences of delegates of residents' meetings. The organs of self-government in rural districts are meetings of peasants, the communal people's council, and the head of the commune. The independence of operation of the territorial self-government organs remains under the auspices of the *Seym* and is protected by the supervision of the Council of State.

9. The Administration of Justice

a. The judiciary

33. The judiciary

'safeguards the constitutional system of the Polish People's Republic, protects the achievements of the Polish working people, law and order, social property and civil rights, and punishes criminals' (Art. 58 of the Constitution of the Polish People's Republic).

The administration of justice in the Polish People's Republic is carried out by the Supreme Court,[1] the Supreme Administrative Court, and *voivodship* and regional courts[2] – the first and second instances in civil and criminal cases – and by special courts, such as labour and social security courts and other organs of labour jurisdiction. A general reform of the labour judiciary was carried out in 1985.[3] The Supreme Court has its seat in Warsaw. It is divided into Civil, Criminal, Labour and Social Security, and Military Chambers. The Supreme Court is composed of the first President, the Presidents of the chambers, and justices. The Supreme Court is appointed by the Council of State for a term of five years. The judges of other courts are appointed by the Council of State for an indefinite period of time. The judges are independent: they are subject only to the law. The hearing of cases by the courts (with the exception of the Supreme Court) takes place with the participation of lay assessors, elected by people's councils who – in making decisions – have rights equal to those of the judges. The hearing of cases before all courts is open to the public, with exceptions specified by law. The structure and procedures of the organs of administration of justice in individual labour disputes will be elaborated in Chapter XI.

1. The Law of 20 September 1984 on the Supreme Court (Journal of Laws No. 45, item 242).
2. The Law of 30 April 1985 on the ordinary courts system (Journal of Laws No. 31, item 137).
3. The Law of 18 April 1985 on settlement of individual labour disputes (Journal of Laws No. 20, item 85).

b. The Supreme Administrative Court

34. The Supreme Administrative Court was created in 1980 by the Law of 31 January 1980 concerning the Supreme Administrative Court and the modification of the Code of Administrative Procedure. Its function is to decide cases of complaints against decisions taken by the state administration organs. The range of administrative decisions which can be the subject of complaints before the Supreme Administrative Court is defined by the above mentioned law of 31 January 1980. The Supreme Administrative Court has its seat in Warsaw; it also has certain territorial branches in the countryside. The

Chairman and the Deputy Chairman of the Supreme Administrative Court are appointed by the Council of State on the recommendation of the Prime Minister; the justices are appointed by the Council of State on the recommendation of the Minister of Justice. In passing decisions the justices are independent and subject only to the law.

c. The Public Prosecutor's Office

35. The objective of the Public Prosecutor's Office of the Polish People's Republic is to safeguard law and order, to protect social property, and to guarantee the observance of civil rights (Art. 64 of the Constitution of the PPR). The basic organisational structure of the Public Prosecutor's Office embraces the Public Prosecutor-General and *voivodship* and regional prosecutors. The Public Prosecutor-General is appointed for an indefinite period of time and removed by the Council of State. The Public Prosecutor-General is responsible to the Council of State. He also directs all the activities of the Public Prosecutor's Office of the Polish People's Republic.

d. Attorneys

36. The Bar, an important aspect of the administration of justice in the Polish People's Republic, is organised in accordance with the principles of professional self-government: attorneys (and their apprentices) carry on their profession in attorneys' guilds; the self-government organs are attorneys' *voivodship* councils and chambers, the Supreme Attorneys' Council, and the National Bar Congress. The organisation and behaviour of attorneys are regulated by the Law of 26 May 1982 on the organisation of the Bar.

e. Legal advisers

37. Of great importance is the role played by the profession of legal adviser in charge of the legal services of state enterprises and other organisational and economic units. The function of a legal adviser is the strengthening of the legal order, the protection of legal interests of the economic unit employing him, and respect on the part of citizens and other subjects of activities of the unit involved. Legal advisers are associated in self-government groups whose organs are district chambers of legal advisers and a Nationwide Chamber of Legal Advisers under the Law of 6 July 1982 on legal advisers.

Basic rights, freedoms and duties of citizens of the Polish People's Republic

38. The principle of the equality of all citizens before the law lies at the foundation of the political system of the Polish People's Republic; this includes equal rights for both women and men. Citizens of the PPR have equal rights regardless of their sex, birth (in or out of wedlock), education, profession, nationality, race, religion, as well as social origin and position (Art. 67 of the Constitution). The Constitution defines the rights, freedoms and duties of citizens, all of which determine the position of the citizen in the state and society. The list of these rights and duties undergoes transformations in the course of history. The 1980 Social Agreements provided the basis for a new, more profound approach to that problem.

Basic socio-economic civil rights, including the rights of workers (with the right to work pre-eminent) are discussed in Chapter III concerning the Constitution of PPR as a source of law. The basic civil rights promulgated by the Constitution in regard to other spheres of life are:

1. the right of citizens to elect their representatives to the *Seym* and to People's Councils, and the right of eligibility, as well as the right to request reports from deputies and councillors;
2. the right to participate in carrying out social supervision, through consultations and national referendum on key problems of the country's development (a national referendum was held in November 1987);
3. freedom of thought and religion, freedom of speech and of the press, freedom of assembly and of association, including the right to associate in trade unions, freedom of petition to all state organs for redress of grievances and to make suggestions which should be considered efficiently and without delay;
4. the right of personal immunity;
5. the right to security of their homes, secrecy of correspondence, the right of the accused to defence, the right to enjoy the natural environment, and the right to protection abroad by the Polish People's Republic.

The Constitution provides special care for the family and for the education of young people in the public spirit.

The establishment in 1987 of the Ombudsman for Civil Rights (see Para. 27) contributes considerably to the safeguarding of basic human rights in Poland.

§4. ECONOMY, POPULATION, EMPLOYMENT

A. Economy

1. Forms of property

39. There are three forms of property in the Polish People's Republic:
1. socialised property (state-owned and cooperative);
2. individual property (private enterprises, craftsmen's workshops, individual farms);
3. personal property (items intended to meet the personal needs of the owners and their families).

Of major importance for the economy are the forms of socialised and individual property. The recognition of the new form of property – a communal property – is discussed in Poland in 1988.

a. Socialised property

40. All natural resources are state-owned in Poland, as is 44 per cent of the total land area, 80 per cent of the means of production (industrial plants) and 55 per cent of non-productive property (residential buildings, schools, hospitals, etc.). About 2 per cent of the land, 6 per cent of the means of production, and 10 per cent of non-productive property (cooperative apartments) are the property of cooperatives. Thus, the socialised economy has at its disposal all natural resources, about 50 per cent of the land (*i.e.* about 12 million hectares, including more than 65 per cent of woodland), 86 per cent of the means of production, and 65 per cent of non-productive property.

b. Individual property

41. Most land in Poland is individually owned: over 60 per cent of the total area, including 71 per cent of arable land, is owned by more than three million individual peasants. The protection of individual peasant property was strengthened by the 1983 amendment to the Constitution.

Individual ownership of the means of production (private firms, workshops, private trade etc.) accounts for 6 per cent of the total and is increasing along with the development of economic reform in Poland. The development of the non-socialised sector is supported by the state in agriculture, handicrafts and services and in small industry. However, the legal and economic system did not favour, so far, the development of large-scale private property. The legal limit on individual property in agriculture is generally 50 hectares (in the eastern and northern territories – 100 hectares) of land, while in industrial production and commerce enterprises may normally employ no more than 50 workers. The Law of 8 June 1972 regarding handicrafts (as amended in 1982 and 1986) determines the employment limit in craft production and services at 15 employees, plus journeyman, apprentices, retired workers and persons not directly employed in the performance of the handicrafts (*i.e.* those servicing the craft shops). The Law of 31 January 1985 on small industry[1] considerably enlarged the possibilities of private small producers' workshops. In 1988 as a part of the second phase of the economic reform in Poland, a considerable enlargement of individual property and initiative is envisaged: the new law favouring the individual enterprise and initiative has been discussed renouncing previous limitations.

1. See the Law of 31 January 1985 on small production (Journal of Laws No. 3, item 11).

42. Foreign legal and physical persons can obtain the right to perform economic activity on Polish territory under the Law of 1982 regulating operations involving small productions on Polish territory;[1] practically, this law affects primarily the so-called 'Polona-enterprises' – enterprises established in Poland by foreigners of Polish descent, though the law applies to all foreigners. Foreign economic persons may carry out in Poland economic activities within the sphere of small production consisting of:

1. production of goods and extension of services;
2. trade turnover;
3. export of their own production and services and imports needed for such production and services.

Article 21 of that Law stipulates that foreign enterprises utilise the local labour force according to rules generally binding in Poland; the provisions of the Polish Labour Code are applicable to all employment relations entered into by foreign enterprises. A licence from Polish state administrative organs is required for foreign enterprises to conduct economic operation on Polish territory. According to the law, the organ issuing the licence establishes the number of staff who may be employed by foreign legal and physical persons carrying out economic activity in Poland.

In 1986 a law on joint-ventures was adopted.[2] Polish-foreign ventures may be created in order to carry out economic operations consisting of the production of goods and the extension of services, as well as their trade and sale in Poland and abroad. The creation of a joint-venture requires a licence granted by the Minister of Foreign Trade after consultation with the Minister of Finance. A licence is granted primarily when economic operations are aimed at:

a. initiating modern technological and organisational processes in the national economy;
b. supplying goods and services for export;
c. the improvement of supplies of modern and high-quality goods and services to the domestic market.

The participation of Polish partners in the capital of a joint-venture cannot be less than 51 per cent of total capital. In 1988 the amendment to this law is discussed, aiming at considerable alleviating of conditions of operating of foreign capitals in Poland.

1. See the Law of 6 July 1982 on rules for carrying out small-scale production on Polish territory (Journal of Laws No. 13, item 146).
2. See the Law of 23 April 1986 on Polish-foreign joint-ventures (Journal of Laws No. 17, item 88).

2. Economic development of the Polish People's Republic

43. In 1978 Poland ranked tenth in the world in industrial production. The annual average rate of growth of national income was 9.8 per cent in the period 1971–1978, while the average annual rate of growth of industrial production was 10.4 per cent during this period. The total national income reached about 100 billion US dollars in 1978, with per capita national income

about 3,000 US dollars. However, those achievements were to a large extent the result of foreign credits. The economic crisis soon changed this picture of the economy. The change in national income over the period of crisis was as follows (1970 = 100): 1975 – 159, 1980 – 169, 1982 – 140, 1983 – 149, 1986 – 171 (1987 *Statistical Yearbook*, Warsaw). The rate of economic development in the past 40 years as regards capital investment puts Poland in a strong position in the world. It is estimated, however, that in regard to the living standards of the population (level of wages, consumption, household facilities etc.). Poland has only achieved the average international standard (it dropped during the 1980–1982 crisis and as a result of economic sanctions). Therefore, the tasks of developing consumer goods' industries and agriculture which, in spite of having doubled its production over the past quarter of a century does not fully meet social demand, are treated as the most urgent requirements of economic strategy.

44. As a result of the economic sanctions imposed in 1982 on Poland by some western countries, economic ties with CMEA and with individual socialist countries strengthened. International decisions of 1986–1988 regarding Poland's international debts and Poland's entry to the International Monetary Fund open new economic opportunities.

Type of production	Volume of production
Electric power in kWh (billions)	140
Hard coal (millions of tons)	192
Steel (millions of tons)	17.1
Copper (thousands of tons)	388
Passenger cars (thousands)	290
Ships (thousands DWT)	536

45. The dynamics of Polish imports and exports show the following tendencies:

Imports

Socialist countries	Other countries
1970–100	1970–100
1980–194.7	1980–283.3
1986–221.7	1986–184.7

Exports

Socialist countries	Other countries
1970–100	1970–100
1980–206.9	1980–190.8
1986–277.4	1986–172.8

Coal, machines and equipment rank first in Poland's exports, next to consumer durables. Next to machines and equipment – ships, motor vehicles, and complete industrial projects (sugar refining plants, sulphuric acid factories, power plants, etc.) are the major items of Polish exports.

Poland attaches great importance to industrial and scientific-technical cooperation with foreign countries realised by contacts between Poland and large firms of world renown (such as FIAT), and also by appropriate international agreements.

B. Population

46. As regards population (37.5 millions in 1987) Poland ranks 25th in the world, and seventh in Europe (after the USSR, West Germany, Great Britain, Italy, France and Spain). The density of population in Poland is 118 per km^2; it varies depending on the region – in industrial districts (Warsaw, Katowice and Lódź) it amounts to 500–750 persons per km^2, while in some regions to only 40–50 persons per km^2 (Suwałki, Słupsk). Poland is a homogeneous country as regards nationality: the percentage of minorities is estimated at about 1.5 per cent; they have total freedom to develop their own socio-cultural life. In the post-war years the birth rate in Poland was very high; from 1946 to 1987 the population increased by 13.5 millions, *i.e.* by about 50 per cent. A population explosion was recorded in 1950–1956 (by more than 19 per cent on average). Then, in the 1960s, the birth rate dropped considerably, while in the 1970s, in connection with the reaching of maturity by those born during 'the demographic peak', the birth rate soared again to 10.2 per cent in 1983. However, it fell to 6.9 per cent in 1986. A slow ageing of the Polish population is noticeable. In connection with the rapid urbanisation of the country, the urban population grew from 33 per cent of the total population in 1946 to 60 per cent in the 1980s. Unlike the situation at the end of the ninteenth century and in the first decades of the twentieth century, characterised by a high rate of emigration in search of employment, especially of the rural population from the poorest regions, there is no economic need for emigration from People's Poland (there is, however, a difference in living standards between Poland and the richest countries of the world). An undesirable phenomenon of temporary economic emigration was observed in the 1980s, as a result of the socio-economic crisis.

C. Employment

47. In Poland, the policy of full employment results from the principles of the political system and constitutes the basic element of socialist transformation (however, this may be complicated by the implications of economic reforms at the end of the 1980s). Over the years 1945–1956 a policy of extensive employment was pursued, with the employment in developing industries of those migrating on a massive scale from the rural regions. Since the early 1960s, because of the need to restrict the departure of labour from agriculture, employment policy in Poland has gradually assumed an intensive character consisting in the rational distribution and utilisation of manpower. The number of professionally active people in Poland was about 17.3 million in 1986, of whom about 12.4 million were employed in the socialised sector and 4.8 million in the non-socialised sector (including 3.8 million individual farmers). In 1986 employment in the major branches of the economy was as follows:

agriculture	4,896,000 persons
industry	4,915,000 persons
construction	1,315,000 persons
transport and communication	1,057,000 persons
trade	1,476,600 persons
education and training	900,000 persons
health care	757,000 persons
state administration and justice	275,500 persons

About 40 per cent of the professionally active population is employed in industry and construction, about 32 per cent in agriculture and forestry and about 30 per cent in other sectors.

Employment in the widely defined service sector still remains relatively low in Poland – the objective of current economic policy is to increase employment in services to 40 per cent by 1990. Economic reforms favour this trend.

In general, the economic reform introduced over the years 1984–1987 and subsequently should cause far-reaching changes in the employment structure in Poland, aiming at the elimination of existing overmanning in the enterprises. For the time being, the effect of economic reform on the employment of self-managing and self-financing enterprises is assessed as insufficient and overmanning continues to exist.

48. Women account for 48 per cent of all employed persons in Poland. In some fields, such as education, medicine, the lower levels of the judiciary and trade, far-reaching feminisation has occured. Both the total social equality of women, acknowledged by the system, and the demands of the national economy enhance their full vocational participation. On the other hand, attempts are being made to find both legal and economic measures to prevent social degradation of the reproductive and socialising functions of women in the family.

49. There is no unemployment in People's Poland; rather the economy suffers from a growing shortage of manpower. According to the statistics, the number of registered persons seeking employment at the end of 1986 was 4,000 women and 1,000 men while the number of vacant positions was 66,000 for women and 222,000 for men.[1] Both the present situation on the labour-market and forecasts for the period to 1990 indicate that the Polish economy faces a labour deficit, especially in view of the economic plans for

NATIONAL COLLEGE
OF IRELAND
LIBRARY

those years and the expected good economic conjuncture resulting from economic reform. The resolution of these difficulties provides for rational employment of manpower, suppression of existing overmanning, maximalization of labour productivity and efficiency, a wide spread introduction of technological, organisational and economic progress, an incentive wages systems, increased vertical mobility and activation of female reserves of labour.

1. See *Concise Statistical Yearbook* 1987, Warsaw, 1987, p. 57.

50. About 9.5 per cent of persons employed in the national economy have higher (university) education; about 32 per cent have completed secondary school and 28 per cent have basic vocational training. Poland has at present about 400,000 engineers and 67,000 physicians.

51. The average nominal monthly remuneration in the socialised sector of the economy is as follows:

> 1970 –   2,253 zlotys
> 1980 –   6,040 zlotys
> 1984 – 16,500 zlotys
> 1986 – 24,100 zlotys
> 1988 – 47,000 zlotys (preliminary data)

The years 1980 to 1988 were a period of rising inflation. The minimum monthly wage established by the state for 1988 was 9,000 zlotys.

Chapter II. Outline of Evolution of Labour Law in Poland

§1. Labour Law in Poland (1919–1939)

52. The development of Polish Labour Law began when Poland regained her independence after the First World War. Discarding the socially unsatisfactory legal regulations of the former ruling powers, the Polish state – although assuming the form of a landowner-bourgeois republic – adopted in the initial period of her independence several social laws of a progressive nature. The value of these regulations was positively influenced by the revolutionary events of 1917–1919 in Central Europe, by the enactment in the Soviet Union of a revolutionary socialist Labour Law, as well as by the positive impact of the foundation of the International Labour Organisation, of which Poland was a founding member.

53. The major legal regulations of this period differed positively from social relations in Europe at that time. They included:
1. the 1919 law on working hours which made general the eight-hour working day, partially introduced in Poland a year earlier, and the 46-hour working week, as well as additional pay for overtime amounting to 50 and 100 per cent of renumeration;
2. the 1922 law on vacation leave of workers which was one of Europe's first legal acts giving paid annual leave the status of a legal institution. The law introduced a month's leave for white-collar workers, but only eight days' leave for blue-collar workers. Incidentally, the law sanctioned the division of working people into white- and blue-collar workers, which division became firmly established in Polish Labour Law as a *sui generis* socio-legal anachronism;
3. the 1924 Law on employment protection for juveniles and women, exceeding in many of its provisions the international standards of that time, such as the setting of the minimum working age at fifteen, not – as in other European countries – fourteen, introducing certain provisions protecting women against dismissal during pregnancy and maternity leave, etc.;
4. the 1927 decree on labour courts, organising a labour judiciary separate from the general administration of justice and operating with the participation of elected assessors who, at that time, had not yet been admitted to the general judiciary;
5. in the field of collective labour relations a 1919 decree introduced some range of trade union freedom, making trade unions independent of the general administration; the field of collective labour relations was later regulated by the 1937 law on collective agreements.

Along with the protective measures, most urgent for a state starting – after regaining its independence – to lay the foundations of its economy, the key problems of the employment relationship also called for legal regulation. This was done by two simultaneous decrees of 1928 determining separately – in the face of the already established dichotomy between workers – the contract of employment of white-collar workers and the contract of employment of blue-collar workers (earlier, in 1922, a separate law had dealt with the civil service functionaries). The law on the employment relationship established by these two decrees in the form of detailed provisions was later extended by *sui generis* 'general provisions' in the form of a group of provisions on contracts of employment included in the 1933 Code of Obligations constituting a part of the planned codification of Civil Law never, however, implemented in inter-war Poland.

54. The progressive legal regulations of the 1920s broke down in practice during the years of the world economic crisis which, in landowner-bourgeois Poland, was acutely combined with reactionary political changes. Social laws, formally in force, were notoriously violated at that time, particularly those regulating working hours which – from the very beginning – were the subject of fierce attacks by capitalists. This resulted in the 1933 amendment of that law extending the working week to 48 hours and cutting down by half the additional renumeration for overtime work.

At the same time unfavourable changes were introduced as regards vacation leave and in other fields. Poland had not recovered from this socio-political regression resulting from anti-worker measures of the thirties by the time of the 1939 Nazi aggression.

§2. LABOUR LAW IN POLAND PRIOR TO CODIFICATION (1944–1975)

A. Evolution of labour legislation

55. After World War II Poland, emerging from the appalling destruction which affected all fields of life, entered an entirely new political, economic and social situation involving the nationalisation of the means of production and agrarian reform. However, unlike the other countries adopting a socialist system after World War II, Poland took over the pre-1939 legal system. The old laws concerning labour remained effective, though with basic amendments, as well as a totally new interpretation in accordance with the needs and goals of a socialist state. The amendments of social legislation in the early years of People's Poland consisted in the abolition of the unfavourable changes introduced in the 1930s (such as the restoration of the 46-hour working week and the 50 and 100 per cent supplements for overtime work), and in the improvement of workers' rights beyond their former scope, including – for instance – the extension of protection for juveniles and pregnant women, the extension of the vacation leave of blue-collar workers to up to 12 days after a year of employment, and to one month after 10 years of employment.

56. Along with the adaptation of previous provisions to the needs of socialist society, the first thirty years of People's Poland was a period of intensive activity in the field of Labour Law and resulted in many laws of major importance before final codification was complete. The most significant measures undertaken in the early post-war period resulted in new socio-legal institutions spontaneously developing in nationalised industry: the organs of workers' representation and trade unions. The system of social insurance in the Polish People's Republic was also totally reconstructed, both as regards its procedural rules, and the range and level of benefits. An important instrument of the modernisation and development of Labour Law during the 30 year prior to codification were collective agreements, frequently initiating new labour law institutions which, later – after practical testing – gained the status of law. Finally, the jurisdiction of courts and arbitration committees, as well as the considerable achievements of the doctrine of socialist labour law, played an important part in the modernisation of this sphere of the law.

57. The transformation of Labour Law in People's Poland served three basic functions: *protective, organisational,* and *educational.* In socialist Labour Law all these functions are of equal status. This general principle was not changed by the emergence in Poland in the period from 1950 to 1955 of a trend which stressed the administrative and organisational functions of Labour Law, especially in the field of the planned utilisation of the labour force and the strict observance of a formalistic labour discipline, along with the simultaneous temporary reduction in that period of the importance of collective agreements.

58. The legislative process in the field of Labour Law in Poland between 1945 and 1975 was subordinated to the following general goals:
a. the development of collective elements in employment relationships;
b. the raising of the standard of and the extension of the range of workers' rights and benefits, along with the simultaneous abolition of the anach- ronistic division of employees into white- and blue-collar workers;
c. the rationalisation and simplification of labour legislation.

B. Development of collective elements in the employment relationship

59. The expansion of collective elements in labour relations, along with the development of collective elements in the employment relationship, brought about a fundamental qualitative transformation of the essence of Polish socialist Labour Law, although, at certain periods of time, practice did not fully reflect the intentions of the law. Even the first legal acts – the 1945 decree on the organisation of trade union committees and the 1949 law on trade unions, sanctioned the extensive rights which had developed sponta- neously and also the position of workers' representatives and trade unions. A further broadening of the sphere of trade union rights occured through the statutes of individual trade unions and their associations, as well as by collective negotiations; in practice, the problem was to what an extent the trade unions could take advantage of the rights accorded to them. The workers' committees – organs of workers' representation and, at the same time, the basic trade union organs – gained wide functions, including participation in the establishment of internal rules of employment and cooperation in the employment and dismissal of workers, and in general, social supervision. A system of workers' self-government was established in 1956 (its structure and functions were defined by the law of 1958 on workers' self-government); this system operated satisfactorily until the mid-sixties; it then succumbed to a process of formalisation and became an institution to a large extent just 'for show'. The supervision of employment conditions was transferred to the trade unions; initially, by the shaping in 1950 of a social labour inspectorate, a social service carried out by the workers themselves and, later, by subordinating to the trade unions by virtue of a 1954 decree, a professional labour inspectorate which, from that time up to 1981, was carried out by a specialised apparatus of the trade unions of that time; this last structural solution was controversial. The unions also supervised the labour disputes' field. The previous labour courts were abolished and the 1954 decree on workers' arbitration committees established a specific system for settling labour disputes; under this system such disputes were settled in the first instance by arbitration committees in the enterprise organised by the unions; and in the second instance – by the territorially superior organ of the trade union or by a public court of justice. The function of reviewing the effective decisions of the arbitration committees (*sui generis* extraordinary appeals) was carried out by the Central Council of Trade Unions (the central organ of the pre-1980 trade unions). Negotiations on collective agreements, which were concluded for entire branches of the economy by the main boards of branch trade unions with the respective ministers, were an important aspect of trade union activity. Finally, on a nationwide scale, trade unions had the right to exert their influence on economic and social decisions taken by state organs regarding the functioning of the planned economy, and on the shaping of the Labour Law: legal acts in this field were enacted with the agreement of the Central Council of Trade Unions (a pre-1980 organ).

The development of collective elements in the Labour Law of that period was delayed by bureaucratic tendencies in the operation of trade unions of those days, especially of their central authority: the Central Council of Trade Unions.

C. Extension of workers' rights

60. The major improvement of the standard, and the extension of the rights and benefits of workers, along with the simultaneous elimination from the law of the division between white- and blue-collar workers was for the most part already completed prior to the codification of Labour Law. In regard to the employment relationship, the two 1928 decrees on the employment contracts of white- and blue-collar workers were amended by the 1956 decree restricting the admissibility of termination of employment without notice and protecting employment continuity. That decree intro-duced uniform regulation for all workers of the rules governing instant dismissal, restricting this right only to certain specified causes and establishing uniform claims in the event of unwarranted dismissal: claims for reinstatement or compensation. Reinstatement, a concept newly introduced in Labour Law, was acknowledged as especially significant for the system of socialist Labour Law. Compared with the previous situation, the 1956 regulation represented a remarkable advance in employment protection in the Polish People's Republic. The division of employees into white- and blue-collar workers, though removed at that time in regard to immediate dismissals, survived – however – in regard to the termination of the employment contract with prior notice: the period of notice amounting until 1975 to three months for white-collar workers and two weeks for blue-collar workers. The length of the trial period at the start of an employment contract was also differentiated until codification, with three months for white-collar and seven days for blue-collar workers. The Labour Code introduced a differentiation of these periods based on criteria other than the division by the type of worker.

61. Still prior to codification, in 1969, the division between workers was also removed in regard to annual leave, which had previously been one month after one year of employment for white-collar workers, but only after 10 years for blue-collar ones. The 1969 law on workers' vacation leave made the length of leave, with rules indentical for all workers, dependent on the length of employment and the standard of education; this provision was later included in the Labour Code.

62. According to the principles of socio-economic policy of the Polish People's Republic, the protection of women's work and of maternity leave has been considerably extended. The 1972 law increased the length of maternity leave, formerly amounting to three months, to sixteen weeks for the first confinement and 18 weeks for each subsequent confinement. The institution of one year's unpaid leave to look after a young child was first introduced in 1968, and extended in 1972 to three years, enabling a working woman to perform her maternity functions and provide personal care with no formal interruption of her professional career; while maintaining various ties with the firm, a woman, after leave without pay, had the right to resume her former job under previous conditions. This type of protection for working women was later taken over and developed in the Labour Code.

During the 30 years of People's Poland the protection of young people, aimed in the first place at their vocational preparation, has been improved by successive legal acts.

63. The protection of all workers has also been systematically extended: the 1965 law on occupational health and safety laid down a very modern and effective system of protection, and the Labour Code availed itself extensively of the achievements of that law. The principles and level of benefits for workers in the event of accident at work, or an occupational disease, have been improved several times. In the sphere of social insurance too, the 1954 decree already introduced a uniform scheme for all workers and, at the same time, considerably raised old-age and disability pensions. These pensions have subsequently been steadily improved, as regards both their amount and the organisational and legal principles of social insurance. However, the existence and succeeding revivals of so-called 'old portfolios' of pensioners resulted in a generally unsatisfactory level of old age pensions throughout 40 years of post-war Poland.

§3. THE CODIFICATION OF LABOUR LEGISLATION (1 JANUARY 1975)

64. Prior to 1975, Labour Law in the Polish People's Republic was complex and confusing, which seriously hampered its application. The incentive to codification also stemmed from the fact that the other European socialist countries already had Labour Codes, some even 'second generation' ones. Therefore, the codification of Labour Law in Poland became an urgent social and political necessity. The legislative attainments of the 30 years of People's Poland fully prepared the foundations of a new, complete regulation of employment relationships. The Labour Code, in force since 1 January 1975, has been such a regulation.

65. After ten years of operation of the Code it is assumed that, in principle, it has met social expectations; it was not submitted to any general social criticism even in the years 1980–1981. However, some of its shortcomings are apparent, being expressed among other things by centralistic-managerial tendencies characteristic of the political climate in Poland in the mid 1970s. Moreover, in the early 1980s, the Labour Code did not catch up with the changes, especially as regards the requirements of the economic reform and the organisation and the prerogatives of trade unions. Its amendment cannot be avoided, and work on it started in 1984. The general reform of Labour Law in Poland is planned for 1990s.

§4. LABOUR LEGISLATION IN POLAND AFTER 1980

66. After the justified workers' protests and the conclusion of Social Agreements in 1980 there occured a development, but also a particular complexity of collective labour relationships caused by the emergence in 1980–1981 of a pluralistic structure of trade unions (the 'Solidarity' movement, branch trade unions, autonomous trade unions, and many others). Starting in 1982 the process of shaping up of the new trade unions movement has been in progress, their membership being early in 1988 7,5 million, that is over 60 per cent of the total labour force in Poland; workers' self-management in state enterprises is also expanding on new principles. A durable attainment of the years 1980–1988 in Poland has been the understanding by society of the need for authenticity and independence of trade unions, the renovation of workers' self-management, rationalisation of collective negotiations, the legal sanctioning of the notion of collective labour disputes and the creation of legal mechanisms for their solution, including a legal guarantee of the right to strike.

67. After 1981 the developmental trend of Polish Labour Law underwent regression caused by martial law and by the struggle with economic crisis. A dramatic move was the suspension and, in October 1982, the dissolution of all trade unions registered prior to that date (the 'Solidarity' movement, branch, autonomous, and all other trade unions); as per the interpretation of the Supreme Court, also the job security of former trade union activists was abrogated for the duration of the trade unions' suspension. Moreover, the regulations accompanying the introduction of martial law contained a number of restrictions of workers' rights, especially in militarised work establishments and in those of crucial significance for the national economy. After the abolition of martial law in July 1983, the Law of 21 July 1983 providing special legal regulations for the period of overcoming the socio-economic crisis, introduced for a transitory period – up to the end of 1985 – certain special measures involving Labour Law, such as the right of a company's manager to increase the previously shortened working time up to the full maximum in force; and also the right of that manager to extend the period of notice, on the worker's initiative, of termination of employment by six months, in the event of the specific needs of certain work establishments. The process of discontinuation of the above-mentioned remnants of 'crisis Labour Law', whose duration had been legally set down as ending in 1985, began in 1984.

68. The specific feature of the period after 1981 is that, simultaneously with the introduction of the exceptional measures, Polish Labour Law gained some new laws of considerable value, especially as regards collective Labour Law. Those are the two Laws of 25 September 1981 on state enterprises and on the self-management of employees at those enterprises; the Law of 8 October 1982 on trade unions; the Law of 6 March 1981 on the State Labour Inspectorate; the Law of 24 June 1983 on social labour inspection, the Law of 26 January 1984 on workplace remuneration systems, the Law of 16 September 1982 concerning the legal position of employees of the state administration (civil servants), the Law of 18 April 1985 on the settlement of individual labour disputes (the mechanism of settling collective labour disputes was laid down in the law of 1982 on trade unions) and the Law of 24 November 1986 on collective agreements. In preparation are other current amendments to the Labour Code and over the long-term – by 1990s – the entire re-codification of Polish Labour Law.

The outstanding feature of significant laws enacted after 1980 is that they favour the economic reform and its objectives, such as independence, self-managing and self-financing of state enterprises, incentives for individual initiative and enterprise, introduction of market economy mechanisms, radical rise of efficiency and productivity, and are compatible with the demands of the Polish people regarding trade union independence, efficiency of their mechanisms (consultation, collective bargaining, collective labour disputes, the right to strike), the renovation and importance of workers' self-management and the general transition from crisis into the path of undisturbed development and improvement of living conditions.

Chapter III. The Sources of Labour Law

§1. OUTLINE OF THE SOURCES OF LABOUR LAW

69. The source of Labour Law in Poland comprise a wider set of elements than do the common sources of law. For Labour Law, in addition to the common sources of law, is based on specific sources, appropriate only to Labour Law, the acknowledgement of which as sources of law has occured gradually, and the legal nature of which remains the subject of discussion in Labour Law doctrine.

The major general sources of law in Poland are:
– the Constitution of the Polish People's Republic;
– laws and decrees;
– resolutions and ordinances of the Council of Ministers issued on the basis of an authorisation of the laws and for their implementation, as well as;
– ordinances and orders of ministers, issued on the basis of authorisation of the laws and for their implementation.

The latter acts are sources of law, because both the direction and range of regulations are always outlined by a law or, at least, a decree.

The specific sources of Labour Law are:
– the 1980 Social Agreements;
– branch collective agreements;
– internal rules of employment;
– workplace collective agreements and other workplace level standards.

It can be claimed, in general, that legal acts constituting common sources of labour law draw their power – directly or by authorisation – from the will of supreme legislative organs. The sources specific to Labour Law derive their status from the fact that they arise from the joint will of management and workers' representatives at different levels.

70. The core of Labour Law consists of laws, of which the Labour Code is of particular significance. The laws are passed by the *Seym* of the Polish People's Republic, the supreme legislative authority. A decree, on the other hand, is an act with the force of law, issued by the Council of State in the period between parliamentary sessions; it requires subsequent approval by the *Seym*. Decree is a form of legislation now rarely used.

71. Legislative initiative lies with the Council of State, the government, and deputies to the *Seym*. Trade unions may institute legislative proposals through deputies to the *Seym* who represent the unions; unlike in other socialist countries, in Poland the unions do not have the direct right of legislative initiative.

72. Consultation with trade unions. According to the practice strictly observed since 1984 (applied in previous periods too, but not always in a satisfactory way), legal acts in the field of Labour Law are prepared and issued in consultation with trade unions (after hearing their opinion and sometimes after negotiations); nationwide acts – in consultation with the All-Poland Trade Union Alliance (OPZZ, see paras. 365–374) and branch standards with the respective nationwide trade union organisation (Federation, see paras. 363–364).

73. Legislative procedure. Prior to their submission to the *Seym*, drafts of labour legislation are examined in terms of their legal form and their content by the *Seym* Legislative Commission, the Commission for Labour and Social Affairs, and by other competent commissions; they also are the subject of consideration by a Social and Economic Council, a consultative organ to the *Seym*. The drafts submitted at the government's initiative are the subject of prior examination by the Legislative Council, a consultative organ to the Council of Ministers.

74. The Polish constitutional system observes the principle that the regulation of citizens' rights and duties belongs to the exclusive competence of the legislative authority, *i.e.* the *Seym* of the Polish People's Republic. This principle is also applicable to the establishment of workers' rights and duties, and is effective in the sphere concerning the imposition of new duties on workers or restriction of their rights.

75. The Polish Labour Code does not mention custom as a source of law. Academic authors are, however, of the opinion that custom plays a part in the practical functioning of work establishments and in determining the legal status of the workers. Under conditions of economic reform, the role of custom may even grow in the activity of independent, self-managed, and self-financing state enterprises, as well as in private enterprises.

76. In the Polish legal order decisions of the judiciary do not constitute a source of law, as the role of the courts is to implement the law, not to create it. However, the judiciary in general, and the Supreme Court in particular, is of essential importance for the shaping of Labour Law by way of its interpretation. Moreover, in specific situations, such as *e.g.* at the time of martial law, many decisions of the Supreme Court had, as a matter of fact, a norm-creating character.

§2. THE CONSTITUTION OF THE POLISH PEOPLE'S REPUBLIC

77. The highest-ranking source of law, the Constitution of the Polish People's Republic, also called 'the fundamental law', determines the political and socio-economic system of the State, the main organisational structure and the competence of organs of state authority, of the main organs of administration, and certain other state organs; it established citizens' rights and duties and regulated other matters of state.
The Constitution of the PPR was enacted in 1952, but its present shape is the result of amendments in: 1976 (changes in various fields); 1980 (subordination of the Supreme Board of Control directly to the *Seym*); 1982 (creation

of the Tribunal of State and of the Constitutional Tribunal); 1983 (creation of
the constitutional basis for the Patriotic Movement of National Revival
(PRON), constitutional guarantee of individual peasants' landed property,
competence to proclaim martial law and a state of emergency); 1987
(introduction of a national referendum).

In 1987 works were initiated to prepare a substantial amendment or draft of
a new Constitution which should be adopted in 1991/1992 – years of
celebration of 200th anniversary of 3 May 1791 Constitution and 40th
anniversary of the 1952 Constitution.

78. Article 67 of the Constitution reads:
   'The Polish People's Republic – securing and extending the attainments
   of the working people – strengthens and broadens the citizens' rights and
   freedoms';
   thus it lays down what legal doctrine calls 'a principle of dynamism in the
   development of citizens' rights in People's Poland.

The Constitution proclaims the following basic civil rights, at the same time
the basic rights of workers:
– the right to work (Art. 68);
– the right to remuneration according to the quantity and quality of work
  (Art. 58);
– the right to rest (Art. 69);
– the right to health care (Art. 70);
– the right to assistance in case of illness or incapacity for work (Art. 70);
– the right of association, including in trade unions (Art. 84);
– the right of women to equal treatment in all fields of life, including at work
  and in professional activity (Art. 78);
– the right of the staff of an enterprise to participate in its management (Art.
  13);
– the right of citizens to participate in nationwide consultation and in
  referendums in important state matters;
– the right of citizens to lodge appeals, complaints and grievances with state
  organs (Art. 86);
– the right to education (Art. 72);
– the right to enjoy cultural attainments and to creative participation in the
  development of national culture (Art. 73);
– the right to enjoy the values of the natural environment and the duty to
  protect it (Art. 71).
In 1987 the office of Ombudsman for Civil Rights subordinated directly to
Seym was established (see para. 27), as a new guarantee of the observance of
citizens' rights in Poland.

The significance of the Constitution of the PPR as a source of Labour Law
consists in the fact that – proclaiming the basic rights of citizens and workers –
it indicates the main rules governing the entire Labour Law system, outlines
the direction of future legislation and the improvement of present laws, and
also indicates the rules of interpretation of Labour Law.

79. The supremacy of constitutional norms requires that all other legal acts comply with the Constitution. The body responsible for supervising the conformity of laws with the Constitution is the Constitutional Tribunal, created in 1985 (see para. 25).

§3. The Labour Code and Other Laws

A. The Civil Code

80. The Civil Code (effective as of 1965) is of major importance for Labour Law in Poland; in matters not regulated by provisions of Labour Law, the relevant provisions of the Civil Code are applied to the employment relationship, provided they are not inconsistent with Labour Law principles. Also the Code of Civil Procedure (effective since 1965) is respectively applied to Labour Law; provisions of the Labour Law often refer to it in regard to settlement of labour disputes by courts.

B. General characteristics of the Labour Code

81. The Labour Code of the Polish People's Republic is an act of particular significance in Polish Labour Law and is applicable throughout the territory of Poland. It was enacted on 26 June 1974 and became effective as of 1 January 1975. The enactment of the Labour Code was preceeded by the work on codification, conducted for many years, including the past legislative achievements of People's Poland and Polish socio-legal conditions. In 1973–1974 a draft code was presented for consultation with the then existing trade unions, with employees of large industrial establishments, with scholars and Labour Law experts, and with organs of the administration of justice. The final draft code was submitted jointly by the Government and the then Central Council of Trade Unions to the *Seym* for debate, and was subsequently adopted on 26 June 1974.

82. Prior to 1975 Labour Law in Poland was not codified and consisted of many scattered legal acts from various periods of time, ranging from 1918 to 1974, which made it inconsistent and complicated. According to the belief common in Poland, the form appropriate for a national regulation of the Labour Law had to be a Code (the other European socialist countries also have a codified system of Labour Law, with codes in the USSR – 1970/1971, Czechoslovakia – 1965 with subsequent amendments, the GDR – 1977, Hungary – 1967 with subsequent amendments, Bulgaria – 1986, Romania – 1972). Moreover, the 1974 codification in Poland provided an opportunity for substantial improvement of legal solutions in many areas of Labour Law.

83. 1985 marked a decade of operation of the Labour Code. Taken as a whole, it had not been the subject of any major social criticism, so marked in

1980–1981; at that time the need for changing a few of its solutions was voiced and was soon done. The Labour Code remained in force also during the martial law (1981–1983); however, simultaneously with the validity of the Code, martial law regulations controlled a number of issues, especially regarding work in militarised establishments, in a stricter way, different from that indicated in the Code. Also the subsequent Law of July 1983, on special legal regulation during the period of overcoming the socio-economic crisis contained – without abrogating the Code – certain provisions differing from the norms of the Code and scheduled to remain in force to the end of 1985. This (temporarily) incorrect legal situation resulting therefrom, defined as 'labour law disintegration', was criticized by Polish academic scholars. In 1986 this problem practically disappeared.

Two important amendments were introduced to the Labour Code in 1985 and in 1986 by the Law of 18 April 1985 on settlement of individual labour disputes and by the Law of 24 November 1986 on collective agreements.

84. The Labour Code continues to be in force, but a feeling that amendment is necessary prevails, particularly as regards its adaptation to the requirements of economic reform and to the new situation in the trade union movement. After 1990 a general re-codification of Polish Labour Law is expected. A National Committee for Labour Law Reform was appointed in 1988, chaired by Professor Zbigniew Salwa of Warsaw University. In 1984–1986 the pre-amendment work was resumed by the Legislative Council.[1] The trade unions associated in the All-Poland Trade Union Alliance (OPZZ) will certainly play an important role in the amendment of the Labour Code and in the general reform of Labour Law in Poland; it is expected that they will object to and oppose a number of radical governmental proposals and perhaps submit their own counter-proposals (the general position of trade unions is that radical economic reforms should not excessively hurt the workers' rights and living conditions).

1. The results of this work are published. See Z. Salwa and M. Matey (eds.): 'Trends and Premises of the Reform of Labour Law and Social Security', *Ossolineum*, Warsaw, 1987, pp. 203 (in Polish).

C. Integration and differentiation of Labour Law

85. The Labour Code defines the rights and duties of workers *i.e.* persons employed on the basis of an individual contract of employment. This does not imply a general standardisation of the rights and duties of all workers. As a matter of fact, the indispensable differentiation is stipulated by the Labour Code; it is also provided by special laws, executive provisions and collective agreements. However, the Labour Code expresses the general trend to Labour Law integration, *i.e.* it embraces within the sphere of Labour Law all the employment relationships on the basis of which work is performed. It is interesting to note that the Labour Code also includes within its scope persons employed on the basis of appointment and nomination (civil servants); according to the Code, in both cases we are dealing with an employment relationship.

D. Categories of workers covered by the Labour Code

86. The main and most numerous category of persons covered by the Labour Code are workers employed on the basis of an individual contract of employment concluded for an indefinite period of time. Thus, the provisions of the Code refer in the first place to contractual relations.

However, many provisions of the Labour Code also apply to relations established on the basis of appointment, nomination, election and a cooperative contract of employment.

E. Sectors of the national economy covered by the Labour Code

87. The Labour Code embraces workers of both the socialised sector, *i.e.* that based on state and cooperative property, and the non-socialised sector, based on individual property. In 1986 about 12.5 million workers were employed in Poland in the socialised sector and about 4.9 million people worked in the non-socialised sector, including individual farms. These proportions may fluctuate with progressing of the economic reforms.

In the non-socialised sector provisions of the Labour Code apply to persons employed by employers who are individual persons (physical persons), handicraft workshops and private industrial firms. They also apply to foreign-owned small-scale productive firms and to Polish-foreign joint ventures (see para. 42).

F. The structure of the Labour Code

88. The Labour Code is composed of 15 Sections, namely:
  I. General Provisions (Articles 1–21);
 II. Individual Employment Relationship (Articles 22–77);
III. Remuneration and other Benefits (Articles 78–93);
 IV. Duties of Employers and Workers (Articles 94–113);
  V. Workers' Material Liability (Articles 114–127);
 VI. Hours of Work (Articles 128–151);
VII. Paid Leave (Articles 152–173);
VIII. Protection of Women's Work (Articles 176–189);
 IX. Employment of Young Workers (Articles 190–206);
  X. Occupational Safety and Health (Articles 207–237);
 XI. Collective Agreements (Articles 238–241, as amended in 1986);
XII. Settlement of Individual Labour Disputes (Articles 242–265 as amended in 1985);

XIII. Liability for Infringements of Workers' Rights (Articles 281–283);
XIV. Limitation of Claims (Articles 291–295);
 XV. Final Provisions (Articles 296–305);

G. Other labour laws

89. Besides the Labour Code, other important Labour Laws are in force:
– Law of 17 December 1974 on cash social security allowances in cases of sickness and maternity (uniform text after amendments in Journal of Laws No. 30/1983, item 143);
– Law of 12 June 1975 on allowances in cases of work accidents and occupational diseases (uniform text after amendments in Journal of Laws No. 30/1983, item 144);
– Law of 25 September 1981 on self-management in state enterprises (Journal of Laws No. 24, item 123);
– Law of 6 March 1981 on State Labour Inspection (uniform text in Journal of Laws No. 54/1985, item 276);
– Law of 8 October 1982 on trade unions, as amended in 1985 (uniform text in Journal of Laws No.54/1985, item 276);
– Law of 24 June 1983 on social labour inspection (Journal of Laws No. 35, item 163);
– Law of 26 January 1984 on workplace remuneration systems (Journal of Laws No. 5, item 25);
– Laws No. 5, item 25), amendment in June 1988 (Journal of Laws No. 20/1988);
Laws No. 20, item 85);
– Law of 16 September 1982 on the legal position of employees of the state administration (Journal of Laws No. 31, item 214);
– Law of 24 November 1986 on collective agreements (Journal of Laws No. 42, item 201);

§4. ORDINANCES AND RESOLUTIONS OF THE COUNCIL OF MINISTERS

90. In addition to the Labour Code and other laws, other sources of Labour Law include executive provisions, *i.e.* Ordinances and Resolutions of the Council of Ministers and ministerial ordinances and orders issued on the basis of the Labour Code or other laws. The characteristic feature of these executive provisions is the fact that:
1. they are issued upon the authorisation of the Labour Code or other laws;
2. the regulations they contain must not exceed the limits set forth by that authorisation;
3. their purpose is the implementation of provisions of the Labour Code or other laws.
There is a substantial number of executive provisions to the Labour Code (about 50).

Ordinances and Resolutions of the Council of Ministers are issued in agreement with all the All-Poland Trade Union Alliance (OPZZ), while orders and ordinances of individual ministers – in agreement with the nationwide trade union Federation.

§5. THE 1980 SOCIAL AGREEMENTS

91. In the Autumn of 1980, as a result of justified workers' protests, nationwide Social Agreements were concluded in Gdańsk, Szczecin and Jastrzębie (Silesia) between the Government Commission and the Strike Committees. Besides social and labour questions, the Agreements involved economic and political matters of national concern. In the Polish theory of law those Agreements are defined as political acts from which legal effects result – in this sense they are, therefore, characterised as a source of Labour Law.

The Polish state authorities declare themselves being durably bound by the provisions of the 1980 Agreements. Also, the new trade unions that emerged after 1982 refer to those Agreements in their organisation and programmes; they describe themselves as 'heirs of the 1980 Social Agreements'. There are controversies between the government and the political opposition as to the extent to which the Agreements have been implemented.

§6. BRANCH COLLECTIVE AGREEMENTS

92. Collective agreements constitute specific sources of law appropriate for the Labour Law. The Law of 24 November 1986 on collective agreements defines the legal position, contents, parties, procedure for negotiating and concluding, the rules of operation and termination of collective agreements. The law amended a respective section of the Labour Code.

In 1987 collective agreements concluded between 1976 and 1980 are still in force and negotiations aiming at the conclusion of new collective agreements are under way. The validity of old agreements is unwillingly accepted by the new trade unions – those agreements having been concluded by the old unions, *i.e.* those existing prior to 1980, with which the new unions, which emerged after 1982, do not identify themselves. Moreover, the old agreements are not appropriate to the new economic situation and do not reflect conditions of economic reform. In 1987 77 collective agreements concluded prior to 1980, as well as 1,020 supplementary protocols, remained in force.

93. The functions of collective agreements in Poland have undergone considerable transformation over the past 40 years. It can be claimed generally that, prior to the 1974 codification of Labour Law, when labour legislation consisted of numerous, disparate legal acts, collective agreements were the main instrument for the modernisation of Labour Law, its adaptation to the needs of current practice, the experimental introduction of new legal institutions later frequently extended, and for shaping an objectively justified differentiation of Labour Law. Thus, during the pre-codification period, as a result of the shortcomings of labour legislation, collective agreements were perhaps burdened with excessive responsibility, exceeding the fuctions normally performed. The Labour Code has defined the functions and status of collective agreements, limiting their contents to wages and conditions of work connected with the specific characteristics of the particular branch of work or occupation. The Law of 24 November 1986 on collective agreements slightly enlarged the functions and contents of branch collective agreements. (See Chapter X: Collective agreements.)

§7. INTERNAL RULES OF EMPLOYMENT

A. General characteristics

94. The internal rules of employment are acts effective within an enterprise, issued at the level and on the scale of the enterprise, concerning internal order and the procedures to be observed within it.

The legal character of internal rules of employment is not clearly determined. Different views are to be found in legal doctrine. One view sees internal rules as a normative act, because of the fact that they contain regulations of the actions and behaviour to be observed by both workers and management. However, according to other views, the source of the legal force of internal rules, similarly to other occuring in the civil law sphere is a contract concluded as a result of the notification by the enterprise of the rules to every newly-engaged worker – *i.e.* their alleged acceptance. The employment rules play an important part in ensuring order in the workplace, the correct performance of work by the workers' collective, and the observance of workers' rights. The laying down of rules for both management and workers prevents conflict and arbitrary managerial decisions.

Internal employment rules are obligatory in every enterprise employing at least 50 workers except for state offices, institutions, and certain enterprises of a special nature.

B. Contents of internal rules of employment

95. The subjects which can be regulated by internal works rules are restricted to matters of organisation and order in the enterprise; moreover, the rules must be based on the effective legal provisions. According to Article 104 of the Labour Code and the implementing provisions,[1] internal employment rules establish internal order and the procedures to be observed within an establishment and prescribe the duties of the management and of workers is connection with the performance of work. In the latter instance – concerning the duties of management and of workers, the internal rules do not lay down these duties independently, but notify the workers, in a form adapted to the needs of specific jobs, of the duties resulting from the provision of Labour Law.

1. See Order of the Council of Ministers of 20 December 1974 on internal rules of employment and on justification of absence from work and days off (Journal of Laws No. 49, item 299), subsequently amended.

96. The matters required to be defined by the internal employment rules include:

1. the hours and times of beginning and ending work;
2. the starting and ending of work for each shift and for individual groups of workers (including young people and other workers availing themselves of reduced working time) and the procedure for alternation of shifts;
3. breaks in work;
4. an 8-hour night;
5. the duty and method of confirmation by the worker of his/her arrival and presence at work;
6. the methods of safeguarding working rooms and tools after the end of the working day;
7. the conditions of the workers' presence during overtime;
8. the requirements concerning the maintenance of order and cleanliness at the workplace;
9. the procedure for justifying absence from and lateness to work, the granting of time off from work and of leave with the indication of entitled persons, as well as the principles for replacing absent workers and keeping their records;
10. the prohibition of admitting workers in a state of drunkenness;
11. the procedure for acquainting workers with the provisions concerning occupational safety and health and the provisions relating to fire prevention, as well as the regulations concerning restrictions on smoking at work.

Moreover, the provisions concerning internal employment rules require that the rules mention the basic duties of workers and the most glaring forms of their violation. The rules must also inform the workers of the penalties specified by the Labour Code for the violation of labour discipline and order. Finally, the rules must define the principles of implementation by the establishment of basic duties, namely:

1. the allotment of work;
2. the organisation of work and the supply of indispensable tools and materials;
3. providing working and protective clothing and other protective apparatus, and they must contain information on:
1. the date, place, and time of paying remuneration;
2. the types of work at which, according to the respective lists, it is not permissible to employ women and juveniles;
3. the place and time of receiving workers by the manager of the establishment.

In addition, the works rules may also establish certain other provisions concerning the organisation of work.

C. Procedure for establishing internal rules of employment

97. In enterprises where a workers' self-management organ operates, the internal rules of employment are decided on the initiative of the manager by the workers' council. Article 24 of the Law of 25 September 1981 on self-management of state enterprises ranges that resolution among the basic decisive competences of the workers' council. The plan of the regulations is drafted by the enterprise manager in agreement with the local trade union organisation. In establishments where there is no workers' self-management, internal rules of employment are determined by the manager in agreement with the local trade union organisation. The internal rules of employment must be approved, to ensure their compliance with the law, by the superior of the enterprise. So approved, internal rules become effective two weeks after the workers have been notified about them. The notification of the workers regarding the internal employment rules occurs by posting them in an exposed place or in any other approved way. Moreover, every newly-engaged worker must, before taking up work, be notified about the internal employment rules.

§8. WORKPLACE COLLECTIVE AGREEMENTS AND OTHER WORKPLACE LEVEL STANDARDS

98. Workplace collective agreements are concluded in enterprises which are economically sound and possess the financial resources to meet the obligations resulting from such agreements. Agreements are concluded by the director of the enterprise (after he has sought the opinion of the workers' council and obtained a positive opinion of the general meeting of workers) and by the workplace trade union organisations (See Chapter XIII).

99. Workplace wages agreements are concluded in enterprises and establishments which meet the requirements defined by the Law of 26 January 1984 on workplace remuneration system (See Chapter IX).

100. The issuing of other workplace level standards, called 'local standards' is admitted and frequently applied in the enterprises and establishments. Usually, such standards are issued by the director (after consulting the self-management bodies) in agreement with the workplace trade union organisation.

§9. INTERPRETATION OF LABOUR LAW

A. Interpretation by the Council of State

101. According to Art. 60 of the Constitution of the Polish People's Republic, the Council of State is the organ determining the generally applicable interpretation of laws. Special provisions stipulate that 'the function of laying down a generally binding interpretation of laws consists in the explanation of the content of a provision of a legal act whenever it is indispensable for the understanding and application of this provision in a way corresponding to its design and principles, the implementation of which shall serve the respective legal act'.

The rules concerning the establishment of a binding interpretation of laws also refer to international agreements ratified by Poland. In carrying out the function of establishing a binding interpretation of laws, the Council of State aims at strengthening socialist law and order and increasing the clarity of the law and its concordance with the legal awareness of the society. Questions of the interpretation of a legal act are examined by the Council of State either *ex officio*, or on the proposal of the President of the Council of Ministers, the First President of the Supreme Court and the Public Prosecutor General, and also – in the field of the Labour Law – nationwide trade union representatives. The Council of State can specify instances in which a proposal regarding interpretation may be dealt with by the Secretarial Office of the Council of State, with the authorisation of the latter to inform the petitioner for what reasons his/her proposal does not qualify for further processing. Resolutions of the Council of State determining the binding interpretation of laws must be published in *Monitor Polski*, an official Journal.

B. Interpretation by other organs

102. In practice, the most numerous acts in interpretation in the sphere of Labour Law are those issued by authorised central organs. The Minister of Labour and Social Policy acting in agreement with the nationwide trade union movement is competent to issue acts of interpretation, *i.e.* to give explanations in the field of Labour Law and social security. These interpretations are published in the *Official Journal* of the Ministry of Labour and Social Policy. The acts of interpretation issued by the Minister of Labour and Social Policy (in agreement with the trade unions) do not constitute binding interpretations of law and are not obligatory for the organs of justice, but they do have a considerable impact on the application of Labour Law by the state administration and by enterprises.

C. Judicial interpretation

103. The interpretation of law laid down by the Supreme Court in the form of guidelines for interpretation and court practice, of explanations and decisions in legal questions, often entered into the so-called *Book of Legal Principles* of the Supreme Court, is of major importance for the judiciary in labour disputes.

The guidelines for interpretation of the law and for court practice are resolutions passed by the bench of the Labour and Social Security Chamber, by joint chambers, or by the Bench of the Supreme Court – for the purpose of unifying rulings of all courts and other organs whose rulings fall under the supervision of the Supreme Court. The guidelines are published in the official journal *Monitor Polski*. The violation of a guideline by any court may become the basis for the repeal or change of the decision.

Explanations of legal provisions that arouse doubts, or whose application has produced discrepancy in rulings, are provided by groups of seven judges, by the bench of the Labour and Social Security Chamber, by joint chambers, or by the Bench of the Supreme Court.

Decisions in the legal questions arousing legal doubts in a concrete case are taken by groups of three, five or seven judges, or by the Bench of the Labour and Social Security Chamber.

Resolutions of the Bench of the Supreme Court, of the bench of joint chambers, or by the bench of a single chamber acquire with the moment of their passing the status of legal principles. A seven-judge group may decide to impart to its resolution the status of a legal principle. Legal principles are recorded *ex officio* in the *Book of Legal Principles* of the Supreme Court. Legal principles are binding for all the ruling benches at the Supreme Court. The abandonment of a legal principle requires a new decision by way of a resolution of the Labour and Social Security Chamber, of joint chambers, or of the Bench of the Supreme Court.

104. Legal Practice. Interpretations of the Supreme Court reached according to the usual procedure of judicial supervision, *i.e.* decisions of this court as a court of second instance or as a court of appeal in individual cases examined by it are binding only in the given case (unless laid down in the form of Legal Principles). Actually, however, both Supreme Court judgments and the decisions of provincial labour and social security courts affect the application of Labour Law in Poland. The guidelines, explanations, and selected judgments of the Supreme Court are published officially as a Collection of *Judgments of the Supreme Court, Civil Chamber, and Chamber of Labour and Social Security,* issued by the Supreme Court. Selected judgments of the provincial labour and social security courts are usually published by the periodicals of Law and Labour problems. Judgments of the Supreme Court and provincial courts containing theses of basic importance or of a controversial nature usually become the subject of an approving or critical interest by scholars of the Labour Law (glosses).

D. Scholarly interpretation

105. Scholarly interpretation by scholars – Labour Law experts – is not binding, but its influence is considerable because of the authority of jurisprudence. Scholarly interpretation is expressed in theoretical monographs, university handbooks and commentaries in which no concrete case is involved, as well as in analyses of concrete cases and decisions in the form of glosses published in legal and social periodicals: *State and Law (Państwo i*

Prawo), *New Law* (*Nowe Prawo*), *Labour and Social Security* (*Praca i Zabezpieczenie Społeczne*), *Workers' Service* (*Służba Pracownicza*), *Law and Life* (*Prawo i Życie*), *Trade Unionist* (*Związkowiec*), and in a special publication for glosses (*OSPIKA*).

§10. Basic Rules of Labour Law Interpretation

A. Rules of interpretation

106. According to Art. 7 of the Labour Code

'Labour Law provisions shall be interpreted and applied in accordance with the principles of the socialist system and goals of the Polish People's Republic'.

In this way the Code states the superiority of the principles and objectives of Poland as a socialist country, for the main part set down by the Constitution, for Labour Law.

B. Rules of community life

107. Article 8 of the Labour Code sets down the limits of implementation of a subjective right in the field of labour, *i.e.* criterion of qualifying one's action or behaviour as a correct exercise of one's right, or an abuse of the right. These limits are identical with those previously defined in Art. 5 of the Civil Code and with Art. 90 of the Constitution. According to Art. 8 of the Labour Code

'No person may avail himself/herself of a right if its exercise would be contrary to the social and economic intent of that right or to the rules governing the life of the community of the Polish People's Republic. No such act or omission shall be regarded as an exercise of right, nor shall it enjoy protection'.

The content of these rules is not defined by the law but is formed by legal practice in the process of developing socialist relations in Poland. Some of them are formulated by Supreme Court decisions or by jurisprudence.

C. Rules governing the relation between provisions of Labour Code and laws, collective agreements, and individual labour contracts

108. According to Art. 18 of the Labour Code, provisions of an individual labour contract or other legal act establishing an employment relationship (appointment, nomination, election, or a co-operative labour contract) shall comply with provisions of the Labour Law, *i.e.* above all with the Labour Code. Any provisions of such contracts and acts less favourable to the worker than provisions of the law are null and void – the provisions of the Law are applied instead. The question – not settled by the Code – whether and to what extent individual contracts may be more favourable to the workers than the Labour Code – is a controversial problem.

109. Article 240 of the Labour Code (in the wording of the Law of 24 November 1986 on collective agreements) states that

'The provisions of a collective agreement should conform with the provisions of law and with the social and economic policy of the state laid down by Parliament in national socio-economic plans'.

At the same time

'A collective agreement may prescribe in a wider and more advantageous way the rights of workers determined generally and uniformly in provisions of the Code or in other regulations if this is justified by specific conditions of the work or profession, or if it results from the authorisation of the Code or other regulations'.

Thus, a collective agreement can be more favourable than the general legislation, but cannot be less favourable (conformity with law is required).

§11. INTERNATIONAL SOURCES OF LABOUR LAW

110. International agreements and conventions concluded and ratified by Poland are also a source of Labour Law; they apply through internal legislation.
In 1977 Poland ratified the United Nations International Covenant on Economic, Social and Cultural Rights. Poland has ratified 74 conventions of the International Labour Organisation.

111. Poland is a party to a chain of bilateral agreements binding the European socialist countries, such as the 1948 agreement with the Czechoslovak Republic on cooperation in social policy and administration, the 1957 agreement with the German Democratic Republic on cooperation in social policy and social security, the 1961 agreement with Hungary and subsequent agreement with Bulgaria on cooperation in social policy, and the 1958 agreement with Yugoslavia on cooperation in social policy and social security.

112. The Polish system of Private International Law[1] contains the following rules regarding the employment relationship:

'The parties to an employment relationship may submit it to the law of their choice, provided the law is connected with this relationship. In cases when the parties have not made this choice of law, the employment relationship must be submitted to the law of the state in which the parties have their permanent residence or headquarters. If work is, has been or should be performed in the employer's enterprise, the headquarters of the enterprise is decisive instead of the employer's residence or seat. If the parties reside or are located in different states and have not made their choice of the law – then the law of the state, where work is, has been or should be performed is applicable'.

1. Articles 32–33 of the Law of 12 November 1965 on Private International Law (Journal of Laws No. 46, item 290).

Part I. The Individual Employment Relationship

Chapter IV. Definitions, Notions and Concepts

§1. THE INDIVIDUAL EMPLOYMENT RELATIONSHIP

A. Content of an employment relationship

113. On becoming a party to an individual employment relationship a worker is committed to carry out work of a specific kind for the establishment while the establishment is committed to employ the worker for remuneration. As per the definition adopted in the theory of Labour Law in Poland, the content of the employment relationship is the personal performance by the worker of labour in a continuous manner, under the supervision of the employing establishment, on its behalf and at its risk, for the remuneration due from it. The individual performance of work by the worker in a continuous manner while remaining throughout that time under the management of the superior – these are the elements differentiating an employment relationship from a legal relationship of civil law arising on the basis of a commission or a contract to perform a specific task or work.

114. An employment relationship has the character of a civil relationship of obligations, for each party has simultaneously both rights and duties. However, it has specific features, exceeding civil law obligations, for in addition to content involving property it also contains a number of moral elements reflecting the social usefulness of work, protection of the worker as the economically weaker party, the worker's dignity, the right to professional career, etc. A specific feature of the employment relationship is that the obligations of both parties are neither closely equivalent, nor conditioned by the obligation of the other party, *e.g.* the work establishment is bound to ensure safe working conditions regardless of whether workers perform their duties. A specific feature of the employment relationship is also the fact that, besides specifying obligations, it includes elements involving the sphere of collective labour relations – *e.g.* the right to associate in trade unions, the right to have a share in the management of the work establishment by means of employee self-management, the obligation to observe the rules of loyal cooperation within larger workers' groups, and the like.

115. The content of the employment relationship consists of the performance of work for remuneration. The nature of that performance differs depending on whether simple or complex work is involved, executive or managerial work; as a matter of fact, in Polish Labour Law there are no distinct divisions into types of work according to such criteria (the previously existing legal division into manual and non-manual work was finally eliminated from the content of law from the moment at which the Labour Code became effective (1975)).

B. Subordinated work and principle of risk of the establishment

116. The employment relationship consists in subordinated work. The worker acts within the framework of the internal order in force at the work establishment and complies with instructions given by those persons authorised to direct the work process on behalf of the work establishment (the management). The character of the subordination and its limits are defined by law by placing the worker under the obligation to comply with managerial directives regarding labour. The subordination of the worker and the rights of management resulting therefrom involve the labour process and, as a rule, is limited to that range of work laid down in the contract of employment.

The subordination of the worker means that he is not solely responsible for the effects of his work and cannot bear the negative effects resulting from the managerial operations of his superiors. He should, however, take as a rule advantage of the positive effects of the work establishment's operation by means of a properly devised remuneration system. Polish Labour Law recognises the principle that the worker does not bear risk connected with the activities of the enterprise; this is the principle of the work establishment's risk.

C. Concept of partnership groups (brigades)

117. The new concept of partnership groups (brigades) emerged in 1985–1988 favoured by Poland's economic and political authorities. According to this concept workers are encouraged to organise themselves in groups (brigades), chaired by elected leaders. Such groups, being independent production units, take up concrete production tasks on the basis of 'contracts on final result' concluded with managements of enterprises, which on their turn have to ensure means of production and necessary raw materials. The group (brigade) is autonomous as ways, forms and organisation (for instance hours of work) applied for completion of the agreed task are concerned. The group (brigade) shares autonomously the remuneration due for completion of agreed production task among its members, according to their individual share of work; this system results in considerable increase of gains of efficient workers. In the same time the group (brigade) takes full responsibility for non-completion of the agreed task – in that case no remuneration at all or solely minimal remuneration is due to its members. Thus, the concept of partnership groups does not comply with traditional principles of subordinated work and risk of the employer, remaining in force in Poland.

In 1988 about two per cent of the total of workers employed in Poland have been organised in partnership groups; exceptionally in construction industry this part was seventeen per cent. The legal status of the partnership group, (brigade) as well as the legal position of workers – members of the group, were not defined; however the existence of the Recommendation of the Minister of Labour, Wages and Social Affairs of 21 August 1985 on rules of group organisation of work in state enterprises – has to be mentioned, as a not binding advisory material. The implementation of the groups' system is entirely voluntary. Economists generally emphasise advantages connected with the brigades work system; a dramatic rise of work's efficiency and, on the other hand, radical and justified increase of workers' earnings. The emergence of brigades system is sometimes defined as a kind of Labour Law flexibility phenomenon in the socialist country. However, many controversies arise around this concept and little theoretical support is given to it by most of labour law scholars; trade unions so far do not take position in this matter. In 1988 it is difficult to formulate any prognosis as to the extent of future development of this system in Poland.

D. Legal bases of the employment relationship

118. The employment relationship arises on the following legal bases:
– the contract of employment, which in Poland is the prevailing basis for the arising of a labour relationship, regulated in detail by the Labour Code;
– appointment, pertaining to work establishment managers and their deputies and to other persons specified by the law.[1] A specific procedure regulates the appointment of state enterprise directors:[2] they are appointed after a process of competition (see para. 177);
– nomination, embracing executive functionaries of state[3] and, by virtue of special provisions, judges, prosecuting attorneys, militia functionaries and other employees, railway and postal workers, as well as teachers and professors of universities and of the Polish Academy of Sciences;
– election to managerial functions of social and political organisations, trade unions, cooperative organisations; the acceptance of election produces the establishment of the employment relationship for a specified period of time. An employment relationship established by election is dissolved with the moment of extinction of the mandate. Throughout the performance of elective functions the employment relationship with the enterprise at which the elected person worked prior to the election continues. The Labour Code provides for unpaid leave[4] for the duration of performance of the functions resulting from election, and the right to return to previous employment on the cessation of the mandate;
– a cooperative contract of employment involving a labour relationship between the cooperative and its member; this contract is governed by Art. 77 of the Labour Code and by the Cooperative Law.[5]

1. Ordinance of the Council of Ministers of 20 November 1974 regarding definition of managerial positions held by persons employed on the basis of appointment (Journal of Laws No. 45 of 1974, as amended in the Journal of Laws No. 4/1976, item 22).
2. Articles 34–37 of the Law of 25 September 1981 on state enterprises (Journal of Laws No. 24/1981, item 122, as subsequently amended).
3. Law of 16 September 1982 on state administration functionaries (Journal of Laws No. 30/1982, item 214, as amended in the Journal of Laws No. 35/1984, item 187).
4. Ordinance of the Council of Ministers of 20 September 1974 regarding principles for granting leave without pay to workers called by election to the preformance of functions in social organisations (Journal of Laws No. 37/1974, item 218).
5. Articles 181–203 of the Law of 16 September 1982 – the Cooperative Law (Journal of Laws No. 30/1982, item 210, as amended in the Journal of Laws No. 39/1983, item 176).

E. The principle of freedom to work

119. The institution of an individual employment relationship, irrespective of its legal basis, requires the declared consent of the establishment and of the worker. The principle of the freedom to work in Poland was thus formulated in Labour Law theory. Although the Introduction to the Labour Code quotes Art. 19 of the Constitution of the Polish People's Republic that work in Poland is 'a basic right, duty and matter of honour of every citizen', the generally adopted theoretical interpretation is that we may speak merely of a moral duty, not a legal one; this interpretation continues to be in force. Freedom to work also involves a free choice of the type, place and time of work.

120. Certain new elements emerged in this connection with the entry into force of what is known as the 'parasite-control law'.[1] This law requires men aged 18 to 45 who have had no job for the previous three months and who are not students to explain the reasons why they neither work nor study. Persons embraced by this law who do not submit convincing evidence in this respect are entered on a list of persons avoiding work; this creates the possibility that they may be required to perform some public or community work for up to two months in a year. Such work may be organised in the event of *force majeure* or elemental disaster seriously endangering normal living conditions of all the population or part of thereof.

In accordance with the official view that law is not incompatible with the general principle of freedom to work, as its purpose is to arouse in demoralised persons the motivation to voluntarily take up employment, while the work that this law admits within a limited scope is not work performed within the framework of an employment relationship. This law has aroused controversial opinions in Poland.

1. The Law of 26 October 1982 on procedures applicable to persons avoiding work (Journal of Laws No. 35/1982, item 229).

§2. The Worker

121. The term 'worker' refers to a person employed on the basis of an individual contract of employment, appointment, election, or nomination, or a cooperative contract of employment (see para. 118).

122. A worker may be any person who has reached the age of eighteen years. The young person *i.e.* persons who have reached the age of fifteen years but are not over the age of eighteen years may be employed on condition that they have completed at least their basic schooling and present a medical certificate confirming that work of a particular kind presents no risk to their health. The employment of young persons should, with some exceptions, have vocational training as its objective; the legal status of such workers embraces many elements of the status of student. Exceptionally, a person not yet fifteen years of age but over fourteen years and who has completed basic schooling may – on the request of a legal representative – be employed for the purpose of learning a profession; the aim is to avoid a situation in which a young person would already have finished school and be without work, which he might not yet be allowed to undertake. Besides such exceptional situations the employment of persons who have not yet reached fifteen years of age is prohibited.

123. A person who is limited in his capacity to effect legal transactions may become a party to an individual employment relationship and effect any legal transactions connected with that relationship without the approval of a legal representative. However, if the employment relationship is not consistent with that person's welfare, his legal representative may terminate the relationship after obtaining the permission of the court of wards. This rule concerns both minors in the meaning of the Civil Code, possessing limited capacity to enter legal transactions and adults partially legally incapacitated. Indeed, a legal representative of a minor is not entitled to undertake on his behalf any engagements involving an employment relationship.

§3. The Work Establishment

124. The term 'work establishment' refers to an organisational unit employing workers, including a unit not possessing legal personality. More particularly it refers to a state enterprise or any other organisational unit, cooperative or social organisation. Most work establishments in Poland are state enterprises, however, in view of the existence of other organisational units employing workers, it has become customary in the labour law to use a wider term, namely, work establishment, to refer to the employing party.

Attention should be drawn to the fact that in Polish legal language the term 'employer' is used as a rule to indicate a physical person employing workers.[1] An example of such a situation is the employment of domestic help in a household.

1. See Art. 299 of the Labour Code and the Ordinance of the Council of Ministers of 20 November 1974 regarding employment relationships in which the employer is a physical person (Journal of Laws No. 45/1974, item 272).

125. Polish labour law does not clearly specify the legal effects resulting from the employment relationship of the organisational-legal changes occuring in a work establishment (*e.g.* its division or merger). It is believed that such changes do not cause, nor do they justify, immediate termination of employment contracts with workers, nor do they abolish protection against dismissal with notice; only a complete liquidation of the work establishment abolishes protection of workers against dismissal. The effect of bankruptcy of the enterprise on workers' situation is specified by the provisions on bankruptcy.[1]

1. See Law of 29 June 1983 on the soundmaking (improvement) of the economy of state enterprise and on bankruptcy (Journal of Laws No. 36, item 165).

§4. The Director of the Establishment

126. Legal transactions connected with an individual employment relationship are effected on behalf of the establishment by the director of the establishment or by some other worker empowered for this purpose. Where reference is made by law to the director of an establishment, this is construed as including any other persons empowered to act on behalf of the establishment in any particular respect. Thus, for the performance of a legal action involving an employment relationship, the declaration of will of one person is sufficient; however, in state enterprises, in instances involving property, the rule is joint action by two persons. The authority of the director of a work establishment pertaining to matters other than the employment relationship is regulated by the Civil Code, by the Law of 25 September 1981 on state enterprises, by the Law of 29 June 1983 on the improvement of the economy of state enterprise and on bankruptcy, and by other provisions.

127. The director of an establishment represents the latter in relation to its staff of workers and acts on behalf of the establishment in accordance with the principle that managerial responsibility is vested in a single person. This principle, formulated in Art. 4 of the Labour Code, is considered to be the fundamental principle of operation of a scioalist work establishment. Since 1981 however, this principle must be interpreted with the modifications resulting from the provisions on enterprise self-management (see Chapter XV).

Chapter V. The Economic Reform of Mid-1980s and Employment Policy (Right to Work)

128. The employment relationship is a form of realisation of the right to work guaranteed by Articles 19 and 68 of the Polish Constitution. The right to work cannot, however, be claimed through the judiciary. To that right corresponds the obligation of the state to observe an adequate socio-economic policy; Art. 10 §1 and §3 of the Labour Code make this precise in the following way:

'Citizens of the Polish People's Republic shall be assured of work through the constant and comprehensive development of the national economy and a rational employment policy ... Competent state organs shall assist citizens in finding employment corresponding to their vocational skills'.

An element of the right to work is also protection against unfair dismissal.

129. Prior to 1981, that is before the introduction of economic reform, the state's policy of full employment consisted of a centrally elaborated balance of man-power demand and labour suppply; and further of influencing the employment policy of work establishments by administrative measures, by means of employment and wages fund quotas, and also by other measures meant to shape the planned distribution of the labour supply.

The situation on the labour market in Poland has for a long time been one of increased demand for labour and its not insignificant shortage; however, in certain regions of the country, there is a small labour surplus, particularly women's labour. Simultaneously there exists underemployment (overmanning) at work establishments, *i.e.* the under-utilisation of labour and the tolerance of persons the employment of whom is not justified either by the needs of the work establishment or by their suitability, but merely by social considerations (family situation, status of health, etc.).

130. The economic reform introduced in the 1980s led to essential changes in the principles of operation of the economy, ensuring to enterprises autonomy, self-management and self-financing. Autonomy and self-financing mean that enterprises are free to decide on the extent of employment, the hiring of workers and their dismissal (with the observance of the provisions of Labour Law). In 1983–1986 the previous administrative measures applied to work establishments – namely quotas (para. 129) were replaced by economic mechanisms, including the levying from work establishments of payments depending on the sums spent on wages – for the Vocational Activation State Fund[1] (the role of those payments was somewhat similar to a tax on employment). Since 1986, the situation changed in that sense that a tax on extra-normative employment has been established, replacing payments for the Vocational Activation State Fund, which is now financed by state donations. Thus, even with progressing of the economic reform in Poland, the authorities do not renounce the exercising of an economic pressure on enterprises in order to discourage the excessive employment.

The Vocational Activation State Fund is intended for the financing of:

a. vocational training, including that of temporarily unemployed persons,
b. the creation of additional jobs where there are no other possibilities for the employment of jobless persons, of those changing work, and of partially handicapped persons and invalids,
c. local emergency projects organised for creating additional work projects,
d. the development of a system of information for employment services and vocational advice,
e. benefits for temporarily unemployed persons.

> 1. See the Law of 29 December 1983 on the Vocational Activation State Fund (Journal of Laws No. 75/1983, item 334) as subsequently amended.

131. Those entitled to the benefits due to the temporarily jobless are persons able to work and ready to assume it, registered at an appropriate employment exchange, within seven days of registration, if the person concerned has no job and there are no suitable work opportunities available, or if he attends vocational training. Such benefit is not due to a person who has refused the offer of a job for the performance of which he has adequate vocational preparation, or the offer of some adequate substitute work, or a proposal for vocational training essential for obtaining work.

132. The economic reform provides, therefore, that autonomous, self-financing enterprises observe rational employment policy, dismissing superfluous or unsuitable workers (despite the continuing ideological controversy as to whether a socialist country may allow the existence of a labour reserve, *i.e.* limited unemployment, or whether this is inadmissible for ideological reasons). Such moves are also required by the 'improvement programmes' adopted by enterprises on the basis of the Law of 29 June 1983 on the improvement (sound-making) of the economy of state enterprises and on bankruptcy. However, as of the mid-1980s reductions' programmes had not been observed and there continues to be a labour shortage. Work establishments are often unwilling to dismiss superfluous workers fearing that when the economic situation improves and they need more labour, they will be unable to find workers as there will then be a manpower shortage on the labour market. Moreover, trade unions adopt an unfavourable attitude to far-reaching dismissals. Some see the system of protection of workers against unfair dismissals provided for in the Labour Code as an obstacle to necessary reductions; there are plans *de lege ferenda* that, in the case of dismissals within the scope of 'improvement programmes', it may be possible to disregard protection or substantially reduce this protection (these proposals are controversial).

133. The state organs in charge of employment policy are:
a. the Minister of Labour and Social Policy and

b. local employment and social affairs sections (at offices of the *voivodes*, city presidents and heads).

The operations undertaken by these organs include:

a. providing vocational advice and orientation;
b. providing an employment service; this entails collecting from work establishments information about posts available and notifying job-seekers about vacancies and directing them to such work establishments. Recourse to the employment service is voluntary. (During martial law compulsory employment service was instituted in about a dozen *voivodships*; the validity of that decision ceased late in 1985);
c. exchange of manpower resources (clearing);
d. employment of higher and vocational school graduates in accordance with a system enabling work establishments to secure graduates during their studies by allocating to them scholarship funds or by conclusion of preliminary contracts;[1] that system ensures graduates priority in securing work ahead of other persons seeking jobs.

Work establishments have special services dealing with workers' employment programmes.

> 1. See the Law of 14 December 1982 on employment of graduates (Journal of Laws No. 40/1982, item 267 as subsequently amended) and Ordinance of the Coucil of Ministers of 31 August 1983 regarding employment of graduates (Journal of Laws No. 53/1983, item 234).

134. Some categories of persons have the right to employment (which can be claimed through the court) or the right to priority in employment.

The right to employment is enjoyed by:
a. workers whose employment relationship has been ended due to their temporary arrest so long as they have reported for work within seven days of the date at which the quashing of the proceedings or acquittal was final;
b. war and military veterans;
c. occupational invalids or persons not fit for their present work due to accident at work or occupational illness but who are not invalids;
d. wives of servicemen in basic military service;
e. former servicemen released from basic military service.

The right of priority to employment is enjoyed by:
a. workers dismissed without notice through no fault of their own (see para. 167) after the reason of the dismissal has become inoperative;
b. workers dismissed without notice because of contagious disease after the danger of infection has ceased;
c. family members of workers who have died as the result of accident at work or who have become permanently disabled.

The right of priority does not impose on the work establishment a compulsory obligation to employ the person in question; if however, the establishment employs a new worker it has to be one with the right of priority to employment.

Chapter VI. Conclusion and Termination of the Employment Relationship

§1. THE CONTRACT OF EMPLOYMENT

A. General characteristics

135. The contract of employment is the most widely applied legal act constituting an individual employment relationship (the others are: appointment, election, nomination, and co-operative contract of employment). Along with the provisions of Labour Law, the general provisions of the Civil Code regarding contracts are also applicable respectively.

136. Contracts of employment may be concluded for a non fixed or fixed period. A contract of indefinite duration is the most frequently applied contract of employment; it may be terminated with notice given at any time by any of the parties. Fixed-term contracts are:
a. contracts of employment for a definite period – the duration of its validity is determined in advance by specifying a particular date or event (*e.g.* the return to work of another worker absent due to illness);
b. contracts of employment for a period required to carry out a specific piece of work – its termination is linked to the completion of the task.

137. The main characteristic of fixed-term contracts is their termination at the time determined beforehand and the limitation of the possibility of earlier termination by one of the parties.

The law does not provide for a situation in which, after termination of a fixed-term contract, another contract of the same type may be concluded with the worker. The judiciary adopted the thesis that the repeated conclusion of a fixed-term contract constitutes an improper attempt to avoid protective regulations against termination with notice and violated the worker's interests; it must be assumed that the new contract is one of indefinite duration.

The law does not indicate any maximum duration of validity for fixed-term contracts; it envisages, however, in the instance of contracts concluded for a period longer than six months, the admissibility of an agreement that such a contract may be terminated prior to its deadline, with two-weeks' notice. When a contract is concluded for a shorter period, or in the absence of such an agreement, unilateral immediate termination of the contract may occur only for important reasons (see below paras. 165 and 167).

138. Any of the contracts indicated above – both indefinite and fixed-term – may be preceded by a contract concluded for a trial period which shall not exceed two weeks or three months in the case of a worker holding a managerial or other independent post or a post involving material liability for the property entrusted to him. The purpose of a contract for a trial period is to confirm the suitability of a worker before permanently employing him.

In addition to providing for a trial period, the Labour Code introduced a new type in the form of a contract for an initial period which should be applied to workers taking up employment for the first time or who have not worked for at least one year in any establishment. Employment for a trial period and thereafter for an initial period should amount to a total of one year. However, the initial period contract is rarely applied in practice and it has been criticised in the literature as being purposeles. Its elimination from the Labour Code is expected during the process of the next Amendment.

B. Conclusion of a contract of employment

139. According to the Civil Code, a contract is considered to be concluded at the moment when the party making the offer receives a declaration of its acceptance or at the moment when the parties reach an understanding as to all those provisions which were the object of negotiation. The moment of conclusion of a contract of employment is not always identical with the moment of establishing the employment relationship, which may occur later. According to the Labour Code, the employment relationship is established on the date specified in the contract as the date of commencement of the work; and if no such date is specified, on the date on which the contract was concluded. The date of establishment of the employment relationship is of essential significance, for it is then that arise the mutual obligations of the parties; on the part of the worker the obligation to take up work, and on the part of the work establishment the obligation to create conditions enabling its performance.

140. A contract of employment must be concluded in writing. Where such a contract has not been concluded in writing, the work establishment should immediately provide the worker with a written confirmation of the nature and terms of the contract. In requiring a written form the Code does not, however, invalidate an unwritten one. Consequently, if there is no contract in writing and no written confirmation therof, the worker may take his claims involving the employment relationship before a court.

141. The contents of a contract of employment should include the essential elements for determining its character as a contract of employment. According to the Labour Code, a contract of employment must contain an explicit indication of the type and terms of the contract and should more particularly specify:
a. the nature of work and the date of its commencement;
b. the remuneration corresponding to the work;
c. the worker's obligation to observe order and labour discipline.
The contract of employment may also contain, in addition to its essential components, other provisions, for example regarding the site and hours of work; such provisions, inasmuch as they are *accidentalia negotii*, may undergo changes only with the consent of both parties to the contract.

The employment contract may also contain what is known as autonomous clauses which may be denounced by the parties while the contract of employment continues to remain in force.

142. The violation of provisions regarding the conclusion of contracts of employment does not cause the invalidation of the contract. In some instances, however, a contract concluded contrary to law is unconditionally invalid, *i.e.* in the event of employment of a minor under the age of 15 or of a person legally fully incapacitated without the consent of that person's statutory representative, and also in the event that the contract was designed to evade the law (Art. 58 of the Civil Code). In spite of the invalidity of the contract in the instances specified above, the period of actual performance of work under such a contract is treated as within the sphere of the worker's rights as if the relationship were based on a valid contract. This aims to avoid harming persons who have performed their labour duties even without a valid legal foundation.

C. Termination of a contract of employment

1. General traits

143. A contract of employment may be terminated:
1. by agreement between parties;
2. by a declaration of notice by either party;
3. by a declaration of either party without notice;
4. on the expiry of the period for which it was concluded;
5. on the date of completion of the task for which it was concluded.
A declaration by either party terminating a contract of employment either with or without notice should be made in writing. A declaration by the establishment terminating a contract of employment either with or without notice should include an indication of the legal remedies open to the worker.

2. Termination by agreement between the parties

144. Termination of a contract of employment may occur by the same method by which it was concluded, namely by agreement of the parties. Such agreement is possible at any time and may pertain both to contracts concluded for an indefinite period (also during the trial period and the initial period) and to contracts concluded for a definite period or for a period of completion of a definite task or job. Either party may initiate such an agreement – this is legally of no importance. The date of termination of the labour relationship depends entirely on the agreement between the parties.

3. Termination with notice

145. Either party may terminate with notice a contract concluded for an indefinite period, for a trial period, and for an initial period. The moment at which the termination with notice occurs shall be determined by means of two criteria:
a. the length of the period of notice,
b. the date of termination.

a. Periods of notice

146. The period of notice for a contract of employment concluded for a trial period not exceeding two weeks is three working days. The period of notice for such a contract with a worker holding a managerial or other independent post involving material liability for property entrusted to him – is two weeks. The period of notice for a contract concluded for an initial period is two weeks.

147. The length of the period of notice for a contract of employment concluded for an indefinite period depends on the length of the period of employment. The latter refers to work at the same establishment. It may include employment at a previous establishment if the worker changed his job as the result of agreement between the establishment concerned or on the recommendation of a higher level organisational unit, or in other cases prescribed by law.[1] The circumstances justifying the inclusion of periods of previous employment should be noted in the worker's certificate of employment (see para. 189). The period of notice is:
– two weeks if the worker has been employed for less than one year;
– one month if the worker has been employed for at least one year;
– three months if the worker has been employed for at least ten years.
The periods of termination indicated above are minimum periods which may be extended by way of a collective agreement or contract, but cannot be shortened.

1. See the Ordinance of the Council of Ministers of 20 September 1974 regarding inclusion of the previous employment into the duration of work on which depends the length of the period of notice (Journal of Laws No. 37/1974, item 216).

148. The dates of termination are: for a two week period of notice – a Saturday; for one- and three month periods of notice – the last day of the month.

149. During the period of notice a worker is entitled to time off with pay to look for a new job, namely two working days during a period of notice not exceeding one month and three working days during a three-month period of notice.

b. Justification of termination

150. Termination with notice by the establishment cannot be arbitrary. The constitutional right to work and to participation in the management of work establishments as well as personal and social considerations must protect the worker against loss of work. On the other hand, work establishments must have the possibility to regulate the composition of the workforce in a way compatible with the tasks required of them. The system of protection of the worker against unjustified termination with notice provided for in the Labour Code observes both these premises and provides conditions for harmonising the economic-organisational and social functions of that system.

In 1987–1988 in the framework of preparations to the second stage of economic reform in Poland, proposals were formulated, according to which the protection against unjustified dismissal should be reduced or entirely suspended in cases the dismissals were necessary as part of the 'soundmaking' (improvement) programmes of the economy of state enterprises. These proposals were controversial.

151. In view of the practical difficulties and varied trends in judicial interpretations of the term 'unjustified termination with notice', the Supreme Court in the full Bench of the Chamber of Labour and Social Security issued on 27 June 1985 directives for the interpretation of that term.[1] The principal theses of these directives are as follows:
– the principles of the system and the aims of the PPR shall be observed in the interpretation of the definition of 'unjustified termination';
– the assessment of the legitimacy of termination of a contract of employment should be made in consideration of the proper interests of the work establishment and of the values of the worker in the labour relationship. Other circumstances pertaining to the worker, having no connection with the labour relationship, may only in exceptional cases form the basis for the statement that termination with notice is incompatible with the rules governing life in the community;
– the circumstances favouring the protection of the worker against notice shall be considered only with regard to workers discharging conscientiously and carefully their duties and observing labour discipline;
– of decisive significance for recognition of the lawfulness of notice is the nature and importance of its cause. The importance of that cause may preclude the worker's reference to circumstances involving his own interests;
– with regard to workers holding managerial and independent positions stricter criteria for assessing and causes justifying notice are to be applied;
– improper performance of the worker's duties is a justified cause of notice not only when the worker is blame-worthy, but also when he is not. However, a single minor infringement of duties shall not as a rule justify notice of termination;
– the reduction of staff in a work establishment is a justifed reason for notice. The body examining workers' disputes is not qualified to examine the

justness and appropriateness of staff reductions. However, circumstances involving a worker's protection may be the reason that notice of termination of an employment contract in a specific case is considered as unjustified and incompatible with the rules governing life in the community;

– the justness of notice does not depend on a previous offer to the worker by the work establishment of another appropriate available job, unless such duty results from existing regulations;

– the reason for notice shall be genuine and specific.

Those directives of the Supreme Court are binding on the courts and must be respected by work establishments.

1. Published in the Rulings of the Supreme Court, the Civil and Administrative Chamber, and the Chamber of Labour and Social Security, No. 11/1985, item 164.

c. Trade union control

152. Termination with notice is subject to trade union control. The opinion expressed by trade unions in such cases is not binding on the work establishment (as is the case in most socialist countries). However, the viewpoint of the trade union is of a major influence on the final decision of the director of the establishment and, what is more, for the worker it constitutes a very important argument in any possible subsequent dispute before the labour court for recognising notice of termination as unjustified. The worker may desire to initiate a dispute in any instance when he considers the notice to be unjustified, regardless of whether the trade union was against the notice, or did not provide an opinion.

While the trade union view is not binding, it is obligatory to contact them according to proper procedure; and if the work establishment fails to do so, this gives to the worker the basis for voicing a claim that the notice was unlawful.

153. Termination is subject to the trade union control from the stage of the intention. When the director of an establishment intends to give notice of termination of a contract concluded for an indefinite period, he must inform the trade union in writing, with the indication of the reason for termination. If the union organisation considers termination to be unjustified it may, within five days of being informed thereof, notify the director of the establishment in writing of its reservations, with an indication of the reasons. If the director of the establishment does not take into account the reservations notified to him within the allotted time by the enterprise union organisation, he must submit the matter to the chairman of a higher level union organisation, who should express an opinion on the reservations within five days.

The director of the establishment has the right to take a final decision on termination with notice no earlier than at this stage, after examining the opinion expressed by the chairman of the superior union organisation or when such an opinion has not been received within the allotted time.

154. These procedures in cases of termination with notice of contracts of employment, laid down prior to the changes that occured in 1982 in the principles of operation and structure of trade unions (including the law on trade unions), currently entail difficulties regarding the range of participation of 'higher level union organisations' which – as present-day Federations – have lost the right to contradict the view expressed by enterprise union organisations. The modification of such procedures is under discussion.

d. Cases of persons particularly protected

155. A contract of employment cannot be terminated with notice with a worker who is on leave or absent for any other legitimate reason, *e.g.* because of sickness (provided that the period entitling the establishment to terminate the contract without notice has not yet expired).

156. Under the various provisions scattered in Labour Law, the termination with notice of a contract of employment shall not take place in the instance of the following categories of workers:
a. pregnant women, those on maternity leave, and those on the three-year child care leave;
b. workers serving as councillors on people's councils;
c. members of workers' councils (self-management organs in state enterprises);
d. social (voluntary) labour inspectors;
e. workers in military sevice;
f. wives of soldiers in military service;
g. war and military invalids;
h. any worker who is less than two years away from pensionable age.
In some of these situations notice may be issued in instances of the liquidation of the work establishment, for serious reasons, or after securing the consent of appropriate organs.

e. Cancellation of conditions

157. If the work establishment does not wish to continue to employ the worker on present conditions but merely wishes to change them, it may serve notice of cancellation of the contractual conditions of employment or remuneration. This is a legal operation of a complex plan whose principal aim is a change of the contract and whose secondary aim (in the event the worker does not consent to the change) is termination of the contract. As regards situations in which the cancellation can be applied, then the Directives of the

Full Bench of the Chamber of Labour of the Supreme Court, referred to in para. 151, read:

> 'Notice of changes in the conditions of employment or remuneration may be justified both by any reason which is also grounds for a termination with notice, or by any other reason adequate for cancellation of these conditions'.

158. Notice of cancellation of the conditions of employment or remuneration is deemed to have been given if proposals for new conditions have been made in writing to the worker – only then does the period of notice begin.

Where a worker refuses the proposed changes in conditions of employment or remuneration, his contract of employment shall be terminated on expiry of the period of notice. If, before half the period of notice has expired, he has not rejected the proposed conditions, he shall be deemed to have accepted them; the letter from the establishment giving notice of the cancellation should contain an indication to that effect. In the absence of any such indication the worker may announce his rejection of the proposed conditions at any time before the expiry of the period of notice.

No notice of cancellation is required in the event of the worker being entrusted, as the result of the needs of the establishment, with work other than that specified in his contract of employment for a period not exceeding three months in a calendar year, on condition that this does not involve loss of pay and corresponds to the worker's qualifications.

With some exceptions, the provisions on protection against termination with notice of contracts of employment are also applied to cancellation with notice of the conditions of employment or remuneration.

f. Legal effects of unjustified or unlawful termination with notice

159. Unjustified termination with notice of a contract of employment concluded for an indefinite period or violation of the rules governing termination with notice (non-application of the written form, non-observance of procedures for submitting the case to the trade union, and also dismissal of a worker covered by special protection) give the worker the right to take legal proceedings for unfair dismissal.

160. The legal effects of the claim differ depending on whether the verdict of the court is delivered:
– before the expiration of the period of notice: in such a case the declaration of the notice of termination is ruled to be without effect. The contract of employment is not terminated, the employment relationship goes on without interruption, and the worker suffers no loss in remuneration;
– after the expiration of the period of notice, when the contract of employment has already been terminated. In such a case the worker shall be

reinstated on previous conditions and losses suffered shall be compensated (see para. 161).

161. A worker resuming employment after being reinstated is entitled to remuneration for the period when he was not employed, subject to a maximum of two months' pay or, when the period of notice is three months' to a maximum of the month's pay. To a worker covered by special protection remuneration is payable for the entire period.

However, compensatory remuneration is reduced by the amount of any remuneration that the worker may have earned by taking up employment during the period in question in some other establishment.

162. An establishment may refuse to re-employ a worker who does not, within seven days of reinstatement, announce his readiness to resume work without delay, unless the foregoing time limit is exceeded for reasons beyond the worker's control.

A worker who has taken up employment in another establishment prior to reinstatement may terminate his contract of employment with that establishment within seven days of reinstatement without giving notice of termination but subject to a three-day warning.

163. Where a worker has resumed employment after reinstatement, his period of employment shall include any period for which he was not employed but for which he was granted remuneration; a period for which he was not granted remuneration is also to be reckoned as providing a basis to certain workers' rights.

4. Termination without notice (immediate termination)

a. General traits

164. The fundamental features of termination without notice applicable to both the work establishment and the worker are the following:
a. it is applicable to all kinds of contracts of employment;
b. it causes termination of a contract immediately after presentation of the declaration of will;
c. it may be applied solely in cases clearly provided for by the law;
d. specific rigours are in force regarding the periods at which it may be applied.
Generally speaking, immediate termination is the result of such misdemeanour on the part of the worker which renders his further employment to no avail, and also the effect of a lasting inability on the part of the worker to perform his work. The severe effects that immediate termination entails for a worker require intervention of the law to ensure workers protection against their immediate loss of job without sufficient cause, and also against the unfavourable consequences in the further career development of the worker

which in labour law are linked to immediate dismissal of a worker through his own fault (see below). This is why the list of justified reasons laid down by the law is of a limited nature.

b. Reasons justifying termination without notice

1. FAULT OF THE WORKER

165. An establishment is entitled to terminate a worker's contract of employment without notice if:
– the worker commits some serious violation of his basic duties as a worker and, more particularly, if he disturbs the order and peace of the workplace, is absent from work without justification, repeatedly makes products of poor quality,[1] reports for work in drunken state, drinks alcohol during working hours, or commits abuses in connection with receipt of social security allowances or other welfare benefits;
– the worker commits an offence that renders further employment at his post impossible, if the offence is evident or has been established by a judgment with the force of law;
– the worker ceases, through his own fault, to have the qualifications necessary for the preformance of his job.

  1. This reason results from Art. 6 of the Law of 8 February 1979 on the quality of products, services and construction units (Journal of Laws No. 2/1979, item 7).

166. Analysis of the reasons justifying termination without notice through the fault of the worker as provided for by law presents many difficulties in practice. Their interpretation is elaborated in numerous court rulings, but many doubts still remain.

Particularly requiring explanation is what constitutes a 'serious violation of the worker's basic duties'. Two problems arise here:
a. how to assess the extent of the worker's misdemeanour;
b. which of the worker's duties are fundamental.
In the first instance it has been accepted that a serious violation of duty is an instance of a wilful blatant carelessness, and not instances of a lesser fault; an extenuating circumstance is the previous blameless performance of his duties by the worker. As regards the second instance, the fundamental duties of the worker are, in principle, the duties specified in Art. 100, §2 of the Labour Code (see para. 180); but duties of essential significance for the proper functioning of the work establishment and the performance of its tasks may also be taken into consideration.

2. ABSENCE OF FAULT

167. An establishment is entitled to terminate a contract of employment without notice:

– if the worker is incapacitated for work by disease and such incapacity lasts:
  1. for longer than three months, in cases where the worker has been employed at the same establishment for less than six months,
  2. for longer than the permitted period of sickness benefit when the worker has been employed at the same establishment for at least six months, or where the incapacity was caused by an accident at work or by an occupational disease;
– if the worker has been absent from work for more than one month for a justified reason other than sickness.

b. Periods and circumstances

168. A contract of employment cannot be terminated without notice through the fault of a worker if one month has expired since the establishment became aware of the circumstances warranting such termination.

A contract of employment cannot be terminated without notice through no fault of the worker if a worker has been absent to care for a child or has been placed in isolation because of a contagious disease for such time as he is in receipt of an allowance on that account. Neither can it be terminated without notice after the worker has reported for work on the cessation of the reasons for an absence for which he cannot be blamed.

d. Trade union control

169. The director of a work establishment takes the decision to terminate a contract without notice after seeking the opinion of the enterprise trade union, which he shall inform of the reasons justifying such termination. When the trade union has reservations as to the grounds justifying termination without notice, it must express its opinion without delay and in any event within three days. While the trade unions view is not binding, it is obligatory to ask their opinion; if the work establishment fails to do so, this gives to the worker the basis for voicing a claim that the termination was unlawful.

e. Duties of the establishment

170. The declaration by an establishment of the termination without notice of a contract of employment should indicate the reason for such termination.

Wherever possible, an establishment should re-engage a worker who, within six months of the termination of his contract without notice through no fault of his own, announces his return to the establishment immediately after the reason has ceased to exist.

NATIONAL COLLEGE
OF IRELAND
LIBRARY

f. Termination without notice by the worker

171. A worker is entitled to terminate his contract of employment without notice if a public health service institution confirms that his work is harmful to his health and if the establishment does not transfer him within the time limit indicated in the medical certificate to some other job appropriate to his state of health and vocational skills. The declaration by the worker of the termination of his contract without notice should be made in writing, with an indication of the reason for such termination.

g. Legal effects of unlawful termination without notice

172. A worker whose contract of employment has been terminated without notice in violation of the provisions governing termination without notice shall be entitled to claim through the courts either reinstatement on previous conditions or the payment of compensation. The choice of which of these to claim lies with the worker.

When termination without notice has been motivated by a reason justifying such termination, but where there have been violations of the formal provisions (relating to the written form of the declaration, the permissible time limit for termination so long as it was not exceeded by more than an insignificant period, the required procedure of submission to trade union oversight, or the indication of the reason of termination) the labour court may reject an application for the worker's reinstatement or the payment of compensation if its acceptance would be against the rules governing life in the community.

173. A worker resuming employment after being reinstated is entitled to remuneration for the time he was not employed, subject to a maximum of three months' pay; in the case of a worker covered by a special protection (see para. 156), remuneration shall be payable for the entire period for which such a person was not employed.

Such remuneration is reduced by the amount of any remuneration that the worker has earned by taking employment in some other establishment during the period in question; provided that the remuneration shall not be less than one month's pay.

174. When a worker claims compensation rather than reinstatement, compensation is payable at the rate of the worker's remuneration for the period of notice. When a worker is granted compensation, the relevant period of employment shall include the period for which he was not employed insofar as it corresponds to the period for which compensation was granted.

5. Extinction of a contract in cases of unnotified desertion of work

175. The term 'desertion of work' does not appear in other legislation; it refers to the abandoning of the workplace by a worker without justification for his absence or without adhering to the procedures for termination of the contract of employment as laid down by law. In view of the frequency of the socially undesirable and economically harmful phenomenon (work establishments faced by desertion have difficulty in finding an immediate replacement since there is a labour shortage in Poland), Polish legislation tries to counteract it by means of legal consequences unfavourable to the worker. These problems are controversial in Polish jurisprudence.

If a worker deserts a job his contract of employment is abrogated (extinguishes). The worker is regarded as deserting his job when he wilfully avoids performing his work or fails to report for work without informing the establishment within the appropriate time limit of the reason for absence. The date of extinction of a contract is deemed to be the date on which the worker ceased to do his job. Extinction has the same legal effects as termination without notice by the establishment through fault of the worker; certain special provisions make the effects wider in scope in order to reduce the number of desertions. The establishment should allow a worker to resume his work if he was unable to justify his absence at the proper time but compiled with this duty immediately after the impediment ceased to exist.

Extinction of a contract also occurs when a worker is absent for three months because of remand in custody.

§2. Appointment and Recall of an Enterprise Director

A. Appointment

176. The director of a state enterprise is appointed by the establishing body (usually a superior economic organisation) or by the organ of workers self-management.[1] In most state enterprises in Poland (75 per cent) directors are appointed by workers' councils; only in enterprises of crucial significance for the economy, a list of which is laid down by the Council of Ministers in consultation with the trade unions, is the director appointed by the establishing body. If the workers' council fails to make use of its powers within a time period allowing the proper, continuous operation of the enterprise, then the director is appointed by the establishing body.

Both the workers' council and the establishing body have the right to present, within two weeks, motivated objections to the decision appointing a director – in that way mutual control of the correctness of the decision is provided. Should the objection be disregarded, the body which submitted it has the right to ask the court for a final verdict.

The director of a state enterprise is appointed for a period of five years or for an undefined period of time.

Actions regarding the employment relationship of the director, and in particular those laying down his remuneration, are taken by the establishing body of the enterprise; with regard to a director appointed by the workers' council, those actions are performed in agreement with that council.

1. See the Law of 25 September 1981 on state enterprises (Journal of Laws No. 24/1981, item 122, as subsequently amended) (see Chapter XV).

B. Competition for the post of director

177. The director of a state enterprise is chosen from candidates for that post after a qualifying competition has been held. The body entitled to appoint a director sets up a commission composed of: three representatives of the workers' council, and one representative each of: the establishing body, the bank financing the operation of the enterprise, the trade unions, political organisations, youth organisations, and the main technical organisations operating in the enterprise. The commission selects candidates on the basis of their abilities to manage the given enterprise, namely their professional qualifications, moral and social attitudes, and ability to co-operate with other people.

The announcement of the competition is public, for example in the press, and must specify the formal criteria for the selection of the candidates. Any person meeting the formal criteria indicated above may submit his canditature. The selection process may consist of a single stage or of several. After termination of the competition the commission selects one or more candidates by secret ballot.[1] In the event of finding more than one candidate suitable, the commission lays down the sequence of the candidatures. The commission presents the results of the competition to the organ appointing the director.

1. See the Ordinance of the Council of Ministers of 30 November 1981 regarding detailed principles for and proceedings at the organisation of the competition for the post of director of a state enterprise (Journal of Laws No. 2/1982, item 12).

C. Recall of a director

178. Directors are recalled by the same bodies and by the same procedure (motivated objections, final decision by a court) as is established for the appointment.

The workers' council may approach the establishing body to recall a director appointed by that body if the director:

a. seriously violates the law by his activity,

b. causes by his inadequacies unsatisfactory economic results of the enterprise.

The establishing body should either take action on the request within two weeks or carry out an inquiry to explain the case. If the inquiry reveals that the objections were justified, the body must comply with the request within seven days. In case of controversy over the results of the inquiry, the workers' council has the right to submit the case to the courts for a final decision.

Exceptionally, in view to remove the impediments and to accelerate the realisation of the economic reform, the Law of May 1988 on special economic powers and authorisations for the government[1] established the right of the Council of Ministers to recall or to suspend in operating a director of a state enterprise who violates the principles and aims of the economic reform; the recalling or suspending must be based on objective criteria of assessment, defined in the same law. The period of effectiveness of the authorisation for the government was limited till the end of 1988.

1. See the Law of 11 May 1988 on special economic powers and authorisations for the Council of Ministers (Journal of Laws No. 13/1988).

Chapter VII. Duties, Rewards and Liabilities of the Workers and of the Work Establishment

§1. Internal Employment Rules

179. The internal procedures and order to be observed within the establishment are laid down by the internal works rules issued by the head of the establishment in agreement with the works trade unions' unit, and in enterprises where workers' self-management operates – by the workers' council on the motion of the director of the enterprise (see paras. 94–97).

§2. Duties, Rewards and Liabilities of Workers

A. Duties of workers

180. It is the duty of a worker to perform his labour in accordance with the contract of employment; he is obliged to carry out his work conscientiously and carefully, observe work discipline and comply with the instructions given him in connection with his work. The performance of work is a complex process consisting – for example – of the fundamental duties of the worker specified in the Labour Code:
a. to conform to the hours of work observed in the establishment and use the working time as effectively as possible;
b. to endeavour to achieve the best possible results at work and, to this end, display appropriate initiative;
c. to comply with the internal employment rules and internal order observed at the establishment;
d. comply with the provisions and rules governing occupational safety and health and the provisions relating to fire prevention;
e. to have regard for the welfare of the establishment, take good care of its property and use it in accordance with the purposes for which it is intended;
f. to keep state and business secrets;
g. to observe the rules governing life in the community.

B. Rewards and distinctions for workers

181. Workers making a particular contribution to the performance of the tasks of the establishment by an exemplary discharge of their duties, the display of initiative at work, and the improvement of labour productivity and quality may be granted the following rewards and distinctions:
a. cash rewards;
b. written commendations;
c. public commendations;

d. certificates of appreciation;

e. other distinctions provided for in each individual branch of industry or establishment.

Rewards and distinctions are granted by the manager after seeking the opinion of the work's trade union unit. A copy should be included in the worker's personal file.

C. Liability for breaches of order and labour discipline

182. Workers who fail to comply with the rules of order and labour discipline, the internal works rules, the provisions governing occupational safety and health, and the provisions relating to fire prevention, are liable to admonition or reprimand.

Workers who fail to comply with the provisions on occupational safety and health or the provisions relating to fire prevention, are absent from their work without good cause, report for work in drunken state or drink alcohol during working hours are also liable to a cash penalty which – for a single offence or for a day's unjustified absence cannot be higher than the worker's remuneration for one day; moreover, cash penalties cannot amount to more than one-tenth of the remuneration payable to the worker.

No penalty may be imposed after two weeks from the date when the worker's breach of his duties bacame known, or after three months from the occurence of the breach.

183. A penalty is imposed by the director of the establishment, who shall inform the worker of the penalty in writing. A copy of the letter is placed in the worker's personal file. The manager may bring this fact to the knowledge of the staff. He also may decide not to impose a penalty in minor cases or if he considers other forms of educational influence to be sufficient.

A worker may appeal within three days of being informed that a penalty has been imposed. The decision accepting or rejecting the appeal should be taken by the director of the establishment in agreement with the works' trade union unit; where an appeal is not rejected within fourteen days of its submission, it shall be assumed to have been accepted.

184. After a year of blameless work a penalty should be deemed cancelled, the entry relating to it should be struck off the records and the copy removed from the worker's personal file. This may also be done at an earlier date.

D. Material liability for damages

185. The principle of the limited material liability of workers applies. A worker who, either by failing to discharge his duties or by failing to discharge them properly, has caused damage to the establishment incurs liability for damage within the limits of the effective loss and in respect of the normal consequences of the act or omission.

Where an agreement has been reached between the establishment and the worker concernd as to compensation, its amount may be reduced, but not by more than one-third, in the light of circumstances; this amount may also be reduced by a court, but not by more than one-fifth.

When a worker has stolen public property or has wilfully caused damage in any other way, he shall compensate for it to the full value of the property concerned.

E. Liability for property entrusted to a worker

1. Individual liability

186. When a worker is entrusted with:
a. cash, securities or valuables,
b. tools, instruments or similar objects, protective clothing, working clothes or personal protective equipment,
c. any other property,
with the duty to return them or account for them, he is liable for the full extent of any damage occuring to such property, but he may be released from liability if he can prove that the damage occured for reasons beyond his control, and more particularly, as the result of the failure by the establishment to provide the conditions enabling him to safeguard the property entrusted to him.[1]

1. See also the Ordinance of the Council of Ministers of 10 October 1975 regarding the conditions of material liability of workers for damage caused to the property entrusted to them (Journal of Laws No. 35/1975, item 191).

2. Joint material liability

187. Workers may by arrangement assume joint material liability for property entrusted to them collectively with the duty to account for it; the arrangement should be based on a contract concluded by them with the establishment, defining the joint material liability. Workers shall be liable in such proportions as are defined in the contract. However, if it is found that all or part of the damage was caused by certain workers, only those workers shall be liable.[1]

1. See also Ordinance of the Council of Ministers of 4 October 1974 regarding joint material liability of workers for the property entrusted to them (Journal of Laws No. 40/1974, item 236).

§3. Duties and Liabilities of the Establishment

A. Duties resulting from the employment relationship

188. An establishment is particularly obliged to:
a. acquaint workers taking up employment with their duties, the manner in which the work is to be done, and their basic rights;
b. organise the work is such a way as to ensure that working hours are fully utilised and that the workers achieve a high level of productivity and a proper standard of work;
c. ensure the observance of order and labour discipline;
d. ensure safe and healthy working conditions and arrange for systematic workers' training in occupational health and safety;
e. pay remuneration at the proper time and in the proper way;
f. enable workers to improve their professional skills;
g. provide workers starting employment after training at vocational school or after completing higher education with such conditions of work as will facilitate their adaptation to the proper performance of their work;
h. cater to the workers' welfare and cultural needs insofar as resources are available for this purpose;
i. apply objective and fair criteria in the assessment of workers and the results of their work;
j. contribute to the formulation at the establishment of rules governing life in the community.
In matters relating to welfare and cultural activities, rewards for workers, the improvement of professional qualifications, and formulating rules governing life in the community, the head of an establishment should collaborate with the works' trade union organisation.

The establishment should sponsor socialist competition at work and afford conditions conducive to the development of workers' inventions and efficiency schemes.

B. Duty to provide a certificate of employment

189. Upon termination or extinction of an employment relationship, the establishment should immediately provide the worker with a certificate of employment which should contain particulars of the worker's period of employment, the nature of his work, the position held, the amount and elements of remuneration, the qualifications acquired at the establishment, the manner by which his employment relationship was terminated (as a result of agreement, with notice, without notice through the fault of, without notice without fault) or the circumstances of its extinction and particulars relating to the future cumulation of employment periods (see para. 147).

The contents of a certificate of employment should be limited to factual data, omitting elements of assessment. A certificate has to serve to establish the formal situation of the worker at a future workplace. It should be prepared in every instance without need for the worker to demand it.

C. Duty to provide a testimonial

190. If the worker so requests, an establishment should provide him with a testimonial as to his work.[1] Testimonials are usually required by a future employer from persons who are to be employed in managerial or independent posts or posts connected with material liability; the objective of such an opinion is the assessment of the worker's former work. A testimonial should particularly contain information as to:
a. the worker's record at work, any special achievements and any rewards or distinctions granted,
b. any disciplinary penalties imposed and not deleted from his record,
c. reasons for termination of the employment relationship, either with or without notice.

If a testimonial does not correspond to the conditions specified by law, the worker concerned may – within three days of receiving it – apply to the director of the establishment to have it rectified. If his application has not been considered within seven days the worker may, within fourteen days of receiving the testimonial, apply to the head of the superior organisation to have it rectified. After examining the matter in agreement with the higher level trade union unit, the superior organisational body may correct the testimonial given or oblige the establishment to give a testimonial of an appropriate content; this must be considered within fourteen days of receipt of the worker's application. This last mechanism of appeal to 'superior instances' laid down in the Labour Code in 1974 has practically never been applied since the introduction of the economic reform and the change in principles of operation of trade unions, in view of the loss of competence of the 'superior instances' both of economic organisations and of trade unions. A change of that mechanism is envisaged, probably to involve the entrusting of this function to labour courts.

1. See also Ordinance of the Council of Ministers of 30 November 1974 regarding work certificates and testimonials (Journal of Laws No. 45/1974, item 269).

D. Compensation for prejudice linked to certificates and testimonials

191. A worker is entitled to claim compensation for any prejudice caused by an establishment by its failure to issue a certificate of employment or testimonial at the proper time or by its issue of an improper certificate or testimonial. This compensation is payable at the rate of the worker's remuneration is respect of any period for which he was not employed on accqunt of such failure, subject to a maximum of six weeks. The award of compensation entitles the worker to have the certificate or testimonial changed.

E. Liability for infringements of workers' rights

192. Any person acting on behalf of an establishment who:
a. terminates an employment relationship with a worker without notice in a manner manifestly contravening the provisions of Labour Law,
b. imposes a penalty on a worker for breach of order or labour discipline that has not been provided for in Labour Law,
c. contravenes the provisions on hours of work or the protection of the work of women and young persons,
d. fails to pay remuneration at the appointed time, reduces its amount, or makes deductions without valid grounds,
e. fails to grant the worker vacation leave or reduces the length of that leave without valid grounds,
f. fails to provide the worker with a certificate of employment or a testimonial,
g. fails to carry out an enforceable decision of judicial body,
is liable to a fine (amounts of fines rise with the inflation).

Any person who, being the head of an establishment or a manager of a group of workers, or acting on behalf of the head of the establishment:
a. fails to comply with the provisions and rules of occupational safety and health,
b. fails contrary to his duty to inform a labour inspector, public prosecutor or other competent authority at the proper time of an accident at work or an occupational disease, conceals such an accident or disease, or submits untruthful information, evidence, or documents,
c. fails to carry out at the proper time the order of a labour inspector,
d. hampers the labour inspectorate and more particularly prevents a visit of the inspectorate to an establishment, or does not provide the inspectorate with the necessary information,
e. takes over for exploitation or starts a new or reconstructed establishment without notifying the labour inspector; or takes without the consent or opinion of the appropriate organs a decision involving health and safety at work,
is also liable to a fine (amount rising with the inflation).

193. In all the cases specified in para. 192 fines are imposed by labour inspectors. The accused person, his counsel or the public prosecutor may lodge an appeal against a labour inspector's decision within seven days of its publication or delivery to the appropriate territorial body for minor offences; that body may either uphold the decision or quash it and issue a new decision. A decision against which no appeal has been lodged within the due time, or a decision given on appeal is final.

Supervision of decisions taken by labour inspectors is exercised by the Chief Labour Inspector; as part of that supervision he may quash the final decision of an inspector if it is contrary to the law or manifestly unjustified. When a decision is quashed, a case is referred for examination to the appropriate territorial body for minor offences. A final decision may be quashed within three months of its becoming final; this time limit does not apply to cases where a decision is quashed to the sole advantage of the accused.[1] Another violation of labour norms may also be an economic offence (Arts. 217 and 218 of the Penal Code) or an offence against the life and health (Arts. 152, 160 and 164 of the Penal Code).

1. See also the Law of 6 March 1981 on State Labour Inspection (Journal of Laws No. 6, item 23, as subsequently amended), and the Ordinance of the Council of Ministers of 20 September 1974 regarding proceedings before the Labour Inspectors on infringements against the worker's rights (Journal of Laws No. 37/1974, item 220).

Chapter VIII. Hours of Work, Holidays, Annual Leave

§1. WORKING HOURS

A. General characteristics

194. The reduction of working time is an essential aspect of workers' living conditions; Poland, having observed until recently a full six-day work week, remains in this sphere somewhat behind other countries, including its neighbours. Efforts to improve the situation resulted in the introduction in 1974 of six free Saturdays a year, and in 1975 – 12 free Saturdays a year; and later, as the result of the 1981 Social Agreements, from 34 to 38 free Saturdays a year with no reduction in remuneration. However, any reduction in working time should be accompanied by an improvement of labour organisation and better utilisation of production potential; this takes place too slowly in Poland and does not give satisfactory results. This is why there has occured a regression in the reduction of working time after the temporary progress of 1981 (recognised as having been premature). Assessments of the economic situation in Poland indicate that without a fundamental increase in labour efficiency and organisational improvement the re-establishment of trends aiming at significant reduction of working time will encounter difficulties.

B. Length of working hours

195. Working hours are those during which the worker is at the disposal of an establishment, either at the establishment itself or at some other place designated for the performance of work.

1. Evolution in recent years

According to the Labour Code (Art. 129) working hours shall not exceed eight hours a day or 46 hours a week. Thus, in principle, the Labour Code recognises a six-day working week (five days of eight hours and a six hour Saturday). However, as early as 1974 and 1975, six and then twelve free Saturdays a year were introduced, with the obligation of compensatory work on other days of the week.

In 1981, with no change in the Labour Code, working time was determined in socialised work establishments by Ordinance of the Council of Ministers:[1] an average of 42 hours a week, adopting as the basis a four-week period of calculation embracing three weeks of five-day working amounting to 40 hours a week, and one week of six-day working amounting to 48 hours; the number of free Saturdays amounted to 38 in a year, namely three free Saturdays a month. A similar extension occured at a later date by subsequent ordinances of the Council of Ministers to cover the years 1982, 1983 and 1984.

In 1985 the principle of 38 free Saturdays a year was maintained in most establishments; however, heads of establishments were authorised[2] with the introduction of free Saturdays to extend working time to nine hours a day and 48 hours a week in periods of increased production service tasks, while reducing it during periods when requirements were less intense, maintaining on average a 42 hour week over the period of calculation.

1. Ordinance of the Council of Ministers of 16 February 1981 regarding working time and principles for the introduction at socialised work establishments of additional days free from work (Journal of Laws No. 3/1981, item 15).
2. Ordinance of the Council of Ministers of 1985 governing rules of the application of working time at socialised work establishments for the years 1986–1988 and changes of certain principles involving working time (Journal of Laws No. 59/1985, item 299).

2. Length of working hours for 1986–1990

196. The possibility of applying a 46-hour work week was reinstated in 1986 for the period 1986–1990.[1] Directors of establishments of crucial significance for the national economy (a list of which has been laid down by the Council of Ministers)[2] or for the defence capability of the country, and public utilities were authorised to establish an eight-hour day, 46-hour week, if the implementation of tasks embraced by the national socio-economic plan for the years 1986–1990, principally involving the supply of raw materials, food economy, operational (priority) programmes, and also government orders, export production involving implementation of international agreements, and production for local market supplies, would be impossible in regular technical and organisational conditions. The application of increased working time may occur on condition that there is proper organisational-technical and material-cooperation preparation of production. Before deciding on it the director of the establishment must undertake an analysis of the technical-organisational and financial status of the enterprise and notify appropriate bodies of the enterprise self-management, political organisations, trade unions of its findings.

Thus in most socialised enterprises average working time of 42 hours a week is in force for the 1986–1990 period provided that, in establishments of crucial significance for the national economy or for the defence capability of the country, and in public utilities, extended working time of 46 hours a week and eight hours a day may be applied (as provided in Art. 129 of the Labour Code).

1. Ordinance of the Council of Ministers of 21 February 1986 on an increased extent of working time in certain work establishments for the years 1986–1990 (Journal of Laws No. 6/1986, item 34).
2. Ordinance of the Council of Ministers of 5 February 1983 laying down the list of establishments of crucial significance for the national economy (Journal of Laws No. 9/1983, item 47 with subsequent amendments).

C. Reduced length of working hours

197. The working hours of those employed in particularly arduous jobs or in unhealthy conditions may be reduced. The reduction may consist in a shortening of the daily or weekly hours of work or in the provision of breaks. Numerous such reductions have been introduced for various groups of workers by ordinances of the Council of Ministers issued in agreement with nation-wide trade unions representation.

§2. OFFICIAL HOLIDAYS

198. Holidays officially established by law[1] are as follows:
– 1 January   – New Year
– Easter Sunday
– Easter Monday
– 1 May   – State Holiday
– Whitsuntide Sunday
– Corpus Christi Day
– 22 July   – National Holiday
– 1 November   – All Saints Day
– 25 December   – Christmas Day
– 26 December   – Boxing Day (Second Day after Christmas)

1. The Law of 18 January 1951 on days free from work (Journal of Laws No. 4/1951, item 28. Amendment: Journal of Laws No. 51/1960, item 297).

§3. OVERTIME WORK

199. Work in excess of the normal hours fixed for a given branch of activity or a given establishment is deemed to be overtime. Such work is permitted only in the event of:
a. rescue operations required to protect human life or health, or to protect property, or deal with a breakdown,
b. special requirements of the establishment.
Also considered to be overtime is that work performed according to the provisions establishing the length of hours of work for 1986–1990 (see footnote 1 to para. 196) in excess of the working time quota laid down in other provisions.

200. Overtime worked in connection with special requirements of the establishment shall not exceed 120 hours in any calendar year for any individual worker. The Council of Ministers is authorised to establish, in agreement with the nation-wide trade union representation, higher limits of overtime hours admitted for determined establishments or branches of economy during a limited period of time. Not included in limits of overtime hours are hours worked on free Saturdays.

The decision on working in overtime hours is taken by the director of the work establishment in agreement with the trade union organisation, account being taken of the needs of the work establishment and the kind of the production and service performed.

201. A worker employed on overtime is entitled to a supplement to his normal remuneration at the rate of:
– 50 per cent of remuneration corresponding to individual grade in the case of the first two hours of overtime in any day;
– 100 per cent of such remuneration in the case of work done during any subsequent hours or at night, or on a Sunday or public holiday (provided that the worker is not granted any other day off during the week).
Workers holding managerial positions or other independent posts may be employed, if necessary, over and above normal working time without thereby being entitled to supplementary remuneration.[1] The same applies to workers whose hours of work can, in view of the nature of their job and their working conditions, be determined only by the extent of their tasks.

1. See Ordinance of the Council of Ministers of 20 September 1974 regarding definition of managerial and other independent positions for the purpose of entitlement to extra remuneration for overtime work and determination of duration of the trial period (Journal of Laws No. 37/1974, item 215).

§4. Work at Night, on 'Free Saturdays', Sundays and Holidays

A. Night work

202. Night work is any period of eight hours between 9 p.m. and 7 a.m. Within these limits the period of night work may be determined in the internal works rules or by the director of the establishment in agreement with the works' trade union. Usually, workers are entitled to a higher rate of remuneration for work done at night.

B. Work on 'free Saturdays'

203. Work on 'free Saturdays' may be ordered or voluntarily undertaken by workers with the consent of the director of the establishment only under conditions of:
1. rational utilisation of working time during the other days of the week,
2. adequate organisational-technical and material preparation of the work carried out on the free Saturday or other additional day free from work.

C. Work on Sundays and Holidays

204. Work is deemed to be performed on a Sunday or holiday if it is done between 6 a.m. on that day and 6 a.m. on the following day. Such work is permitted only in the cases specified in Art. 139 of the Labour Code. Workers are entitled to another day off during the week.

§5. SPECIAL SYSTEMS OF WORKING TIME

205. At establishments of a special kind, or with work of a special kind, special systems of working time may be devised, as determined in Arts. 141–145 of the Labour Code and in special regulations.

§6. ANNUAL LEAVE

A. The amount of leave

206. Workers are entitled to an annual uninterrupted period of vacation leave with pay at the rate of:
1. 14 working days after one year's employment;
2. 17 working days after three years' employment;
3. 20 working days after six years' employment;
4. 26 working days after ten years' employment.
The period of employment on which the amount of the leave depends includes:
– a period of training at a basic or vocational school subject to a maximum of three years;
– a period of training at a secondary vocational school subject to a maximum of five years;
– a period of training at a secondary vocational school for primary school graduates – five years;
– completion of a general secondary school – four years;
– completion of a specialised secondary school – six years;
– completion of higher education – eight years.

207. The period of employment on which the amount of leave depends includes periods of any previous employment and periods of training, irrespective of any interruption. However, a period of previous employment cannot be included if the worker's contract of employment in an establishment has been terminated as the result of desertion of work.

B. The acquisition of the right to leave

208. The period of employment on which the acquisition of the entitlement to leave depends includes any period of previous employment, unless interruption has lasted for longer than three months, or the employment relationship has been terminated with notice by the worker himself. Such a worker becomes entitled to leave after one year's work.

A worker whose employment relationship has been terminated by the establishment without notice through the worker's fault or one who has deserted his job becomes entitled to leave after having worked for one year in a new job, but then only in an amount of leave corresponding to the categories immediately below that to which he had been entitled before the work relationship was terminated or extinguished. The reduction in the amount of the leave applies only to one calendar year.

C. Granting of leave and its utilisation

209. A worker is entitled to leave after completing one year of work and subsequently in the course of each calendar year. The establishment grants leave to a worker in the course of the calendar year during which he becomes entitled to it.

If the worker so requests, leave may be granted by instalments. At least one instalment should consist of not less than ten consecutive calendar days.

210. Leave is granted in accordance with a vacation plan which is drawn up by the director of the establishment in consultation with the works' trade union, with due regard to workers' requests and the need for maintaining the normal rhythm of work. A worker's leave dates may be altered if he so requests for any valid reason; it may also be altered on account of special requirements arising in the establishment if the worker's absence were to disrupt seriously the progress of work.

An establishment should not recall a worker from holiday unless his presence is necessitated by circumstances that could not have been foreseen when his leave began; the establishment should defray any expenses incurred by the worker as a direct consequence of being recalled from leave.

Leave not taken in accordance with the vacation plan should be granted by the end of the first quarter of the following year.

D. Remuneration for the period of leave

211. While on leave a worker is entitled to the remuneration that he would have received had he been working during that time. Variable elements of remuneration may be calculated on the basis of average remuneration over three months preceding the month in which the leave begins; when remuneration fluctuates, this period may be extended to 12 months.

§7. Leave without Pay

212. If the worker so requests for any valid reason, the establishment may grant a leave without pay if the normal progress of work would not be disrupted thereby. Where unpaid leave is granted for longer than three months, the parties may provide for the possibility of recalling the worker from leave for a valid reason.

If a social organisation so requests, an establishment should grant a worker who has been asked to assume office by election unpaid leave for the duration of such office. Childcare leave is discussed below (see paras. 282–284).

Chapter IX. Remuneration for Work and Benefits

§1. REMUNERATION FOR WORK

A. The concept of remuneration for work

213. In Poland remuneration is a form of participation of the worker in the distribution of social revenue, more specifically in that part of social revenue intended for consumption (the so-called individual consumption fund). The worker participates in that distribution in conformity with the quantity and quality of his work. The theoretical concept of the remuneration may evolve with progress of economical reforms in Poland. In a socialist country remuneration fulfils two basic functions:
1. the alimentation function, as the source of maintenance of the worker and his family,
2. the motivation function, stimulating the worker to increasing labour efficiency.

Besides remuneration in its direct sense there are:
1. payments for readiness for work, if the work has not been performed for reasons depending on the work establishment,
2. guarantee payments for duration of leave, see para. 211,
3. compensation (*e.g. per diems* for service trips, refund of travel costs),
4. sickness benefits from the work establishment (see para. 239),
5. social welfare payments (*e.g.* payments for the worker's vacation, housing grants, etc.).

B. Decentralisation of wages policy in the economic reform of the 1980s

214. For many years past two tendencies collided in Poland: those aiming at centralisation of remuneration, *i.e.* the central establishment of the amount of remuneration by state organs, and at its decentralisation *i.e.* negotiation of the amount of remuneration at the level of the establishment or their determination by means of individual contracts of employment. The economic reform of the 1980s recognises decentralisation of wage determination as one of its fundamental principles. That decentralisation is taking place gradually, at a rate considered by many people to be too slow. It is served by:
1. a change in the principles of enterprise and management (autonomy, self-management and self-financing),[1]
2. the adoption in 1984 for most work establishments, especially state enterprises, of the introduction of what are called workplace remuneration systems,[2] and
3. a new model of collective labour agreements created in 1986.[3]

However, state authorities reserve to themselves measures to prevent excessive wage increases which would result in disturbing the market equilibrium and in general inflation. This purpose is served by establishing, in cooperation with the national trade union organisation, long-term National Socio-Economic Plans and annual Central Annual Plans, laying down the average increase of remuneration within an appropriate period of time covered by the plan.

However, in the mid-1980s, the economic management of the country did not succeed in keeping the agreed rate of prices' and wages' increases; every year those increases exceeded considerably the negotiated and planned level. Trade unions make efforts to ensure that the increases of wages (and those of pensions) keep pace with the rise of prices. In 1987 the inflation seemed to get out of economic control. This was the reason for granting 'special economic powers' to the government in May 1988,[4] in force till the end of the year, aiming at the restraining of the inflation and accelerating the economic reforms.

1. See Law of 26 February 1982 on financial economy of state enterprises (Journal of Laws No. 7, item 54, as subsequently amended).
2. See Law of 26 January 1984 on the rules of creation of workplace remuneration system (Journal of Laws No. 5, item 25). A substantial amendment of this law was prepared in 1988.
3. See Law of 24 November 1986 regarding collective agreements (Journal of Laws No. 42, item 201).
4. See Law of 11 May 1988 on special powers and authorisations for the Council of Ministers (Journal of Laws No. 13/1988).

C. Elements of remuneration for work

1. Basic remuneration

215. In the remuneration of workers we find some principal elements (basic remuneration) and additional elements (bonuses, extra remuneration). The basic wage depends on the grade of the worker and the rate of pay. The basic remuneration rates for each grade are laid down in tables of categories in establishments. These rates can be determined by the span method. The basic wage rate in the lowest category cannot be lower than the currently valid minimum wage (in 1988 the minimum wage was 9.000 zl a month).

2. Remuneration systems

216. Depending on the labour measure appropriate to a given type of work, there are the following remuneration systems:
a. remuneration for the duration of work (monthly, weekly, daily, by the hour), applied as a rule to administrative work and to productive work the effect of which cannot be measured,
b. remuneration according to the effects of work (piece-work, bonus rates). The piece-work system may be simple or progressive, when the rate is increased as a specified quantity of production or operation is exceeded.

Piece-work may be individual or collective. There are also combined remuneration systems, *e.g.* time-bonus, or piece-work-bonus. Quite special rules are applied to wages in partnership groups' (brigades) organisation of work system.

3. Work norms

217. Piece-work remuneration is based on the existence of work norms which determine the duration of time necessary for the performance of certain determined operations or production in specific organisational-technical conditions. Work norms are laid down according to current standards of technique or labour organisation, taking into account the most rational work methods. A change of work norms is admissible and necessary as technical and organisational improvements ensuring increased productivity are progressively introduced; the fact that work norms are exceeded is not a reason for changing them if the results are due to increased personal effort on the worker's part or to his greater efficiency at his job.

4. Bonuses

218. Bonuses are additional remuneration of a variable amount; their objective is to ensure material incentives for the worker when remuneration by the time or piece-work system does not adequately stimulate increasing labour productivity. The following bonuses are applied:
1. for high quality of work,
2. for economy of materials,
3. for labour productivity,
4. for timely performance of work,
5. for production compatible with export requirements,
6. for improvement of the production process and better work organisation, and some others.
The fulfilling of one or more conditions is required for right to a bonus. On the other hand certain factors also generate a reduction or limitation of the right to a bonus. These factors are laid down in regulations usually referred to as bonus-granting regulations; they may take the form of a legal act (law, ordinance), a collective agreement, workplace wages agreement or a workplace collective agreement.

5. Extra payments

219. Extra payments are usually fixed in amount. They may be either for particularly arduous work – these are allowances for difficult or harmful working conditions. They may also be granted for a greater range of responsibilities: their monthly rate cannot be lower than 10 per cent of the lowest remuneration; or for vocational skills including allowances for education, for scientific degrees, for knowledge of foreign languages; or finally for length of seniority.

6. Jubilee awards

220. If they meet the conditions provided for by the law, workers are entitled to 'jubilee awards'. The amount of a jubilee award after ten years of work amounts to 100 per cent of remuneration and increases after every succeeding five-year period of work by 50 per cent; and, starting with 25 years of work by 100 per cent of remuneration.

D. Instruments for establishing remuneration

1. Remuneration laid down under provisions of law

221. The remuneration of workers belonging to what is called the non-material sphere of production, financed from the state budget, is laid down by way of unilateral legal acts of state organs in agreement with trade unions. Wages of employees of the state administration, higher schools and the Polish Academy of Sciences, and teachers are *inter alia* established in this fashion.

2. Branch collective agreements

222. Under the law of 1986 on collective agreements (see para. 214 n.3), collective agreements determine 'conditions for the remuneration of workers and allocation of other benefits connected with work'. Provisions of such agreements should conform to law and to the social and economic policy of the state laid down by the Parliament in the national socio-economic plan. They should also be compatible with the principles of policy of remunerations and other benefits connected with work which are laid down by the Council of Ministers in agreement with the national inter-union organisation for the purpose of realisation of the central policy of remunerations and benefits laid down in the national socio-economic plan.[1]

1. See Resolution of the Council of Ministers of 17 August 1987 on the rules of shaping wages, remunerations and other benefits in collective agreements in the period 1987–1990 (*Monitor Polski* No. 26, item 206).

223. With regard to workers employed at work establishments authorised to apply workplace remuneration systems, the lowest rates of the basic remuneration and principles for their allocation are laid down in a branch collective agreement. The agreement may also provide for other components of remuneration, especially those justified by the nature of work in the given branch of work or profession, or by other special needs and elements dependent on the effects of work.

With regard to workers employed at work establishments not applying their own workplace remuneration systems, the branch collective agreement determines detailed conditions of remuneration and the award of other payments connected with work in the given branch of work or profession.

Remuneration allowances and other benefits are determined in the branch collective agreement by the percentage system reckoned from the lowest remuneration valid in January of the given year, or from the lowest remuneration laid down in the agreement.

3. Workplace collective agreements (workplace remuneration systems)

224. Workplace remuneration systems, as components of the workplace collective agreement, apply to workers employed at state enterprises, at cooperatives operating on the basis of economic accounting, and in trading companies with a share of social capital, with the exception of establishments covered by liquidation or bankruptcy proceedings, and of certain special categories of workers, *e.g.* young persons employed for the purpose of learning a profession. The Council of Ministers may extend the range of application of workplace remuneration systems to cover other types of workplace.[1]

1. See also Law of 24 June 1988 amending the Law of 26 January 1984 on the workplace remuneration systems (Journal of Laws No. 20, item 134).

225. Workplace remuneration systems lay down detailed conditions of remuneration and other payments connected with work. The application of provisions of branch collective agreements pertaining to remuneration and other payments specified in collective agreements may occur only when the workplace has the necessary financial means in conformity with the principle of the self-financing of enterprises.

The workplace remuneration system may apply higher levels of remuneration and payments than the lowest laid down in the branch collective agreement if the work establishment has the appropriate resources in accordance with the principle of self-financing, and if it applies the work norms correctly (see para. 217). However, the application of wages and payments above the lowest laid down in branch collective agreements is not permissible in work establishments covered by proceedings aiming at an improvement of their economy (called 'sanation' programmes) or by liquidation or bankruptcy proceedings.

4. Periodical review of the situation involving remuneration

226. The 1986 law on collective agreements engages the Council of Ministers, in agreement with the national trade union organisation, to

undertake every two years – in the context of the economic situation of the country – an analysis of the extent of wages and other payments provided for the separate branches of labour and the professions and the examination of possibilities for raising the level of remuneration or payments.

E. Remuneration for time not worked or for defective products

227. While not performing work the worker retains his entitlement to remuneration only where provisions of the law permit it, even though Polish Labour Law generally acknowledges the principle that risk is borne by the work establishment. For periods not worked remuneration is payable to a worker at the rate of his personal grade if he was ready to work but was prevented by reasons attributable to the establishment. If the worker is idle through his own fault, no remuneration is paid. If the worker is employed at a job that is subject to weather conditions, he may be entitled to remuneration for idle periods caused by such conditions. When a worker is otherwise idle, the establishment may entrust him with other appropriate work for which he should be paid the remuneration attached to it but not less than the remuneration corresponding to his own grade. However, if he is idle through his own fault, he can only be paid remuneration corresponding to the work done.

228. No remuneration is paid for defective products or unsatisfactory services if the worker is at fault; wages are appropriately reduced when the quality of products or services is lessened as the result of unsatisfactory work performed by the worker. Where deficiencies are remedied by the worker, he may be paid remuneration appropriate to the quality of the product or service, but not for time worked to remedy defects.

F. Protection of remuneration

229. Remuneration should be paid at least once a month, except in the case of elements of remuneration that are payable for longer periods of time. If the worker so requests, he should be allowed to inspect any documents concerning the calculation of his remuneration. Remuneration should be paid at the place, date, and time specified in the internal rules of employment or in wages regulations.

230. After deduction of income tax and pension contributions, only the following debts may be deducted from remuneration and in the following order:
1. amounts due by virtue of an enforcable order to cover maintenance payments or other debts,
2. cash advances made to the worker,
3. cash penalties.

Deductions may be made within the following limits:

a. in case of attachment due to maintenance payments in amounts up to three-fifths of remuneration,

b. in case of attachment due for other debts and cash advances up to one-half of remuneration.

Except in cases indicated by law, deductions to cover maintenance payments may be made by a specialised establishment even without recourse to the attachment procedure at the creditor's request and on production by him of an enforceable document. The same rule applies to deduction of sums awarded against a worker in favour of socialised economic units. The provisions of the Code of Civil Procedure and those relating to the administrative attachment of cash payments apply respectively.

Payments other than those mentioned above may be deducted from a worker's remuneration only with his written consent.

§2. Benefits and Payments in Cases of Justified Absence and Time off

A. Justified absence from work and benefits

1. Justified absence from work

231. Polish Labour Law provides for and justifies situations when a worker is unable to report for work. If the reason for such inability is known beforehand, the worker should notify the work establishment of it. In other instances he shall notify the work establishment of the reason for absence and the expected time of its duration on the first day of that absence and not later than on the following day, either personally, by means of other persons, or by mail. Failure to meet these conditions is acceptable only in exceptional cases. A justification of absence from work does not automatically provide the right to benefits. The right to benefits is only due in instances to be discussed below.

232. Among the accepted reasons justifying absence from work or lateness are specifically:[1]

a. incapacity for work as the result of the sickness or isolation of the worker due to a contagious illness;

b. temporary removal on the basis of a medical decision if the work establishment does not employ the worker at another job compatible with the state of his health;

c. treatment at a spa if its duration is accepted in a medical certificate as a period of incapacity for work due to sickness;

d. illness of a family member demanding personal care by the worker;

e. the need to care for a child aged under eight years.

When absence is for reasons indicated in a., b., c. and d. the worker shall submit to the work establishment an appropriate medical certificate.

1. See Ordinance of the Council of Ministers of 20 December 1974 regarding internal rules of employment and principles for justifying absence from work and the granting of time off (Journal of Laws No. 49/1974, item 299; amended in 1975, 1977, 1981, 1982, 1983, 1985).

2. Incapacity for work and benefits arising

a. General remarks

233. While absent from work because of temporary incapacity for work, workers are entitled to the following benefits:[1]
a. in case of incapacity for work as the result of sickness – to sickness benefits or rehabilitation allowances,
b. during maternity leave – to maternity benefits,
c. for care of a child or a sick family member – to care benefits.
Sickness benefit is paid by work establishments which provide it from their own wage funds.[2] Sickness benefits, although paid for by work establishments are considered as social security allowances. Since they bear sickness benefit costs, work establishments are authorised to analyse, with the participation of the works' trade union and public health services, the extent of sickness absenteeism and its causes and to undertake prophylactic measures. Moreover, work establishments are authorised (together with organs of the Social Security Board) to confirm whether workers receiving sickness benefits actually use their absence for curative purposes.[3]

Maternity and care benefits are also paid by the work establishment but on behalf of the Social Security Board from which it subsequently obtains a refund. Thus the cost of such benefits is borne by the Social Security Board. In the instance of workers in non-socialised establishments, all these benefits, including sickness benefits, are paid directly by the Social Security Board.

All those allowances are due by reason of employment, regardless of the basis of the employment relationship. They also cover certain other groups of persons, *e.g.* persons engaged in out work for socialised work establishments.

1. This is governed by the Law of 17 December 1974 on cash allowances from social security in cases of sickness and maternity (uniform text after amendments in the Journal of Laws No. 30/1983, item 143).
2. See Ordinance of the Council of Ministers of 6 June 1983 regarding principles for the calculation of social security benefits and for covering expenses for those benefits (Journal of Laws No. 33/1983, item 157).
3. See Order of the Minister of Labour, Wages and Social Affairs of 30 December 1974 regarding control of a correct utilisation of medical certificates giving release from work (*Monitor Polski* No. 37/1974, item 263).

b. Temporary incapacity for work and sickness benefit

1. TEMPORARY INCAPACITY FOR WORK

234. Temporary incapacity for work entitling a worker to sickness benefit paid by the work establishment includes:
a. sickness during the period of employment and in some instances up to three months after the termination of employment, confirmed by a medical certificate,
b. incapacity to perform work on the basis of a decision of a public health organ made within the framework of control of contagious diseases,
c. treatment at a medical establishment for alcoholism.

2. CONDITIONS ENTITLING TO SICKNESS BENEFIT

235. A worker employed for an indefinite period acquires the right to sickness benefit regardless of the duration of his employment. A worker whose contract of employment has been concluded for a trial period, for a specified time period or for the time of completion of a specific task – acquires the right to sickness benefit after having worked for at least one month, unless his incapacity for work was caused by an accident at work, a vocational disease, or by other causes provided for by law.

236. Incapacity for work caused wilfully by participation in a fight or as the result of another wilful offence or misdeed does not give the right to sickness benefit. In the instance of incapacity for work caused by abuse of alcohol, sickness benefit is not due for the first three days of that incapacity.

If, during sickness or absenteeism, a worker performs some other gainful occuptaion, or some arduous operation that may extend the period of his disability; or if he takes advantage of his medical release from work in a way incompatible with the purpose of that certificate, he loses the right to sickness benefits for the entire duration of that release.

237. A worker who, for the reasons indicated above has lost the right to benefit, will have his sickness benefit reduced by 25 per cent for any further period of incapacity during a period of one year. The same applies to a worker absent for even a single day, who deserts work (see para. 175) or with whom the employment relationship has been terminated without notice through his own fault. That reduction does not apply if the incapacity for work is due to an accident at work or an accident on the way to or from work, or occupational disease; or if it occurs during pregnancy.

3. THE PERIOD OF BENEFIT

238. Sickness benefit is due for the duration of the incapacity for work due to disease (confirmed by medical release from work) or by the incapacity to perform work for other reasons indicated in para. 234, but for not longer than six months; and if incapacity for work is caused by tuberculosis – for not longer than nine months.

If, after the lapse of that period, a worker continues to be incapable of work due to disease, and further treatment or rehabilitation provide hope of recuperation of work capacity, the payment of sickness benefit may be extended for the duration of that treatment – but for not longer than a further three months.

The 'benefit period' includes periods of continuous incapacity for work caused by the same disease or by other diseases and also periods of incapacity to perform work for reasons provided for by law. Also included into the 'benefit period' are periods of previous incapacity for work caused by the same disease interrupted by not more than 30 days.

4. AMOUNT OF SICKNESS BENEFIT

239. Monthly sickness benefit amounts to:
1. 100 per cent of remuneration – for workers who have been employed for more than eight years,
2. 80 per cent of remuneration – for workers who have been employed for three to eight years,
3. 75 per cent of remuneration – for workers who have been employed for less than three years.

When establishing the duration of employment on which the level of sickness benefit depends, previous periods of employment are also taken into consideration.

Sickness benefit is paid for every day of incapacity for work, without excluding days off.

Sickness benefit for the first three days of illness amounts to 50 per cent of remuneration, with the exception of diseases specifically enumerated by the Minister of Health.[1] The list of those diseases is very extensive, so that the restriction to 50 per cent plays no major role in practice.

   1. See Ordinance of the Minister of Health and Social Welfare of 24 March 1983 regarding the list of diseases for which sickness benefits shall not be lowered (Journal of Laws No. 15/1983, item 77).

240. In certain instances sickness benefit amounts to 100 per cent of remuneration, regardless of the period of employment of the worker. Those instances are:
a. from the first day of incapacity if this occured due to an accident at work, an accident on the way to or from work, or due to an occupational disease;
b. from the first day of incapacity due to disease during pregnancy;
c. for the duration of uninterrupted incapacity for work lasting for over 30 days, starting on the thirty-first day of that incapacity.

The basis for the assessment of sickness benefit is the average monthly renumeration paid to the worker for the period of three calendar months preceding the month in which the right to benefit arose.

5. REHABILITATION ALLOWANCE

241. If a worker, after having exhausted his sickness benefit, continues to be unfit for work, while further rehabilitation treatment prognosticates the restoration of work capacity, he is entitled to a rehabilitation allowance in the amount of 75 per cent of remuneration (or 100 per cent of remuneration if incapacity arose from an accident at work, an accident on the way to or from work, or due to occupational disease) – for a period essential to recovery of the capacity for work, but for not longer than twelve months. The right to a rehabilitation allowance is decreed by medical commissions for disability and employment affairs. Rehabilitation allowances are paid by the work establishment, deducted from the establishment's contributions to social security – so that, in the final instance, expenses for rehabilitation allowances are borne by the Social Security Board (unlike sickness benefits which are fully borne by the work establishment).

3. Maternity allowances

See para. 281.

4. Absence from work for child care or care of a sick family member

242. During a justified absence from work due to a need to care for:
a. a child aged up to eight years, in the event of:
  i. the unexpected closing of the nursery, kindergarten or school the child attends,
  ii. maternity or sickness of the spouse of the worker permanently caring for the child, or his/her stay at a medical establishment;
b. a sick child aged up to 14 years;
c. another sick family member,
the worker is entitled to a care benefit.

A family member in the understanding of c. includes the spouse, parents, parents-in-law, grandparents, grandchildren, brothers and sisters, and children aged over 14 years if they live in a common household with the worker. The children specified under a. and b. are the worker's own children or those of his/her spouse, adopted children, and also children of some other person taken for fostering.

If both parents are at work, care benefits are due to the mother of the child and to the father only if the mother is away from their normal place of residence or is unable to care for the children because of illness or maternity.

243. Care benefits are due for no longer than:

a. 60 days in a calendar year, if children are being cared for:

b. 14 days in a calendar year, if the care is of other family members.

Jointly, for both these reasons, benefits may be allocated for a period not longer than 60 days in a calendar year, regardless of the number of family members and number of children.

Care benefits are not due if, in addition to the worker, there are other persons in the household who may ensure care; this is not applicable, however, to a working mother's care of a sick child up to two years of age, for such a child needs the mother's individual care.

244. The monthly care benefit amounts to 100 per cent of remuneration. Reductions apply in the same manner as for sickness benefits (see para. 237). Care benefits are paid by the work establishment, but deducted from contributions which it makes to the Social Security Board, so that the cost is borne by the latter.

245. Justified absence to care for a child or a sick family member may last longer than the duration of the period for which the care benefit is due for that reason – and it remains a justified absence. A worker is not paid wages for such a period. It should be borne in mind that, in event of a justified absence longer than one month, the work establishment has the right to terminate the employment relationship without notice (see para. 167) if the duration of care benefit has ended.

B. Time off from work

246. In the event that it becomes necessary to deal with certain personal or social matters, or others not connected with professional work, the worker may receive time off from the work establishment within the limits and according to the principles determined by provisions of law.[1]

Meetings and debates of a social character (*e.g.* involving trade unions) may be organised only outside working hours; with shift work they should be organised in a way reducing lost working time to a minimum.

1. See Ordinance of the Council of Ministers of 20 December 1974 regarding internal rules of employment and principles for justifying absence from work and granting of time off (Journal of Laws No. 49/1974, item 299, subsequently amended).

247. A work establishment is obliged to release a worker from his work while continuing to pay wages:

1. for the performance of the functions of:

    a. a councillor or member of a people's council's commission;

    b. a lay judge;

    c. a member of the territorial body for dealing with minor offences;

    d. a member of the conciliatory committee at the work establishment;

    e. an expert appearing in court or before an administrative body;

2. for purposes connected with the performance of the general duty of defence;
3. for answering the summons of administrative, court, or other bodies;
4. for undergoing compulsory medical examinations;
5. for the performance of work specified in regulations or participation in training;
6. to enable the performance of functions of a member of the executive of a political, social or other organisation provided for in statutes, and participation in sessions of organs of such organisations and in their work as determined in provisions of law;
7. in other instances provided for by law (see n.1, para 232).

A work establishment may release a worker but without continuing to pay wages to workers taking part in sports activities as provided for by law, and in other occasional or vocational instances specified in legal provisions.[1]

1. See Ordinances of the Council of Ministers of 20 December 1974 regarding internal rules of employment and principles for justifying absence from work and granting of time off (Journal of Laws No. 49/1974, item 299, subsequently amended).

248. A worker may be granted time off for as long as necessary for taking care of some important personal or family matter; he has the right to remuneration for that time but he must make up the time lost.

The worker is entitled to time off while keeping his right to remuneration in instances of:
1. the wedding of the worker – two days,
2. the birth of the worker's child – two days,
3. the wedding of a child – one day,
4. the death and funeral of the spouse, child, father, or mother – two days,
5. the death and funeral of a sister or brother, mother- or father-in-law, a grandmother or grandfather, or of another person maintained by the worker or taken care of by him – one day.

§3. DEATH GRANTS

249. When a worker dies during his employment relationship, or while in receipt of a sickness benefit after termination of his employment, his family is entitled to receive a death grant from the establishment at the rate of:
a. one month's remuneration if his period of employment was less than ten years,
b. three months' remuneration if his period of employment amounted to at least ten years,
c. six months' remuneration if his period of employment amounted to at least twenty years.

The period of employment here includes any periods during which work was performed, irrespective of any interruptions or of the manner by which the employment relationship was terminated.

A death grant is payable to the following members of the worker's family:
a. his/her spouse,
b. other family members in the understanding of social security provisions.
A death grant should be shared equally among qualified members of the family. However, where there is only one family member qualifying for a death grant, it shall be paid to that person at the rate of one-half of the appropriate amount.

NATIONAL COLL_ _
OF IRELAN_
LIBRARY

Chapter X. Protection of Work

§1. THE NOTION OF 'PROTECTION OF WORK' IN POLISH LABOUR LAW

250. The field of protection of work in Polish Labour Law embraces at least four basic spheres:
1. occupational safety and health,
2. operation of the labour inspectorate,
3. protection of the work of women,
4. protection of the work of young people.
Although the last two spheres also embrace those exceeding the 'protection of work' in its exact meaning *e.g.* the specific rules of employment of both those categories of workers, the prohibition against discrimination against women in employment, leave granted to take care of young children, provisions specifying the purpose of vocational preparation in the employment of young people – it is common practice in Poland to treat those problems as part of labour protection in a wide understanding of this concept.

§2. OCCUPATIONAL SAFETY AND HEALTH

A. General remarks

251. The Constitution of the Polish People's Republic guarantees in Art. 70, as a fundamental civic right the right to protection of health, also substantiated by a steady improvement of conditions of occupational safety and health. A work establishment is charged with the duty to ensure that its workers are afforded safe and healthy working conditions. The discharge of this duty is an integral part of the establishment's activities: for this purpose appropriate use should be made of achievements in science and technology.

In the opinions of the State Labour Inspectorate, of trade unions, and in the general social assessment, the condition of occupational health and safety does not attain in many Polish work establishments a standard that might be deemed fully satisfactory. This is caused partly by the acute economic crisis that has occured in the 1980s.

B. Rules and provisions of occupational safety and health

252. In Polish Labour Law the notions 'rules' and 'provisions' of occupational safety and health are used. Considering that provisions can never reach a state of completeness, it is indispensable to refer to 'rules' which consist in the necessity of application of safety measures compatible with rational anticipation and up to modern standards of technological science and experience. The source of such 'rules' can be both the provisions of law (if such do exist) and also court rulings, experience, custom and, perhaps, principles of what is known as common sense. The absence of detailed provisions of law does not exempt a work establishment from the observance of 'rules' of occupational safety and health.

Provisions of a general nature governing occupational safety and health are issued by the Minister of Labour and Social Policy, in agreement with the Minister of Health and Social Welfare, and after agreement with the All-Poland Trade Union Alliance; provisions governing particular branches of industry are issued by competent ministers in agreement with the Minister of Labour and Health and with the agreement of branch trade union Federations.

C. General measures of occupational safety and health

253. According to the Labour Code, plans for the construction of new factories and of modification of industrial establishments must take account of occupational safety and health requirements, or improve the existing occupational safety and health conditions. A labour inspector takes part in the inauguration of a factory that has been newly constructed or modified.

Machines and technical equipment must be so designed and constructed as to ensure safe, healthy and suitable conditions of work and reduce the arduousness of working conditions. They must be assessed from the aspect of occupational safety and health before they are allowed to become operative. Machines and tools not complying with such requirements must be fitted with appropriate safe guards.

254. The establishment must provide its workers free of charge with protective clothing, personal protective equipment and other protective appliances, as well as with appropriate health and hygiene equipment and the necessary facilities for personal hygiene.

255. The factory management has to acquaint its workers with the rules and provisions of occupational safety and health relating to the work for which they are engaged. It is not permitted to hire a worker for employment for which he does not have either sufficient knowledge of the rules and provisions of occupational safety and health or the necessary skills.

Persons holding managerial posts must have due knowledge of the rules and provisions of occupational safety and health and of other provisions relating to the protection of labour.

256. The director of the establishment is responsible for the standard of occupational safety and health in that establishment. This responsibility applies also to the heads of departments of the establishment, foremen and other persons supervising groups of workers. On the other hand, organisational units above the level of establishments should, in the course of their activities, take account of the requirements of such establishments in connection with the provision of safe and healthy conditions of work.

257. It is a basic duty of every worker to observe provisions and rules governing occupational safety and health. Staff surveys of working conditions should be periodically carried out in establishments.

D. Preventive measures and medical care

258. It is the duty of an establishment to take steps to prevent occupational diseases and other illnesses connected with environmental conditions of work; for this purpose an establishment has to investigate systematically and measure factors harmful to health. These activities of an establishment should be carried out in co-operation with the public health service.

259. Work establishments have the duty to direct workers to medical examination of the following types:
– prophylactic, covering candidates for work and workers,
– preliminary, covering candidates for work and workers transferred to work stations arduous or harmful to health,
– periodic, covering workers exposed to operation of factors harmful to health, or employed at arduous work,
– control, covering workers with a disease lasting more than 30 days and those exposed to operations of ionizing radiation.

260. If a worker is found to have symptoms of an occupational disease, it is the duty of his establishment to examine the causes of the disease and the nature and extent of the danger and to immediately proceed to eliminate this cause. Where the necessity to do so is medically confirmed, the establishment must transfer the worker to other work not exposing him to the hazard of this occupational disease, for a period determined by a health service organ.

If a worker has become unfit for his previous job because of an accident at work or an occupational disease – and has not been classified as belonging to any disability group – then the establishment must transfer him to some other appropriate work, or if such a tranfer is impossible, contact the local employment placement service in order to ensure the worker a suitable job in another establishment.

Where a transfer in any of the above mentioned cases results in a lower rate of remuneration, the worker is entitled to a compensatory allowance for the period of his transfer, subject to a maximum of three months, or in some cases of six months.[1]

1. See Order of the Minister of Labour, Wages and Social Affairs of 14 November 1974 regarding the award to workers transferred to another post due to symptoms of an occupational disease of equalization benefits for a period of up to six months (Journal of Laws No. 47, item 292).

E. Accidents at work and occupational diseases

1. Accidents at work

261. An accident at work means a sudden event produced by an external cause which has occured in connection with work:
a. during or in connection with the performance of the regular operations or recommendations of superiors,
b. during or in connection with the performance by the worker of operations in the interest of the work establishment,
c. during the time the worker remains at the disposal of the work establishment.
On the par with an accident at work is an accident suffered by the worker:
a. during a service trip, unless the accident was caused by behaviour of the worker which had no connection with the performance by him of the tasks he was entrusted with,
b. in connection with the performance of service in self-defence formations at the work establishment or in the establishment's fire service,
c. at the performance of tasks ordered by the work establishment's political and vocational organisations, and also during participation in community work organised by them.
Also, accidents on the way to and from work provide a basis for specific insurance benefits.[1]

1. See Law of 12 June 1975 regarding benefits due in the case of accidents at work and occupational diseases, as subsequently amended (uniform text in the Journal of Laws of 1988 No. 30, item 144).

262. In the event of an accident at work it is the duty of the establishment to determine immediately the circumstances and causes and to take appropriate protective measures. The establishment should immediately notify the labour inspector, the public prosecutor, and its superior organisation of any accident at work which has resulted in death or serious injury or which has involved two or more persons.

The procedure to be followed in the event of an accident at work is determined in special provisions.[1]

1. See Order of the Council of Ministers of 5 December 1974 regarding determination of circumstances and causes of accidents at work, as subsequently amended (uniform text in the Journal of Laws of 1983 No. 55, item 244).

2. Occupational diseases

263. Occupational diseases are those arising in connection with the performance of a particular job or due to the conditions in which that job was performed, provided these diseases are specified in special regulations.[1] The differences between an accident at work and an occupational disease is that in the latter case there is not the element of suddenness: a disease develops as a continuous process and is usually revealed after some time has passed.

1. See Order of the Council of Ministers of 18 November 1983 regarding occupational diseases (Journal of Laws No. 65, item 294).

3. Benefits in cases of an accident at work or of an occupational disease

264. Accidents at work and occupational diseases provide a basis for benefits[1] provided by work establishments and by the Social Security Board.
The benefits due from work establishments embrace:
– a single payment in the event of permanent or lasting damage to health or the death of a worker;
– a compensatory benefit for a worker whose remuneration has been reduced because of a permanent or lasting damage to health; this applies to workers who have not been classified as belonging to any disability group and who do not receive any disability pension;
– compensation for objects ruined or damaged as the result of an accident.
The benefits due from the Social Insurance Board embrace:
– a post-accident disability pension (differing from a regular disability pension);
– a post-accident family pension (differing from regular family pensions).

1. See the Law of 12 June 1975 governing benefits due in connection with accidents at work and occupational diseases, as subsequently amended (uniform text in the Journal of Laws of 1983, No. 30 item 144).

265. Workers are not entitled to the above benefits if the sole cause of the accident at work was proven violation by the worker of regulations pertaining to the protection of life and health, or if the accident was brought about by him wilfully or due to blatant neglect.

Neither are benefits due to a worker who – when intoxicated – contributed significantly to the accident.

4. The rate of accidents at work in Poland

266. In 1985 there occured in Poland a total of 212,469 accidents at work of which 1,258 were fatal. The rate of accidents at work per 1,000 employed persons amounted in 1985 to a total of 17.52, 0.10 of them fatal. Among the causes of accidents are, in order of frequency:
a. absence, improper organisation or non-observance of occupational health and safety regulations,
b. incorrect organisation of work stations,
c. poor condition of technical-production equipment,
d. faulty work organisation,
e. absence of supervision,
f. absence or poor condition of personal protective equipment,

g. absence of training,
h. alcohol.

§3. LABOUR INSPECTION

A. The State Labour Inspectorate

1. Organisation of the State Labour Inspectorate

267. The State Labour Inspectorate is organised as a public service body charged with the supervision and control of labour law observance, and specifically of the rules and provisions governing occupational safety and health.

It is subordinated to the Council of State. Supervision of its activity is performed as laid down by the law[1] by the Chairman of the Supreme Board of Control and by the trade unions.

The State Labour Inspectorate consists of the Chief Labour Inspectorate and district labour inspectorates, and of labour inspectorates acting within the territorial competence of district labour inspectorates.

1. See the Law of 6 March 1981 on the State Labour Inspectorate amended in 1985 (uniform text in the Journal of Laws of 1985, No. 54, item 276); also the Resolution of the Council of State of 27 October 1983 regarding the award of statutues to the State Labour Inspectorate (*Monitor Polski* No. 36, item 201).

2. Council for the Protection of Labour

268. In order to ensure trade union control of the State Labour Inspectorate, the Council for the Protection of Labour was created as an organ authorised to programme and control operations of the State Labour Inspectorate, to carry out periodic assessments of its activities, and to resolve problems of protection of labour on a nationwide scale. The Council is appointed by the Council of State from among candidates proposed by the government, the trade unions, and other social organisations.

According to statute, trade union members should comprise more than one-half of the Council's members. Part of the membership should be appointed from among representatives of the field of science. The chairman of the Council is appointed from among candidates nominated by the trade unions.

3. Tasks of the State Labour Inspectorate

269. The tasks of the State Labour Inspectorate specifically include:
a. supervision and control of the observance by employers of Labour Law, especially of the rules and provisions regarding occupational safety and

health, provisions concerning the employment relationship, remuneration, working time, leave, protection of women's work, employment of young persons, etc.;

b. ensuring the observance of occupational safety and health provisions in the planning of the construction, reconstruction and modernisation of work establishments, machines, other technical equipment and technologies to be operated;

c. participation in the inauguration of constructed or reconstructed work establishments or parts thereof;

d. control of observance by employers of occupational safety and health requirements in the designing and production of machines, equipment and tools, as well as in the making of products and packagings, the use of which might cause risk to health and life;

e. analysis of the causes of accidents at work and of occupational diseases and preventive actions in this respect;

f. co-operation with environmental protection bodies in the control of observance by work establishments of provisions involving the counteraction of hazards to the environment;

g. ruling in cases of offences against workers' rights and participation in the respective proceedings;

h. the issuing of opinions on drafts of legal acts involving Labour Law and initiating legislative work in these matters;

i. initiating ventures and research in the field of Labour Law observance, specifically of occupational safety and health measures;

j. developing advice and technical information aiming at the elimination of hazards to workers' health and life.

4. Instruments of operation of the State Labour Inspectorate

270. For the performance of their tasks labour inspectors are vested with the following rights:
– to visit work establishments without previous notice at any time of the day and night in order to control the observance of the provisions of Labour Law, specifically those regarding occupational safety and health;
– to demand information and submission of documents in matters covered by the operation of the Labour Inspectorate;
– to order the director of a work establishment to eliminate all ascertained violations of the rules and provisions governing occupational safety and health;
– to order the work establishment or part thereof to cease an activity which presents risks to workers' safety and health;
– to submit protests or issue demands for the elimination of violations identified and to make the guilty persons bear the proper consequences.

271. An appeal may be lodged by the director of a work establishment to the district labour inspector against an order of a labour inspector. An appeal does not result in suspension of the implementation of an order unless the labour inspector himself suspends it pending the hearing of the appeal, so long as the activities of the work establishment do not pose direct hazards to the life or health of workers.

5. Liability for infringements of workers' rights

See paras. 192–193.

B. Social Labour Inspection

272. The social control of working conditions is performed by social labour inspectors,[1] elected by the workers themselves from among employees of the work establishment.

The social labour inspectorate as a social service represents the interests of all workers and is managed by the trade union organisations of the establishment.

   1. See the Law of 24 June 1983 on social labour inspection (Journal of Laws No. 35, item 163, as subsequently amended).

273. The scope of operation of the social labour inspectorate embraces control of the observance by the work establishment of the provisions of Labour Law, collective agreements and internal rules of employment, specifically in matters of occupational safety and health, the protection of women's work and the employment of young people, as well as in the control of technical and sanitary arrangements.

274. A social labour inspector has the following instruments of operation available:
- the right to visit all premises covered by the scope of his operation;
- the right to draw the attention of directors of work establishment to shortcomings in the sphere of occupational safety and health and make entries in the book of complaints and recommendations;
- the right to issue directors of enterprises with recommendations in writing aiming at the elimination of short-comings within specified time period or to recommend stoppage of work; the trade union organisation at the establishment should be notified of such recommendations.

Recommendations of a social labour inspector have the character of administrative decisions. The director of a work establishment has the right to file an appeal against such a recommendation to the appropriate labour inspector who will issue the final decision or undertake what legal measures are available to the State Labour Inspectorate. In this sense the social labour inspectorate acts as an auxilliary of the State Labour Inspectorate.

§4. Protection of Women's Work

A. The principle of equal rights of women and men in employment (the non-discrimination clause)

275. The Constitution of the Polish People's Republic guarantees (Art. 67) full equality of the rights of citizens regardless of sex, birth, education, profession, nationality, race, creed, social origin and status.

The principle of equality of rights of women and men is emphasised in Art. 78 of the Constitution, according to which

> 'a woman in the Polish People's Republic has the same rights as a man in all spheres of state, political, economic, social and cultural life. The guarantee of equal rights is provided by:
> 1. the right to work and remuneration equal to that of men, ensured by the rule of equal pay for work; the right to rest, to social security, to study, to honours and distinctions, and to the occupation of public positions;
> 2. protection of mother and child, protection of pregnant women, paid leave before and after delivery, extension of the network of maternity wards, nurseries and kindergartens, developement of the network of servicing and catering establishments.
> The Polish People's Republic strengthens the position of women, especially of mothers and career women in the community'.

Poland ratified ILO Convention No. 111 on Discrimination (in employment and occupation), as well as ILO Convention No. 100 on Equal Remuneration (men and women).

B. Special protection of women's work

1. Purpose and subject of protection

276. The specific psychophysical properties of women and their fulfilment of maternity functions require their protection against excessive physical effort and other aspects of work which may damage their health. This protection embraces:
a. prohibition of the employment of women in specified jobs or jobs with arduous features,
b. compulsory transfer of women to other work during pregnancy,
c. maternity leave,
d. leave enabling care over young children,
e. protection against termination of employment during pregnancy, maternity leave, and child-care leave,
f. other interruptions of and release from work.

2. Prohibited work

277. As a general principle it is forbidden to employ women in especially arduous work or work causing health hazards. More far-reaching restrictions are in force in the case of pregnant women; these depend on the length of pregnancy *i.e.* up to the sixth month and after the sixth month of pregnancy; as well as in the case of nursing women; and more generally they involve all women at child-bearing period. There are no exceptions, those problems being regulated in the list of jobs prohibited to women established by the Council of Ministers after agreement with the All-Polish Trade Union Organisation.[1]

There also exist provisions restricting the disposal of the work of women in certain instances. Thus, for example no pregnant woman may be employed overtime or at night work; there can be no exception to that rule. There are also other prohibitions of a relative nature, meaning that they may not be applied if the interested woman expresses her consent. Thus, no pregnant woman or woman taking care of a baby under one year of age may be given an assignment outside her permanent place of work without her consent. Also, no woman taking care of a baby under one year may, without her consent, be employed overtime or at night work.

1. See Order of the Council of Ministers of 19 January 1979 regarding the list of works prohibited to women, amended in 1984 (Journal of Laws No. 4/1979, item 18, change in the Journal of Laws No. 44/1984, item 233).

3. Compulsory transfer to other work during pregnancy

278. The obligation of a work establishment to transfer a pregnant woman worker to other work occurs in situations when:
1. she is employed at a job that is prohibited to pregnant women,
2. a public health service organ finds that she should not be employed at her previous job in view of her pregnancy[1] when the previous job is not on the prohibited list but may present risks to the health of the woman and to the developing foetus.

The 'transfer' may involve a decrease of the required intensity of the previous work. In cases when transfer to other work results in a reduction of wages, the woman is entitled to a compensatory allowance. After cessation of the causes justifying transfer to some other work, the establishment must employ the woman at the work specified in her contract of employment.

1. See directives of the Minister of Health and Social Welfare of 12 November 1976 regarding the method of issuance of a medical statement on the necessity of transfer of a pregnant woman to another work (Offical Journal of the Ministry of H. a. S.W. No. 22, item 76).

4. Maternity leave

279. During the period of confinement a worker is entitled to maternity

leave combined with the payment of a maternity allowance. The extent of maternity leave is:
- 16 weeks for the first confinement;
- 18 weeks for each subsequent confinement;
- 26 weeks when a woman is delivered of more than one child in any given confinement.

At least a two-week maternity leave should be taken before the expected date of confinement and at least:
- 12 weeks after confinement if leave amounts to 16 weeks;
- 14 weeks after confinement if leave amounts to 18 weeks;
- 22 weeks after confinement if leave amounts to 26 weeks.

A part of maternity leave not taken before confinement should be granted afterwards up to the total amount of leave.

If a child is stillborn or has died during the first six weeks of life, the woman is entitled to eight weeks' maternity leave after confinement. A woman delivered of more than one child in any given confinement is entitled to the amount of maternity leave corresponding to the number of children remaining alive. If a newborn child requires hospital care, a woman who has taken eight weeks' maternity leave after confinement may take the remainder after the child has been discharged from hospital.

280. Polish Labour Law also provides for 'leave on the same conditions as maternity leave'. This is due to a woman who has taken a foster child and has care of it and applied to a court for the initiation of proceedings for the adoption of that child. This leave is for fourteen weeks or until the baby reaches the age of four months. However, when taking a child up to one year of age for fostering, leave of four weeks is due.

281. While on maternity leave a woman is entitled to maternity allowance amounting to 100 per cent of her remuneration. This is calculated on the basis of the average monthly full remuneration paid to the female worker for the three calendar months preceeding the beginning of maternity leave, excluding prizes and elements of remuneration which do not have a permanent character.[1]

1. See the Law of 17 December 1974 on cash allowances from social security in cases of sickness and maternity (uniform text after amendments in the Journal of Laws No. 30/1983, item 143).

5. Child-care leave

282. Female workers employed for at least six months can, after the expiration of maternity leave, take child care leave, the duration of which is up to three years, but for not longer than until the child is four years old. Moreover, a woman taking care of someone else's child can also take advantage of such leave in situations determined by law,[1] or the child's father, if the mother does not take advantage of such leave and agrees that the father does so; and also, in specified cases – another member of the child's family.

In cases of the chronic disease, disability, or retarded mental development of a child, a woman may take advantage of a longer child care leave until the child is ten years' old.

1. See order of the Council of Ministers of 17 July 1981 regarding child care leave (uniform text in the Journal of Laws No. 2/1985, item 10, as subsequently amended).

283. A woman taking advantage of child care leave is entitled to a child care allowance during 24 or 36 calendar months. That allowance amounts to 100 per cent, 75 per cent or 50 per cent of the lowest basic monthly remuneration paid in Poland, depending on the level of the per capita income of the worker's family. A single worker taking care of child is entitled to an allowance increased by 100 per cent and by an extra amount laid down in detailed regulations. The child care allowance is not due if the family's per capita income is higher than the amount laid down in detailed regulations, or if the woman during child care leave takes up some gainful occupation, the wages for which are higher than the amount laid down in these regulations.

Child care allowances are paid by the work establishment which grants child care leave – from the social security funds.

284. During child care leave a woman may take up a professional, gainful, or training occupation within limits determined by detailed regulations.

The work establishment must re-employ a worker after termination of the child care leave in a position equal to the one held previously, or in another compatible with her qualifications at remuneration not lower than the one paid before leave.

6. Protection against termination of employment during pregnancy, maternity leave, and child care leave

285. The establishment may not terminate a female worker's contract of employment either with or without notice while she is pregnant or on maternity, child care leave, unless there are grounds for terminating her contract without notice through her own fault.

When a woman is pregnant or on maternity leave, the consent of the works' trade union committee is required for such termination. When the works' committee refuses its consent, the director of the establishment may appeal to its organisational superior which should settle the case in agreement with the appropriate trade union. Since 1982 the mechanism of that 'appeal' was not applied in view of the new situation in trade unions and the independence of enterprises in conditions of economic reform (*i.e.* the absence of competence of the higher trade union structures with regard to those organisations in the enterprise and the absence of units administratively supervising enterprises).

In certain conditions the termination of employment with a pregnant woman or one on maternity or child care leave is admitted, *i.e.* when the establishment is being liquidated.

7. *Other interruptions of and release from work*

286. A woman breast feeding her child is entitled to two half-hour breaks in the course of her work which are regarded as time worked. If a woman so requests, these breaks may be taken at one time.

A woman with a child under 14 years of age is entitled to two days off with pay during the course of the year. The same entitlement may be enjoyed by a male worker who is the sole guardian of a child under 14 years of age. A worker may also be absent from work because of the need to care for a child according to the rules laid down in paras. 242–244.

§5. SPECIAL PROTECTION OF THE WORK OF YOUNG PERSONS

A. Purpose and subject of protection

287. The special protection of work of young persons includes individuals aged from 15 to 18 years. The reason for this is considerations of health, for the bodies of young people are immature and still developing. Moreover, the aim of protection is to guarantee the possibility of further study and to prevent young people simply from taking up gainful employment without consideration of future career prospects. Thus the prime objective in the employment of young persons is to ensure the priority of study over work. Protection entails:
a. the fixing of a minimum age of employment,
b. the prohibition of employment other than that aiming at vocational training,
c. the enumeration of jobs prohibited to young people,
d. special regulation of the working time and leave.

B. Minimum age of employment

288. It is forbidden to employ a person who has not reached the age of fifteen years. Young persons (between fifteen and eighteen years) may be employed only when:
a. they have completed at least basic schooling,
b. they present a medical certificate that work of a particular kind presents no danger to their health.
In very exceptional cases special provisions permit the employment of persons who have not reached the age of fifteen years but who have

completed their basic schooling[1] and to employ young persons who have not completed their basic schooling.[2]

1. See Order of the Minister of Labour, Wages and Social Affairs of 21 October 1974 regarding employment of persons under 15 years of age (Journal of Laws No. 43, item 260).
2. See Order of the Minister of Labour, Wages and Social Affairs of 16 July 1979 regarding employment of young persons who have not completed basic schooling (Journal of Laws No. 16, item 103).

C. Prohibition of employment other than that aiming at vocational preparation

289. It is the rule that young persons without professional qualifications may be employed only for the purpose of vocational preparation. Vocational preparation takes place either in the form of learning a profession for two or three years, after which the young person gains the title of skilled worker; or in the form of training of from three months to one year, as an unskilled worker. A contract of employment concluded for the purpose of vocational training should specify the nature and duration of such training and the rate of remuneration. Such a contract may be terminated with notice but only in the event of:
a. the young person's failure to discharge the duties deriving from his contract or his duty to complete instruction despite the education provided for him;
b. liquidation of the establishment;
c. a reorganisation of the establishment to an extent making it impossible to continue vocational training;
d. the young person's unsuitability for the work for which he is receiving vocational training.
The rules and conditions governing vocational training of young persons and their remuneration during that time are determined in special provisions.[1]

In exceptional circumstances young persons may be employed on the basis of a contract of employment providing for vocational training:
a. at light, seasonal or occasional work,
b. at simple tasks, work not involving the operation of any machines.

1. See Order of the Council of Ministers of 20 September 1974 regarding vocational preparation of young persons and their remuneration (Journal of Laws No. 37, item 219, amendments in 1984 and 1985).

290. It is the duty of a young worker to continue his education until the age of eighteen years, unless he has acquired professional qualifications through training at school. More particularly he is required to:
a. receive further education in the fields covered by basic schooling if he has not completed primary education,
b. receive further education in a vocation or in the fields covered by general schooling.
The establishment should release him from work for such time as is necessary to take part in continuing education.

D. Work prohibited to young persons

291. A list of jobs prohibited to young persons,[1] including specific prohibitions designed to protect the young persons' health and life and also certain prohibitions having educational considerations in view. The prohibitions pertain to any employment, both that connected with vocational training or undertaken for gainful purposes; however, some exceptions are permitted with regard to young persons of at least sixteen years of age, if employment in certain prohibited work is an aspect of their vocational training.

To ensure the protection of young persons' health, the work establishment shall submit them to an initial medical examination, with periodic health checks carried out during the period of employment. If a physician finds that a particular job presents a risk to a young person's health, the work establishment shall change the nature of the work, and if this is impossible, it shall immediately terminate the contract paying compensation equal to remuneration for the period of notice of termination.

1. See Order of the Council of Ministers of 1958 (Journal of Laws No. 64, item 312, amendment in the Journal of Laws of 1970 No. 10, item 86).

E. Specific regulations of working hours and vacation leave of young persons

292. The working hours of a young person under sixteen years of age cannot exceed six hours a day, and in the case of young persons over sixteen years – eight hours a day. Any period of training, irrespective of whether it is received during working hours, is included in the working hours of a young person, up to a maximum of 18 hours a week.

No young person may be employed overtime or at night work. The holiday leave of young persons is longer than in the case of adult workers, and its conditions are more advantageous: twelve working days after six months, and 26 working days after one year of work. In the calendar year if a young person reaches the age of eighteen years, he is entitled to leave of 20 working days.

A young worker who is attending school should be granted leave during the school vacation. If a young worker studying at a school for working people so requests, his establishment should grant him leave without pay during the school holidays provided that such leave, taken together with his regular leave, does not exceed two months.

Chapter XI. Settlement of Individual Labour Disputes

§1. GENERAL PROBLEMS

293. Workers can seek to vindicate individual claims arising from employment by recourse to the labour courts. Before submitting a claim to the labour court a worker may – on a voluntary basis – take advantage of conciliation proceedings at the workplace. The means for settling individual labour disputes in Poland, as in other socialist countries, may be described as a combined social-juridical mechanism; the social element is ensured by easy access to conciliation procedures and by the participation of lay judges in court proceedings. It must be admitted, however, that after the 1985 reform of the system of settlement of individual labour disputes, the principal stress has been laid in the Polish system on the role of courts, while in certain other socialist countries the principal role is played by the social element, namely the trade unions.

294. It is strongly recommended that labour disputes, at each stage of the dispute, be settled by agreement. However, it is inadmissible to conclude an agreement that would be incompatible with law or with the rules of life in the community.

295. Polish labour legislation does not recognise any divergence between the conflict of rights and conflict of interests. The Labour Code merely indicates that beyond the competence of labour courts are disputes involving:
1. the establishment of new working and wage conditions,
2. the application of work norms,
3. service housing and accomodation at workers' hostels.
Polish Labour Law admits the notion of individual and collective labour disputes (of all the socialist countries, only Poland has the latter concept), without however providing detailed definitions of these concepts. The system of settlement of individual labour disputes is regulated in general outlines in the Labour Code and in detail in a separate law[1] and in the Code of Civil Procedure.[2] The system of settling collective labour disputes is regulated in the law on trade unions[3] and will be discussed below in Chapter XIV.

1. See the Law of 18 April 1985 on the examination by courts of cases involving Labour Law and social security (Journal of Laws No. 20, item 85).
2. Code of Civil Procedure of 1964. In 1985, Chapter III, Title VII of Book I of that Code was amended to read: 'Proceedings in cases concerning Labour Law and social security'.
3. See the Law of 8 October 1982 on trade unions (uniform text in the Journal of Laws of 1985, No. 54, item 277).

296. The rules for settling individual labour disputes in Poland have since World War II undergone numerous changes in both concept and legal regulation. Up to 1954 the labour courts operated in their pre-war form. In 1954 a universal system of workplace arbitration committees were introduced as the sole organs competent to deal with labour disputes (labour courts were liquidated); appeals from judgements of workplace arbitration committees were examined by central trade union branch organs.

That system, compatible with the trends prevailing at that time in all socialist countries, is today considered to be erroneous and incompatible with the Polish Constitution. It deprived workers of the right of settling disputes by courts, as guaranteed by the Polish Constitution, and helped to distort the proper role of trade unions. That system was changed after 20 years, in 1974, when labour and social security courts were again called into being as a system of courts separated from the general jurisdiction. Between 1974 and 1985 labour and social security courts settled claims in the second instance; in the first instance workplace arbitration committees functioned operating however on different principles from the previous ones. Special bodies outside the workplace were created for settling disputes involving termination of employment; they were known as appeal committees for labour affairs, composed of a social element but functioning under the chairmanship of a professional judge. The disruption of that system was caused in the early 1980s by the situation in Polish trade unions – trade unions then no longer assumed the role they were intended to fulfil in the bodies examining labour disputes in the first instance. Finally, the 1985 reform established a system of settlement of individual labour disputes in both instances by labour courts. Since then they have lost their character as a separate labour jurisdiction, becoming chambers of Labour and Social Security of the judiciary.

§2. CONCILIATION PROCEDURES AT THE WORKPLACE

297. Conciliation committees must be appointed in socialised establishments employing more than 50 workers. They may also be appointed in establishments employing fewer than 50 workers.

298. Conciliation committees are appointed from among workers employed at the workplace, though the following persons cannot be a member of a conciliation committee:
a. the director of the establishment or his deputy,
b. the chief accountant,
c. the legal council,
d. the head of departments dealing with personnel, employment and wages.

299. A workplace conciliation committee is appointed jointly by the works' trade union organisation and the workers' council. If there is no trade union organisation or workers' council at the establishment, then it is appointed by either one, and if neither exists – by the whole staff. The organs appointing the conciliation committee lay down the rules and procedures for the appointment of the committee, the duration of its term in office, and the number of its members. The conciliation committee elects from among its members a chairman and his deputies and lays down the rules for the conciliation proceedings. The law does not specify any rules of procedure for the workplace conciliation committee, which may select procedures most suitable for conciliation. However, the Minister of Labour and Social Policy, in agreement with the Minister of Justice, may issue recommendations regarding the appointment, organisation and operation of conciliation committees at the establishments and standard rules for conciliation procedures.

300. Conciliation proceedings in disputes involving workers employed at socialised establishments employing fewer than 50 workers, where no local conciliation committees operate, those employed at non-socialised establishments, and those holding positions of:
a. director of the establishment or his deputy,
b. chief accountant,
c. legal counsel,
d. head of the department of personnel, employment and wages affairs are held by conciliation committees of labour courts.
The rules and procedures of operation of such committees are governed by special provisions.[1]

1. See Order of the Minister of Justice of 17 June 1985 regarding conciliation committees of labour courts (Journal of Laws No. 28, item 123).

301. The establishment shall ensure to a workplace conciliation committee proper premises and the technical means to enable its adequate operation. The expenses connected with the operation of the committee are also covered by the establishment. Those expenses also embrace the equivalent of remuneration lost by a worker through absence from his work in connection with participation in conciliation proceedings.

The discharge of duties of a conciliation committee member is a social, voluntary function. However, a member preserves the right to remuneration during absence from work in connection with participation in the activities of the committee.

302. The conciliation committee should endeavour to settle the case by an agreement within fourteen days of the day of submission of the application.

In cases involving termination, extinction or institution of the employment relationship, conciliation proceedings are terminated by the force of law within fourteen days of the submission of the application by the worker; and in other cases – within 30 days of the submission of the application.

303. The purpose of the conciliation proceedings is to reach an agreement. The agreement should be entered into the minutes of the session of the bench and signed by the parties and by members of the bench. It is inadmissible to conclude an agreement incompatible with law or with the rules of community life.

When an establishment has not implemented an agreement, it should be executed under the provisions of the Code of Civil Procedure, provided the court has established its executory title.

A worker may apply to the labour court within 30 days (within fourteen days in cases involving termination, extinction or institution of the employment relationship) of the date of conclusion of the agreement and demand its recognition as invalid, if he believes that the agreement violates his justified interests.

304. If proceedings before the conciliation committee do not result in the conclusion of an agreement, the committee – upon the demand of the worker – should convey the case immediately to the labour court. The application of the worker for a settlement of the case before the conciliation committee is reckoned to replace the statement of claim. The worker, instead of submitting his demand, may himself submit the statement of claim to the court.

§3. LABOUR COURTS

305. Individual labour disputes are settled:
- in the first instance – by Regional Labour Courts, being separate organisational units of the regional courts, and
- in the second instance – by Labour and Social Security Courts, being separate organisational units of the *voivodship* (provincial) courts.
Labour courts are composed of one judge, who acts as the chairman, and two lay judges.

Disputes involving the establishment of new working and wage conditions, the application of work norms or service housing and accommodation at workers' hostels do not fall within the jurisdiction of labour courts.

306. Besides the workers themselves, proceedings in cases involving Labour Law may be instigated on behalf of the worker by social organisations, especially trade unions.

A worker may present his own case to the court, with no counsel; he may himself report the contents of the appeal measures and other legal documents and also corrections and amendments to them to the court.

A representative of the worker may be an advocate or a representative of the trade union or a worker of the establishment where the claimant is or was employed.

307. Proceedings in labour disputes are free of any court fees. As far as the expenses connected with the procedure are concerned, the court in the ruling terminating the proceedings decides them by applying the appropriate provisions on court expenses in civil cases, with the proviso that the worker himself may be made to pay such expenses only in particularly justified cases.

308. A claim against termination of employment with notice should be lodged with a labour court within seven days of the day of delivery of the letter notifying termination. A claim for re-instatement or for compensation should be lodged within fourteen days of the day of delivery of notification of termination of employment without notice or of the day of cessation of the contract of employment. A claim for institution of a contract of employment should be lodged within fourteen days of the day of delivery of notification of refusal of hiring. If a worker has not submitted his claim in due time, the labour court may, on demand of the worker, re-instate the expired time limit, provided there exist credible circumstances justifying such.

309. The court shall recognise as inadmissible the reaching of an agreement, withdrawal of a claim or appeal, as well as renunciation or diminishment of the claim, if it would be incompatible with law or with rules of community life, and also in instances when such action would violate a legitimate interest of the worker.

310. To ensure rapidity of proceedings in labour disputes, the Code of Civil Procedure requires the date of the hearing to be fixed in such a way that no more than two weeks should elapse from the date of submission of the claim or termination of clarifying operations to that of the hearing, unless there occur unsurmountable obstacles.

311. The labour court, when issuing its decision, examines claims that result from the facts quoted by the worker even in instances when the claim was not embraced by the demand of the worker, or if it was submitted to an extent lower than justified by the results of the proceedings.

312. From the sentence of the court of first instance, *i.e.* a Regional Labour Court, an appeal may be filed to the court of the second instance, *i.e.* the Labour and Social Security Court of a *voivodship* (provincial) judiciary. The review may be based on the following principles:
1. violation of law through its erroneous interpretation or improper application,
2. invalidity of the proceedings,
3. non-elucidation of all circumstances essential for the settlement of the case,
4. discrepancies between the essential findings of the court and the contents of the material collected in the case,
5. other transgressions of procedure if they might have affected the result of the case,
6. new facts and evidence which a party could not have presented in the first instance.
The appeal is filed with the court which issued the initial decision within two weeks of the delivery to the plaintiff of the decision with its justification.

313. From each final sentence may be submitted an appeal for extraordinary review to the Supreme Court. The basis of an extraordinary review is a glaring violation of law or interest of the Polish People's Republic. Extraordinary reviews may be submitted before the lapse of six months from the date on which the appellate judgment has become final and valid or

reviews based on the objection of violation of the interest of the PPR also after that deadline. Those competent to file an extraordinary review to the Supreme Court in cases involving Labour Law are:
1. the Minister of Justice,
2. the First President of the Supreme Court,
3. the Procurator General of the Polish People's Republic,
4. the Minister of Labour and Social Policy,
5. the All-Poland Trade Union Alliance (OPZZ),
6. the Chairman of the Supreme Board of Control – in cases involving benefits due for accidents at work and occupational disease.

§4. LIMITATION OF CLAIMS

314. Claims arising from an employment relationship are limited to a period of three years from the date on which the claim became enforceable. The period of limitation cannot be curtailed or extended by legal transaction.

A claim by an establishment for compensation for damage caused by a worker as the result of his failure to discharge his duties must be pursued within one year of the date on which the establishment became aware that the damage had been caused but in any event not later than three years after the occurence of the damage.

Claims confirmed by final judicial decisions or by agreement are excluded after ten years from the date on which the decision became final or the agreement was concluded.

A period of limitation does not begin and a period that has begun is suspended for such period as there is any impediment, if a claimant is prevented by *force majeure* from prosecuting his claim.

A claim that is barred by limitation may not be prosecuted unless the person against whom the claim is directed renounces the advantage he enjoys from limitation. The court takes account *ex officio* of the expiry of a period of limitation; it may disregard the expiry of limitation if the delay in the prosecution of the claim is justified by exceptional circumstances and is not excessive.

Part II. Collective Labour Relations

Chapter XII. The Trade Unions

§1. GENERAL ASPECTS

A. History of trade unions in Poland

1. 1919–1939

315. The history of the Polish trade union movement before regaining independence in 1919 is closely connected with the history of trade unions in the countries of central and eastern Europe, particularly those participating in the partition of Poland (Russia, Prussia and Austria). The first legal regulations determining the position of trade unions in independent Poland were passed in 1919. However, in 1932 because of the erosion of democracy in Poland, the trade unions were subject to the provisions concerning associations and therefore their independence was limited. There were three main trade union organisations in Poland between the First and Second World Wars: the Organisation of Occupational Associations with socialist tendencies, the Polish Occupational Federation with nationalist tendencies and the Christian Occupational Federation; there were also a few less important organisations.

2. 1945–1980

316. After the Second World War the trade union movement in Poland was united at the Unity Congress in 1949. The Federation of Trade Unions, representing the whole movement, was established. As a result the Trade Union Law of 1 July 1949 was passed. The Law of 6 February 1945 on establishing union councils was also still in force. The Trade Union Law of 1949 abrogated the provisions of the inter-war period limiting workers' rights to associate in trade unions and submitting trade union activities to the supervision of the administrative authorities. At the same time, however, the law entrusted the central organ of the united trade unions – the Central Council of Trade Unions – with keeping a register of trade unions: a newly established trade union acquired the status of a legal person from the moment of registration (this mechanism was criticised by the International Labour

Organisation and was altered in 1980). The organisational structure of the trade unions, during the 30 years during which the law of 1949 was in force, was based on grounds of so-called democratic centralism, which in practice, as the independence of the lower levels of trade union organisation was limited, acquired the features of bureaucratic centralism. The bureaucratic fossilisation of the trade unions, as well as the fact that they gave priority to their functions as co-organisers of the production process over their functions of defending workers' rights and interests, were the main subjects of the criticism raised against the trade unions in Poland in 1980. As a result, the Federation of Trade Unions collapsed, its executive organ, the Central Council of Trade Unions, was dissolved and a profound transformation took place within the trade union movement.

3. 1980–1982

317. The Social Agreement, negotiated between the government and the Strike Committee in Gdańsk in August 1980, provided for the establishment of independent and self-governing trade unions. According to the Social Agreement trade unions should observe the principles laid down in the Constitution of the Polish People's Republic; avoid playing the role of a political party; safeguard social property of means of production; recognise the leading role of the Polish United Workers Party in the State; and not impair the established system of international alliances. As a result of the Social Agreement the following types of independent and self-governing trade unions were established by the end of 1980:
1. the social-occupational movement Solidarity, consisting of – according to its own figures – about 9 million members,
2. autonomous trade unions, consisting of about one million members,
3. the old branch trade unions, continuing their activity in a new guise, consisting of – according to their own estimates – about five million members.

Because of deepening political and economic crisis in Poland and the announcement of martial law on 13 December 1981, the activities of all trade unions as well as other social organisations was suspended. The Trade Union Law of 8 October 1982 contained a provision, according to which registration of trade unions occuring before the Law came into force was no longer binding. That meant the dissolution of all previously existing trade unions, including Solidarity as well as branch and autonomous trade unions. The property of all trade unions was placed under the commissary management of the State.

4. The years since 1982

318. The Trade Union Law of 8 October 1982 began a new phase in the history of trade unions in Poland. The new trade unions, emphasising their self-government and independence from the State administration at present consist of over seven million members. With their embattled attitude to economic and social matters they have increasingly gained the confidence of Polish society. They have also extended international contacts and their representativeness is recognised by the International Labour Organisation (1987).

The new trade unions were initiated in work establishments[1] and after having their statutes registered by courts they pursued their activities for a long time only at the workplace with no higher level of organisation. It was only in 1984 that trade unions began to establish nationwide organisations,[2] usually in the form of federations, of which 116 have been established till 1987. Federations were created on occupational grounds, though in a somewhat chaotic manner: sometimes several federations act in one branch of the economy; in other cases, *e.g.* mining, several federations formed a type of super-federation, not however covering the whole branch. Some unions organised themselves as nation-wide occupational unions (17 till 1987), for instance the Polish Teachers Union. Others have not joined federations; they still act alone, as trade unions solely at the level of the enterprise.

A flexible form of national inter-union representation began to emerge in 1984,[3] for the common defence of workers' rights and interests against administrative authorities. The emphasis was laid on the flexibility of structures, so guaranteeing that they would not undergo a process of bureaucratisation. Initially the so-called Board of Federations' Chairman functioned; it was convened *ad hoc* and debated under the presidency of the Chairman of the Federation which convened it. The national inter-union body known as the All-Poland Alliance of Trade Unions was established at the First Congress of Trade Unions in Bytom in November 1984. During the next two years that form of nationwide representation and the principles of its activities were shaped in a way adequate to the requirements of trade union members and to the needs resulting from the new meaning and comprehension of the functions of self-governing and independent trade unions.

The Second Congress of Trade Unions, held in Warsaw in November 1986, declared itself the Congress of Polish Reborn Trade Unions, approved the establishment of the All-Poland Alliance of Trade Unions and endowed that body with a Statute of new content. The Congress voted to accept the Programme of the Polish Reborn Trade Unions for the next four years. The Congress reelected Alfred Miodowicz as the Chairman of the All-Poland Alliance of Trade Unions (with 61 per cent of the vote; his previous inclusion in the Polit-Bureau of the Polish United Workers Party was thought controversial by a part of the trade unions' electorate). The Congress also elected Deputy Chairmen of the All-Poland Alliance of Trade Unions, of whom four were elected in the first round of voting and three got the required majority of votes in further rounds of voting; one post of Deputy Chairman remains unfilled because the required majority of votes was not obtained by any candidate. Discussion at the Congress was sharp, substantive and concerned the programme of social and economic development of the country as well as impediments, which might become seeds of social unrest (the worsening of the financial situation of working people in Poland resulting from economic crisis, growing inflation and hardships of the economic reform).

1. Legal problems connected with the emerging of new trade unions in work establishments were regulated by the Resolution of the Council of State of 12 October 1982 on the principles and means of emerging of new trade unions' organisations in work establishments (Journal of Laws No. 34, item 222). Moreover, a Social Consultative Committee of the Council of State, under the chairmanship of Prof. Z. Salwa from Warsaw University, was formed in order to render individual advice concerning organisational and legal matters to persons intending to create a trade union organisation in their work establishment. That committee, after having performed its mission, dissolved itself in 1984.
2. Legal regulations were provided for in the Resolution of the Council of State of 12 April 1983 on the principles and means of creation of nationwide trade union organisations (Journal of Laws No. 21, item 92).
3. Legal basis was provided by the Resolution of the Council of State of 26 November 1984 on application of provisions concerning the initial activities of the nationwide interunion organisation (Journal of Laws No. 54, item 276).

B. The goals of trade unions

319. The programme, voted by the Trade Union Congress in November 1986 reads:

'The principle function of trade unions is the defence of working peoples' interests... We were restored to life because of the needs of working people – to defend workers' interests. We gather trade unionists of various outlooks on life and various lineages. We unite working people of town and country, workers and intellectuals. Representatives of all trade unions existing in Poland after August 1980 are among us. We are united by a concern for the future of our country and the well-being of our families'.

320. Trade unions pursue their activities on the basis of statutes which must be compatible with the Constitution of the Polish People's Republic and with other statutory law. In particular, trade union statutes should confirm that the unions recognise: the social ownership of the means of production as the fundamental principle of the socialist system, the leading role of the Polish United Workers Party in the construction of socialism, as expressed in the Constitution of the PPR, as well as the constitutional principles of the foreign policy of the PPR.

321. Trade unions represent the occupational interests of workers in dealing with management, state and economic administration, social organisations and in contacts with trade unions of other countries.

Trade unions represent and protect the interests and rights of workers as regards working conditions, wages, social and cultural facilities, specifically in the area of:

1. rational employment policy, including determination of rights and duties arising from the contract of employment,
2. remuneration for work and fringe benefits for workers,
3. health and safety at work as well as cultural working conditions,
4. working conditions for women and young workers,
5. social benefits for workers and their families,
6. recreation, sports, tourism and holiday facilities,
7. health protection of workers and their families,
8. sickness benefits, old-age pensions, disability pensions and other social security benefits,
9. meeting workers' housing needs,
10. the level of prices and the market situation, and living costs of workers and their families,
11. educational and cultural development within the working community,
12. protection of the natural environment.

Trade unions participate in the elaboration and achievement of objectives in the socio-economic development of the country; they work towards increasing the national income and its equitable distribution. Specifically, trade unions cooperate with enterprise management and with the self-managing bodies acting in such establishments in creating favourable conditions for performing the tasks required of the establishment, introducing technological and organisational progress, expanding workers' inventiveness and their contribution to rationalisation and improving the quality and effectiveness of work, economic efficiency, and health and safety at work. Trade unions perform educational work with a view to developing professional ethics and encouraging conscientious attitudes towards workers' duties and towards observance of the principles of community life.

322. The dilemma concerning the priority of either protective or production functions in the activity of trade unions, well known in socialist countries, has been firmly resolved by the Polish reborn trade unions on behalf of the protective functions; this was clearly emphasised at the Trade Union Congress in Warsaw in November 1986. At the same time trade unions took a rational attitude: 'We understand that to distribute material goods equitably, we must first produce them. We do not want to distribute poverty, but to participate in increasing production in order to distribute it equitably later', reads the Programme.

C. Self-government and independence of trade unions from administrative authorities. Voluntary membership

323. The Law of 1982 guarantees self-government to the trade unions. Self-governing trade unions have the right to determine independently and lawfully:

1. their objectives and programme of their activities,
2. their statutes and other internal rules and regulations concerning their activities,
3. their organisational structure,
4. the rules of electing union executive boards and other executive bodies.

324. The Law of 1982 guarantees independence of trade unions from state and economic administration. The statutory activities of trade unions are not subject to supervision or control by state administrative bodies. The State and economic administration should refrain from any and all actions which might result in the limitation of the trade unions' independence or in the restriction of their lawful activities.

325. Membership of trade unions is voluntary. The trade unions strictly observe this principle. They emphasise that they are not interested in 100 per cent membership (as was the case before 1980). The volume of membership attained (over 60 per cent of those workers having the right to associate in trade unions in 1987) is fully satisfactory and allows for the realisation of their functions and objectives.

The Law of 1982 guarantees that no person may suffer negative consequences either because of his/her membership in a trade union or assumption of functions within it as an elected official; or because of non-membership. Specifically, membership cannot be a condition of obtaining or keeping employment or for promotion. The trade unions represent their members and non-members in the same way. However, certain kinds of social action and cultural activities organised by the trade unions are available only for members, or members may benefit from them on more favourable conditions.

D. Trade union unity or pluralism

326. The Trade Union Law of 1982 does not impose trade union unity in Poland. On the contrary, some of its provisions clearly refer to a situation in which there is more than one trade union organisation in a work establishment. However, temporary regulations under this law provide that 'within a certain period of time whose termination will be determined by the Council of State, no more than one trade union organisation may operate at the workplace'.

Circles connected with the political opposition in Poland opt for trade unions pluralism. However, strong arguments, supported by the attitude of trade unions represented by the All-Poland Alliance of Trade Unions, are put forward on behalf of the principle 'one trade union in one work establishment', referring to recent negative experience of competition and hostility between various trade union organisations in a single work establishment, which damage workers' interests.

Some ideological tendencies in Poland have developed the thesis that in the second half of the 1980s there exists a 'socialist pluralism', whose principles have not been fully formulated yet.

E. The extent of the right of association

327. Persons working on the basis of a contract of employment, regardless of their position or of the specific basis of contract, as well as persons doing commissioned work and those working on the basis of an agency contract are vested with the right to associate in trade unions, provided they are not employers themselves. Retirement, whether on account of old age or disability, does not prejudice the right to associate in trade unions, neither does temporary unemployment while seeking a new job.

328. Certain categories of workers are exempt from the right to associate in trade unions. The list, enumerated in detail in the law includes categories of workers employed in national defence, in the Ministry of the Interior, the state administration, the judiciary and others.

F. The formation of a trade union

329. The right to form a trade union is ensured by the Law of 1982, provided the provisions of this Law are observed. No prior authorisation is required.

Persons intending to form a trade union elect a founding committee and adopt statutes. The number of persons in a founding committee of a nation-wide trade union organisation, on the day the statutes are presented for registration by the Court cannot be smaller than 30, and the number of persons forming a work place trade union must be at least ten.

A trade union may be formed for workers employed in a given branch of work, in a given type of employment or profession, in a given enterprise consisting of a number of establishments, or in a work establishment.

330. A trade union acquires legal personality and the right to pursue its activities on the date of its registration by a court: in case of the workplace trade union organisation by the local provincial court, in case of the nation-wide organisations or inter-union organisations – by the Warsaw Provincial Court.[1]

The Court may refuse to register a trade union if its statutes indicate that the organisation in question is not a trade union as defined by law, or if the provisions of the statutes are incompatible with the law. Alterations to the statutes should be immediately notified to the Court by the trade union concerned; until a ruling on the inclusion of these changes on the register, the original statutes remain binding.

1. See the Order of the Council of Ministers of 15 October 1982 on procedures for registration of trade unions (Journal of Laws No. 34, item 225).

145

G. The dissolution of a trade union

331. The Court strikes a trade union off the register:
1. in the case of a statutory resolution to dissolve the trade union,
2. if a trade union's membership remains lower than 50 persons for over three months.

This kind of issue is decided on the basis of the provisions of the Code of Civil Procedure in non-contentious procedures. An appeal against the ruling of the Court can be lodged with the Supreme Court.

332. If the Warsaw Provincial Court finds that the activity of a given trade union body is in flagrant contradiction to the law, it must set a three-month deadline for this body to adjust its activities to the law. These proceedings are instituted at the request of the Procurator General of the Polish People's Republic.

If a trade union fails to meet the above requirements prior to the expiration of the deadline, the Warsaw Provincial Court may:
a. impose a fine to be paid individually by members of the trade union body,
b. demand that the union leadership hold new elections to that body on pain of suspending that body's activities.

If these measures prove ineffective or if trade union activity proves to be incompatible with the Constitution of the Polish People's Republic and with other laws, the Warsaw Provincial Court may, at the request of the Procurator General of the Polish People's Republic, rule that the trade union concerned be struck off the trade union register. A trade union struck off the register should immediately discontinue its activities and, within three months of the decision to remove it from the register should dissolve itself in accordance with the procedure provided for in its statutes.

§2. Rights and Responsibilities of Trade Unions

A. Consultation

333. Trade unions have the right to express their views concerning:
– drafts of socio-economic plans,
– proposed bills and decisions concerning the rights and interests of working people and their families, including the living conditions of retired people,
– guidelines or drafts of legislative acts and decisions involving the rights and interests of working people and their families.

Trade union participation is ensured in drafting bills and preparing decisions which are of vital interest to working people and their families.

334. Trade unions have the right to put forward proposals and resolutions for new legislation or regulations or to modify existing provisions concerning the rights and interests of working people and their families. The organ of state – and also the Council of State and the Council of Ministers – to whom such proposals have been submitted is obliged to notify the trade union of its attitude to a proposal within one month (and the director of the workplace – within two weeks) and, should this attitude be negative, to substantiate it.

B. Social agreements and collective agreements

335. Trade unions have the right to conclude agreements on cooperation with state and economic administrative organs. Such agreements may be concluded at national level through all intermediate levels down to workplace level.

Trade unions have the right to conclude collective agreements of national scope, as well as collective contracts at enterprise level. In branches not covered by collective agreements, working conditions and wages are established in agreement with the trade union.

C. Other rights and responsibilities

336. Among other trade union rights and responsibilities the following are particularly worthy of note:
- trade unions carry out social control of the observance of Labour Law and undertake initiatives for the improvement of health and safety at work;
- trade unions organise social labour inspection and supervise the activities of the State Labour Inspectorate;
- trade unions cooperate with the Health Service, particularly with the industrial health service; they can organise and operate their own nursing homes and the like;
- trade unions supervise termination of employment at the employer's initiative; they may submit their reservations and negative assessments;
- a national representation of the trade unions (OPZZ) has the right to submit an extraordinary review against any valid judicial decision concerning Labour Law and Social Security Law; it also may submit to the Supreme Court proposals regarding the issuing of guidelines for the interpretation of Labour Law and Social Security Law and may demand explanation of provisions in these branches of law;
- trade unions have the right to assess the working conditions, wages and welfare of workers; to that end they are guaranteed full information on the social and economic situation throughout the country and at workplaces, subject to the obligation to observe the secrecy of classified state, economic and other official information;
- trade unions defend the rights and interests of retired workers; they take part in supervision of the Social Security Board;
- trade unions have the right to pursue their own research programmes within their statutory areas of competence, as well as to pursue publishing and editorial activities for trade union purposes;

– trade unions participate in the extension and dissemination of education and culture, they organise sports and recreation after work, run their own rest homes, supervise Workers' Holiday Fund and cooperate with the Garden Allotment Association;
– trade unions can pursue economic operations.

337. State and economic administrative bodies are responsible for the creation of the necessary conditions for the exercise of trade union rights. Employers should grant leave of absence without pay to workers elected to trade union offices. Management should grant occasional time off on full pay for trade union activities connected with the exercise of union functions if they cannot be performed outside working hours.

§3. STRUCTURE OF TRADE UNIONS

A. Trade union workplace organisations

338. The trade union organisation at a workplace performs the functions of trade unions through their statutory bodies. The statutory bodies of a trade union organisation at workplace level are as follows:
a. the General Meeting
b. the Executive Board
c. the Auditing Committee
Trade union officials in organisations at workplace level are usually elected for a term of office of two years.

339. Trade union organs at workplace level are elected. Trade union statutes usually specify the following principles of election:
– the number of candidates is not limited,
– individual candidates are voted upon,
– the ballot is secret,
– a trade union official may be re-elected only once,
– no trade union function may be performed by a person holding a managerial post in the workplace administration,
– the chairman of the Executive Board is elected by the General Meeting by secret ballot.
Members of trade union organs may be dismissed from the office to which they were elected before their term of office expires in the case of neglect of duties or infringement of the provisions of trade union statutes and resolutions. Decisions concerning dismissal are made by the General Meeting after hearing the member concerned.

340. Trade unions statutes usually provide that the trade union may defend the individual rights of non-union members if such a worker applies for aid.
Statutes also provide that in a case of collective dispute the trade union has the right to organise a strike or other form of protest, in accordance with the

provisions of the Trade Union Law. The strike is considered by statutes as the ultimate measure, which may be applied only after all other methods of resolving the dispute have been exhausted.

341. According to the Law of 1982 on trade unions in establishments where more than one trade union exists, each one pursues its activities with respect to its own members. The organisations concerned may agree that their functions be performed to an extent agreed by a joint body representing all the trade unions. A worker who is not a union member may authorise one of the existing trade union organisations to defend his rights, subject to its prior consent.

Since the Trade Union Law has been in force, *i.e.* from 1982 up to the time of writing this situation has not arisen because of the still binding transitional provision, according to which 'within a period of time whose termination will be specified by the Council of State – only one trade union organisation shall operate at a workplace'.

342. An employer cannot terminate an employment contract with a worker who is a member of the executive of a trade union organisation at the workplace, throughout the duration of his term and for one year after its expiration, unless there are reasons justifying dismissal without notice. When the trade union organisation forms part of a national trade union organisation (a federation), termination of the contract of employment may take place only after the prior consent of the statutorily designated body of that organisation.

B. Trade union federations

343. In most cases the workplace trade unions have established national trade union bodies for a given branch of activity or occupation (federations). However, up to 1987 a certain number have not joined these national federations: 600 thousand (of about seven million) members are associated in trade union organisations not represented at national level.

There were 116 trade union federations of 26 sectors of the economy in Poland in 1987. Certain branches have several federations; some of the existing mining federations have established a super-federation.

Although a federation is the most popular form of national trade union organisation, there are also seventeen other forms, *e.g.* the National Polish Teachers' Union.

344. Statutes of the trade union federations are highly differentiated. They all respect the independence of their federated workplace trade unions; some federation statutes contain a provision according to which the federation's resolutions are not binding on those workplace unions which do not accept them.

C. The National Inter-Union Organisation – the All-Poland Alliance of Trade Unions (OPZZ)

1. Aims of the OPZZ

345. The All-Poland Alliance of Trade Unions (OPZZ) represents its member organisations, the federations and the trade union organisations associated with them.

According to the Statute of the OPZZ, passed at the Congress of Trade Unions in November 1986, the goals of OPZZ are, in particular:
1. the defence of the rights and the protection of the social, occupational, welfare, cultural, health, work and environmental interests of workers, pensioners and their families;
2. the promotion of social activity and occupational ethics, and the protection of workers' dignity;
3. participation in the formulation and realisation of socio-economic goals through the creation of durable achievements by the Polish nation and socialist motherland and increasing national income and its equitable distribution;
4. the unity of the trade union movement and its integration;
5. the strengthening of the position of the Polish trade union movement in international associations and organisations;
6. cooperation with trade unions in other countries. striving for social progress, human rights, democratic freedoms and peace and friendship between nations.

346. The All-Poland Alliance of Trade Unions (OPZZ) strives after for the attainment of its goals by *inter alia*:
– organising cooperation of trade unions presenting a common stance to state authorities, the state administration and economic organs, as well as political and social organisations and associations,
– supporting the lawful activities of member organisations on authorised grounds with measures determined by Trade Union Law (*e.g.* the strike),
– acting in support of social agreements,
– trade union supervision of the observance of workers' rights and intervention in that area,
– appropriate activities of trade union representatives in Parliament, advisory bodies of the state and economic administration as well as in political, social and professional organisations,
– undertaking legislative initiatives through trade union members who are Parliamentary deputies,
– carrying out analytical and research activities,
– consultation and participation in drafting legislative acts, decisions and plans in the socio-economic field which concern the rights and interests of working people; lodging resolutions for legislation, decisions and plans, or their amendment,

– performing mediation functions in disputes between member organisations when authorised by the latter.

347. OPZZ is a member of the World Federation of Trade Unions. It may become a member of other international trade union associations and organisations. It may also negotiate agreements with foreign trade union organisations concerning the trade union rights of Polish citizens employed abroad.

Representativeness of OPZZ was acknowledged by the International Labour Conference in Geneva in June 1987 and re-affirmed in 1988.

2. The structure of the OPZZ

348. The Statute of the OPZZ guarantees that by joining the OPZZ the independence and self-government of member organisations, *i.e.* the federations are not reduced. Member organisations have equal rights and duties in the OPZZ.

349. The All-Poland Alliance of Trade Unions has the following organs:
– the Congress of Trade Unions,
– the Council of the OPZZ,
– the Executive Committee of the OPZZ,
– the Auditing Committee.
The term of office of these organs is four years.

350. The Congress of Trade Unions is the supreme body of the OPZZ; its functions consist of, among others, determination of the programme and main direction of OPZZ activities, voting its Statutes, the election of the chairman and deputy chairmen of the OPZZ (by secret ballot). The Congress is convened every four years; the convening of an Extraordinary Congress takes place within two months of the date of lodging a resolution by a simple majority of member organisations.

351. The Council of the OPZZ is the supreme body in the periods between the sessions of the Congress. The Council's sittings are convened by the Chairman or deputy Chairman of the OPZZ; they are held as needed, but at least every six months. The Council of the OPZZ consisted of 242 members in 1987.

352. The competence of the Executive Committee of OPZZ includes directing OPZZ activities in the periods between meetings of the Council of the OPZZ. The Executive Committee gathers in case of need, but at least once a month. It consisted of 60 members in 1987.

353. The Chairman and Deputy Chairmen of the OPZZ cannot fulfil the same functions in a federation. The same executive position in OPZZ bodies can be held for not longer than two terms.

354. Provincial (*voivodship's*) Alliances of Trade Unions exist in particular provinces in order to realise the goals and tasks of the OPZZ. The Provincial Alliances are appointed by the Council of the OPZZ following a resolution of trade union organisations acting on the territory of a given province to that effect.

In order to prepare opinions for OPZZ organs in matters falling within its statutory competence, the Council and the Executive Committee appoint permanent and temporary committees and subject teams; for instance, the Committee for Amendment of the Labour Code was appointed in 1987.

3. Property of trade unions

355. The property of the OPZZ consists of:
1. membership dues,
2. donations, legacies and grants,
3. income from economic and other statutory activities.

The property of the OPZZ was also enlarged by the property of all trade unions dissolved in 1982.[1]

1. See Order of the Council of Ministers of 30 April 1985 on the property of former trade unions (Journal of Laws No. 25, item 107).

Chapter XIII. Collective Agreements

§1. GENERAL PROBLEMS

A. Evolution of collective agreements in Poland

356. Collective agreements in Poland have undergone characteristic evolution. During the inter-war period they were negotiated in significant work establishments and their legal mechanism was regulated by the Law of 14 April 1937 on collective labour agreements.[1] The Law, with later amendments, remained binding until 1975, when it was abrogated by the Labour Code. During the early post-war years collective agreements in Poland were still negotiated in work establishments and contained important provisions adapting pre-war labour legislation to the new social and economic situation in socialist Poland. 1948 witnessed the beginning of a period of centralisation and direct guidance of economy that continued until 1956; this was a period of decline of collective agreements which were replaced by administrative regulation of the employment relationship. A period of decentralisation, which restored the economic and legal importance of collective agreements, began in 1956. The introduction of the Labour Code in 1975, a voluminous legal act exhaustively regulating the whole area of labour relations, again reduced the importance of collective agreements whose coverage *ratione materiae* was reduced. However questions of workers' remuneration and working conditions connected with the particularities of individual sectors were regulated for entire industries by collective agreements; up to the end of the 1970s 77 of them had been negotiated. These agreements, after certain amendments, are still binding in 1987; they will be replaced by new collective agreements in the near future. New agreements will be negotiated on the basis of the Collective Agreements Law of 24 November 1986.[2] These new collective agreements are being negotiated in 1987–1988.

1. Journal of Laws of 1937, No. 31, item 242.
2. See the Collective Agreements Law of 24 November 1986 (amendment to the Labour Code), Journal of Laws No. 42, item 201.

B. Legal character and legal situation of collective agreements

357. Collective agreements constitute a source of law of a peculiar character, typical of Labour Law. Their specific feature consists in the fact that they constitute bilateral negotiated acts, realised by an agreement between trade unions and economic administrative organs. The bilateral character of the act puts it in a privileged position compared to unilateral legal acts, as:
a. two parties of the agreement are interested in its execution,
b. the collective agreement guarantees higher legal certainty, as it cannot be changed by one of the parties, in contra-distinction to unilateral legal acts concerning Labour Law.

§2. Collective Agreements at Industrial Branch Level (Branch Collective Agreements)

A. Contents of a collective agreement

1. Normative contents of an agreement

358. Jurisprudence distinguishes three basic elements of a collective agreement:
1. the normative element,
2. the element containing mutual obligations and duties,
3. other provisions of a miscellaneous character.

359. Collective agreements are negotiated for workers employed at work establishments belonging to a given branch of activity or occupation; occupations for which agreements can be concluded are determined by the Council of Ministers in agreement with the national inter-union organisation, the OPZZ.

360. A collective agreement determines:
– the conditions of workers' remuneration and other benefits connected with the work,
– the working conditions resulting from the characteristics of the branch of work or occupation, including the rights of workers justified by the character of work in the given branch of work or occupation,
– the principles and means of guaranteeing health and safety at work, as well as social, welfare and cultural conditions,
– the mutual obligations and duties of the parties to the agreement involving the rules and means of its implementation.

361. The provisions of collective agreements should conform to provisions of law as well as to the social and economic policy of the state laid down by the Parliament in the socio-economic plan.

An agreement may specify broader and more advantageous workers' rights than those provided generally and uniformly by the Labour Code and other laws, if this is justified by specific conditions of a job or occupation or if it results from the authorisation of the Code or other laws. However, a collective agreement may not prove less advantageous to workers or more restrictive than general regulations provided by law.

2. Wages and remuneration

362. For enterprises and work establishments, whose favourable economic situation allows the conclusion of a workplace collective agreement (see below paras. 377–381), the branch collective agreement, when laying down conditions of wages and remunerations determines the minimum rates as well as the rules of granting them. The agreement can also determine other components of wages and remuneration,[1] particularly those justified by the character of work in the given branch of industry or occupation or by other specific requirements or elements depending on the effects of work.

For workers employed in enterprises or other work establishments which, for economic reasons, cannot afford to conclude a workplace collective agreement, the branch collective agreement determines detailed conditions of wages, remuneration, and other benefits connected with their work.

1. See the Resolution of the Council of Ministers of 17 August 1987 on the rules of shaping wages, remunerations and other benefits in collective agreements in the period of 1987–1990 (*Monitor Polski* No. 26, item 206).

3. Assessment of implementation and interpretation

363. The parties concluding a collective agreement may establish methods for periodic assessment of its implementation and decide on their mutual obligations in regard to the observance of the agreement.

The interpretation of the content of a collective agreement is laid down jointly by the parties to the agreement. Such interpretation is also binding on parties subsequently acceding to the agreement.

B. Parties to a branch collective agreement

364. In the process of negotiating and concluding a branch collective agreement the employer's side involves the branch economic administration, directors of enterprises and workers self-management (it should be noted that in this case, the workers' self-managment acts on the employer's side). The workers' side is represented by the trade unions.

More particularly, branch collective agreements are concluded:[1]
– on the employer's side: by the appropriate branch minister, after coordinating the contents of each agreement between the representatives of interested enterprises (see para. 365) and the representatives of a national trade union organisation (federation),
– on the workers' side: by a national trade union federation; if several federations exist in a given branch, they may appoint joint representation for the purpose of negotiating and concluding the agreement.

Any of the parties may take the initiative for concluding agreement.

1. See: The Collective Agreements Law of 24 November 1986, amendment to the Labour Code (Journal of Laws No. 42, item 201).

365. The representatives of the enterprises concerned, appointed by the appropriate branch minister on behalf of the employers side in order to harmonise the contents of the agreement with the trade unions should adequately represent the organs of enterprises in the given sector. The organs are as follows:

1. workers' self-management bodies: the general assembly of the workers and the workers' council (see paras. 407–416),
2. the director of the enterprise.

Thus there is a joint representation of directors of enterprises and workers' councils.

After these representatives and the trade unions have agreed the contents of the agreement, the minister asks all organs of the enterprises concerned (their directors and workers' councils) for their views concerning the conclusion of the agreement. This view should be provided within 30 days. If the enterprise bodies do not issue a positive opinion of the agreement, the minister organises consultation with their representatives in order to consider the reservations; this does not delay conclusion of the agreement for the remaining enterprises in the given sector. After this adjustment the collective agreement is signed by the appropriate minister.

366. If in a given branch there are few trade union federations and no joint representation for conclusion of an agreement has been appointed, each federation concludes the agreement separately. The agreement is considered to be concluded after it has been signed by all trade union federations existing in a given branch.[1]

1. See the Order of the Council of Ministers of 30 April 1987 on particular procedures for conclusion, termination and registration of collective agreements (Journal of Laws No. 15, item 90), issued in agreement with the All-Poland Alliance of Trade Unions (OPZZ).

C. Registration of the branch collective agreement

367. Registration of a collective agreement by the Minister of Labour and Social Policy, which should be done within three months of the day on which the agreement was submitted for registration, is a condition of its coming into force.

368. Before registration the Minister of Labour and Social Policy examines the conformity of the agreement's provisions to law and to the social and economic policy of the state. If he finds that the agreement fails to conform to the provisions of law, any of the parties to the agreement may apply to the Supreme Court for resolution of the dispute. If the Minister of Labour and Social Policy finds a discrepancy between the agreement and the social and economic policy of the state, the dispute should be settled, following a request by any of the parties, by a commission, half of whose members are appointed by the government and half by the All-Poland Alliance of Trade Unions (OPZZ).

369. The Minister of Labour and Social Policy enters a collective agreement into the register and includes it in the set of collective agreements; then he notifies the parties to the agreement and the All-Poland Alliance of Trade

Unions of registration and announces it in the *Official Journal* of the Ministry of Labour and Social Policy.

The branch minister publishes the agreement in a circulation ensuring a sufficient number of copies to all trade union organisations concerned and to work establishments.

370. Throughout the period of coordination of the draft agreement by the parties, during the registration process and during the settlement of a dispute concerning an alleged discrepancy, the law on collective agreements forbids recourse to collective dispute prodecures and the right to strike (see below paras. 392–399).

D. Binding force of the branch collective agreement

371. The work establishment is obliged to notify its workers of the coming into force, notice to terminate or termination of an agreement. It is also obliged to facilitate access to a copy of the agreement on demand, and to explain its contents.

The agreement enters into force at the time indicated in it, but not earlier than on the day of its registration. From the day of its entering into force, the provisions of the agreement replace the corresponding conditions of contracts of employment resulting form previously valid agreement regulations.

372. A collective agreement should be made in writing. It may be concluded for an indefinite period or for a definite period; in the latter case the parties may extend its validity for a specific period or for an indefinite period – extension should be made prior to the expiration of validity of the agreement.

373. An agreement applies to all workers employed in enterprises and establishments covered by it, unless the parties decide otherwise in the agreement.

The branch minister and a trade union federation may agree to accede, wholly or in part, to an agreement to which they are not parties.

The Minister of Labour and Social Policy can, on the suggestion of an appropriate national trade union federation – if required by the social or economic policy of the state – expand the coverage of a specific collective agreement.

374. Modifications to an agreement are introduced in the form of supplementary protocols.

E. Termination of a collective agreement

375. The collective agreement may be terminated:
– by consent of the parties at a time determined by them,

– on expiration of the period of notice of termination given by one of the parties; the notice of termination should be made in writing; it cannot be shorter than three months and should expire at the end of a calendar or fiscal year,
– on the expiry of the period for which the agreement was concluded.
In the event of termination or of notice of termination of an agreement, the parties should immediately begin negotiations for a new agreement. Until the conclusion of a new agreement or extension of the validity of the previous one, the previous agreement remains in force unless the parties decide otherwise.

376. If the terms of the projected national socio-economic plan mean that the collective agreement conflicts in some way with the social and economic policy of the state, the law requires the parties to conclude a new agreement or to make appropriate amendments in the existing one. Disputes in this area are subject to resolution by the commission appointed to examine discrepancies between collective agreements and socio-economic policy (see para. 368).

§3. WORKPLACE COLLECTIVE AGREEMENTS

377. Workplace collective agreements may be concluded in enterprises and work establishments pursuing efficient economic activities resulting in a sound economic situation and possessing their own financial resources according to the principle of self-financing. Evaluation of fulfilment, by the enterprise or work establishment, of the conditions required for conclusion of a workplace collective agreement is issued by the establishing organ of the enterprise[1] (the supervising economic administrative organ).

> 1. See: Law of 26 January 1984 on the principles of creation of workplace remuneration systems (Journal of Laws No. 5, item 25), and substantial amendment of 17 June 1988 (Journal of Laws No. 20, item 134).

378. The workplace collective agreement is concluded:
– on the employers side: – by the director of the enterprise or establishment, after seeking the opinion of the workers' council and obtaining a positive opinion from a general meeting of workers,
– on the workers' side – by the workplace trade union.

379. The workplace collective agreement specifies:[1]
1. the tasks connected with the implementation of plans of the enterprise or establishment regarding the creation of conditions favouring increased labour productivity and improvement of operational efficiency and strengthening of labour discipline,
2. the workplace remuneration system elaborating detailed conditions regarding wages and other benefits connected with work,
3. on the basis of and within the framework of the branch collective

agreement, detailed rules regarding working conditions and other matters connected with the implementation of the agreement.

1. See the Law of 24 November 1986 on collective agreements (Journal of Laws No. 42 item 201), as well as Order of the Council of Ministers of 30 April 1987 on detailed procedures for conclusion, termination and registration of collective agreements and conclusion and registration of workplace collective agreements (Journal of Laws No. 15, item 90).

380. The workplace collective agreement may apply higher wages and benefit rates than the minima laid down in the branch collective agreement, if the enterprise or establishment has sufficient financial resources, earned in accordance with the principle of enterprise self-financing, at its disposal. This possibility does not apply to enterprises undergoing economic rationalisation to improve its economic position or in process of liquidation or bankruptcy proceedings.[1]

1. See the Law of 29 June 1983 on the improvement of economy of state enterprises and on bankruptcy (uniform text in Journal of Laws No. 8/1986, item 46).

381. Regulations concerning the conclusion and termination of branch collective agreements are also applied to the conclusion and termination of workplace collective agreements.

Workplace collective agreements are subject to registration by an establishing body (a supervising administrative organ), after ensuring conformity of the workplace collective agreement both to provisions of law and to provisions of the branch collective agreement and after the opinion of the appropriate national trade union federation has been sought. If registration is refused, the parties to the workplace collective agreement and the registrar should immediately begin negotiations aiming to make the agreement conform to law and to the provisions of the branch collective agreement. If the negotiations fail, each party may demand the start of conciliation procedures by a commission appointed by both parties to the dispute (each party appoints half of the commission members), directed by an arbitrator trained in law, who is chosen by the parties. If conciliation does not result in common understanding, each party to the agreement may demand settlement of the dispute by a regional labour court.

Chapter XIV. Collective Labour Disputes and the Right to Strike

§1. The Notion of 'Collective Labour Dispute'

382. The term 'collective labour dispute' entered political and legal vocabulary in Poland in 1980–1981; it soon became the subject of the only such legal regulation in socialist countries, introduced in the law of 1982 on trade unions.[1] The legal solutions adopted in the law of 1982 are based on a draft worked out by a negotiating team composed of government and trade union representatives in 1980–1981 and reflect the experience of that period. At the same time they are considered to be durable solutions, adequate to the new situation and new forms of trade union activities emerging after 1982. Acceptance of the strike as a legal mechanism of social pressure and, at the same time, as a final legal weapon in the effort to settle a collective labour dispute is one of the most characteristic aspects of Polish Labour Law in the 1980s.

1. See the Law of 8 October 1982 on trade unions (uniform text after amendments introduced in 1985, in Journal of Laws No. 54 of 1985, item 277).

383. According to the law of 1982, the parties to a collective labour dispute are trade unions and the appropriate organs of economic administration or enterprise management. A dispute should be resolved by application of the legal mechanisms of negotiation, conciliation and arbitration, determined by the law of 1982.

384. The economic and social rights and interests of a certain group of workers – the entire staff of an enterprise or any part, workers of several enterprises or of the whole branch of industry – may be the subject of dispute.

Though the law of 1982 excludes action of a political nature only with reference to the strike, official interpretation indicates that demands for realisation of political postulates, exceeding the statutory competence of trade unions, cannot be recognised as a collective dispute in the meaning of the law of 1982. Neither does a case in which a large number of workers lodges the same individual claim to a court make a dispute collective – it retains its individual character.

In May 1988 the Law on special economic powers and authorisations for the government,[1] issued with intention to overcome certain impediments in realisation of the economic reform and to accelerate its rate – forbid the initiation of collective labour disputes concerning matters resulting from utilisation by the government of its special economic powers and authorisations, unless the starting of the dispute had been approved by the All-Poland Alliance of Trade Unions (the OPZZ) after previous consultation with the appropriate trade union Federation. This restriction was intended to remain in force from May till the end of 1988.

1. See the Law of 11 May 1988 on special economic powers and authorisations for the
   Council of Ministers (Journal of Laws No. 13/1988).

§2. A THREE-STAGE LEGAL MECHANISM FOR SETTLING COLLECTIVE LABOUR DISPUTES

A. Aims of the mechanism

385. The Law of 1982 on trade unions established a three-stage mechanism
for settling collective labour disputes. The mechanism has several basic aims,
including:
1. resolving the issues in dispute
2. signalling the emerging conflictual situation to the parties and to interested
   bodies and revealing the essence of the conflict.
3. preventing the conflict from spreading.
Certainly, the very existence of such institutionalised channels for resolving
conflict plays a certain preventive role and aids conflict resolution in the early
stages before the emergence of a formal dispute.

The trade unions possess numerous rights helping them to attain their goals
in non-contentious ways, such as consultations, agreements, etc. On the other
hand, however, the very existence of mechanisms for settling collective
disputes, complemented by the right to strike, makes those other forms of
trade unions activity more effective. For instance, when in 1985, 1986 and
1987 they opposed the extent of planned price increases, the trade unions
more than once used their right to enter a collective labour dispute as an
effective argument.

B. Direct negotiations

386. When a collective labour dispute has emerged, the parties are
statutorily obliged to undertake immediate negotiations. These may be
conducted in any manner convenient to the parties – the law does not
intervene in this procedure. Entering into negotiations is a legal duty of the
parties: the main addressee of that duty is the employer (director of the
enterprise), as usually negotiations are begun on trade union initiative. It is
obvious that settling a dispute as a result of such direct negotiations is the
optimal solution.

C. Conciliation

387. If no agreement has been attained in direct negotiations either party
may demand the start of conciliation proceedings, which are optional and
may be omitted (however omission of this stage results in a situation in which
the legal mechanisms for settling the dispute are not considered to have been

exhausted, and therefore a strike is inadmissible). If however, such a demand has been put forward by one of the parties, they are obliged to appoint a conciliation committee consisting of six persons, three from each side. Such a committee is an *ad hoc* body – it is only competent to consider one particular dispute. The law does not intervene in the selection of committee members, nor in the procedure; it merely establishes the time limit within which conciliation should be achieved: within seven days if the dispute concerns one particular enterprise and within ten days if more enterprises are involved. If conciliation fails within the prescribed time limits, the conciliation committee prepares records of differences, indicating the attitudes of both parties. The committee, being a conciliatory body, has no power to make decisions – it may, however, incline the parties to conciliation, suggesting the extent of required concessions or compromise.

D. Social arbitration

388. The third stage of the legal mechanism for settling collective labour disputes consists in mandatory social arbitration. Undergoing social arbitration is a necessary pre-condition of strike action. A further pre-condition of strike action, according to the law of 1982 on trade unions, is a statement by the trade union concerned, prior to arbitration, to the effect that it will not necessarily be bound by arbitration settlement; if no such reservation has been made, arbitration settlement is binding for both parties and strike action is precluded. In numerous disputes trade unions have taken advantage of the possibility of issuing such a reservation.

389. Social arbitration is a rather new and original institution with no precedent in socialist countries. It operates through:
– the Social Arbitration Board of the Supreme Court, competent for cases of collective disputes involving more than one enterprise,
– the Social Arbitration Board of a Provincial Labour Court, competent for disputes involving only one enterprise or factory.
The Boards consist of a chairman, appointed by the President of the relevant court from among judges of that court, and three members appointed by each party. The law recommends the appointment of persons not personally concerned with the subject of the dispute. A board is summoned *ad hoc* for each particular dispute. Locating the boards at courts and making professional judges their chairmen results from the need to ensure that a proper role in arbitration settlement is played by an impartial, independent element possessing legal competence. The law also authorises the boards to take advantage of the aid of experts should a decision require specialist knowledge.

390. According to the rules of proceedings for Social Arbitration,[1] the boards are guided in their decisions by the provisions of law and the rule of community life; they take into account both the interests of the parties and the interests of the state. A majority is required for final decision. A member of the board cannot abstain from voting; however, if he does not agree with the majority, he may declare his minority view while signing the decision.

The Social Arbitration Boards do not administer justice in the same sense in which the courts do; therefore they are not considered a part of the administration of justice. No normal remedies, such as the right to appeal, provided by judicial proceedings, are vested in the parties to Social Arbitration.

1. See the Resolution of the Council of State of 30 December 1982 on rules of procedure before Social Arbitration Boards (*Monitor Polski* No. 1/1983, item 1).

E. Practice of settling collective labour disputes in Poland

391. It should be stressed that the three-stage mechanism of peaceful resolution of collective labour disputes is not a purely theoretical matter in Poland. According to the statistics of the State Labour Inspectorate for 1985–1986, about 800 situations corresponding to the statutory term 'collective labour dispute' arise each year in Poland. The majority of them are resolved by various informal activities and interventions, but a substantial number are examined through direct negotiations and conciliation procedures. A wave of specific collective disputes arose in May 1988 as a result of economic hardship connected with radical economic reform's decisions (prices increases). As far as Social Arbitration is concerned, 29 disputes had reached this stage of the mechanism by 1987; 2/5 of them were concluded with a compromise reached at the Social Arbitration Board, 2/5 were settled by a decision of the Social Arbitration Board and in 1/5 the proceedings continue at the time of writing. At the same time new disputes are being lodged.

The following are examples of collective disputes between *national* trade union organisations and *central* administration:

- *Federation of Ship Repair*: a dispute arose with the former Minister of Labour, Wages and Social Affairs concerning the distribution of working time; in Autumn 1986 arbitration procedure accepted the claims of the trade unions.
- *Federation of Tourism*: a dispute arose with the former Chairman of the Committee for Physical Culture and Tourism concerning increased meat coupon norms for the manual staff of hotels; the dispute was lost.
- *Federation of Open-Pit Miners* (Rock Miners): a dispute with the Government commenced in October 1986 and was aimed at extending the 'Miner's Charter' to the miners employed in granite and basalt quarries (miners employed in sedimentary rock quarries were already covered by the 'Miner's Charter'). The issue had been in existence for many years. Despite recent work on amendments to the Regulation of the Council of Ministers dated 30 December 1981 concerning the 'Miner's Charter', the council of the Federation decided to announce protest action and strike stand-by. On 16 March 1987, as an expression of the protest, all enterprise buildings

were equipped with flags. On 19 March 1987, the Chairman of the Council of Ministers signed a decision which extended to rock miners the provisions of the 'Miner's Charter', thus accepting the rock miners' protest.

– *Federation of Construction Workers*: a dispute arose with the Minister of Construction concerning an unlawful (as maintained by the Federation) limitation of allowances to pensions secured for some professions by the 'Charter of Construction Workers'. The Board of Social Arbitration is in favour of the claim, yet the dispute continues; on 9 May 1988 another round of talks advanced the possibility of a final settlement of the dispute in the near future.

– *Federation of Energy Workers*: a dispute with the Minister of Industry commenced on 20 April 1988 concerning wage increases to the level existing in other industries. Claims have been made to implement the provisions of the 1980 agreements which guaranteed a wage level corresponding to that of steel-mill workers. The dispute was settled on 3 May 1988, with the signing of an agreement in which preferences were made in order to reach a 50 per cent wage increase.

– *Four Federations of Communications Branch*: a dispute arose with the Minister of Transportation, Maritime Economy and Communications concerning an average wage increase in order to make it close to the national average. On 3 May 1988 an agreement was signed before the Board of Social Arbitration which secured additional means for a motivation fund, an increase of exports and improved quality of services.

– *Federation of Municipal Transportation*: a dispute arose with the Minister of Transportation, Maritime Economy and Communications concerning the wage increase and an adjustment to that of other branches. The dispute commenced on 17 March 1988 and was settled with an agreement signed after a strike in Bydgoszcz. The wage increase for municipal transportation workers was made possible through concessions in the excessive wage increase tax and an efficiency improvement programme which have permitted wage rises by some 50 per cent.

– *Federation of Miner's Trade Unions*: a dispute arose with the Government in May 1988 concerning a revaluation of real wages and system of wages determination. According to the Federation, the fixed 30 per cent threshold for wage increases free of the excessive wage increase tax does not secure the possibility of keeping up with the increasingly rising cost of maintaining living standards. Claims were made to increase by 50 per cent the wages in mining. In the course of negotiations it was agreed that, in view of recent decisions fixing the tax-free threshold of wage increases, it was possible to provide a wage rise of 49 per cent on the average. In the final agreement signed on 10 May 1988 it was provided that, after the second quarter, an analysis of wages and living standards costs in mining would be carried out in order to take further appropriate decisions.

The following are examples of collective disputes at the enterprise level:

– *Mechanical Equipment Factory 'PONAR' in Ostrzeszów*: (March – April 1987). A dispute arose concerning a change in the wage system. After having exploited the entire legally-prescribed procedures, including a strike stand-by, the trade union won concessions in an agreement: the wage increase reached was 7,071 zlotys ($1 = 624 zlotys at 6 June 1988), *i.e.* close to that claimed (8,000 zlotys). The dispute was announced after the management stated that wages for 1987 may increase only by 500 zlotys and four per cent of the bonus per employee (the average wage at that time was 19,600 zlotys).

Any wage increase higher than that might have caused bankruptcy of the enterprise due to the danger of exceeding the twelve per cent wage increase threshold and subsequent 500 per cent tax on any wage increase above that, which would result in lost crediting abilities in spite of the high perform-ance of the enterprise. The agreement was signed and announced twenty minutes before the strike was to commence. The strike was declared - according to legal provisions - by the enterprise workforce in a secret ballot in which 992 workers took part (the total enterprise workforce being 1,400 persons) - 721 were for the strike, 109 against and eighteen votes were not valid. In this case, the rules of the economic reform were observed, and the dispute was settled within the enterprise though it necessitated extra work having a total value of about 700 million zlotys (this provision was mentioned in the agreement).

– *Electric Machine Factory EDA in Poniatowa*: (April – October 1987). The dispute concerned a wage increase of 3,500 zlotys. In accordance with the legal provisions, the course of the dispute involved a referendum, strike stand-by and warning strike. The final wage increase amounted to about 1,300 zlotys per worker. In the referendum, 72 per cent of those entitled to vote cast their votes, 92 per cent of whom voted 'for'. Financial means for the wage increase were taken from the part of profits devoted to development and paid in the form of monthly motivation bonuses, but part of them must have been spent on the excessive wage increase tax. Additionally, a proportion of the wage increase was paid due to reduction of employment. It should be mentioned that the Workers Council objected against such allocation of financial means out of profits, but finally changed its attitude after the explanations of the management.

In April and May 1988 and next in August 1988 trade union organisations in enterprises increased the number of collective disputes in view of social discontent with the falling value of real wages and economic difficulties of the enterprises. The majority of these conflicts commenced before the Govern-ment decisions were announced increasing by seven per cent the threshold of wage increase free of the tax on excessive wage increase.

A very characteristic situation emerged in mid-1987 as concerns the coal allowances, traditionally established in mining industry by collective agree-ments. The governmental provision issued in July 1987 aimed to reduce these allowances within the general regulation of coal supply on a national level. Rejecting such unilateral intervention into collective agreements, the All-Poland Alliance of Trade Unions (the OPZZ) submitted the case to the Constitutional Tribunal for examining the compatibility of the governmental provision with the Law on collective agreements. The day preceding the convened sitting of the Constitutional Tribunal the government withdrew the incriminated provision – so the sitting of the Tribunal has been cancelled and the controversy resolved.

§3. The Right to Strike

392. The strike is the ultimate sanction vested solely in trade unions, not in individual workers. It cannot be used without previously exhausting the three-stage peaceful settlement of a collective labour dispute (direct negotiations – conciliation – social arbitration). However, the opinions are voiced by trade unions in connection with 1988 strike incidents that the legal procedure is too complicated and too long – what may incline workers to omit it and engage in illegal strikes.

According to the definition by the law of 1982 on trade unions, a strike consists in voluntary, collective abstention from work in order to defend the economic and social interests of a certain group of workers. Political strikes are inadmissible. When proclaiming a strike the trade union should take into account the commensurability of its demands and any losses resulting from the strike.

393. A strike is proclaimed by the workplace trade union after a majority of staff, including non-trade union members, have accepted the decision in a secret ballot and after the superior trade union (a federation) has approved the decision.

Participation in voting as well as in the strike is voluntary. Each participant in a strike may withdraw at any time, without giving reasons. No one may be forced to take part in or to refuse participation in a strike. It is forbidden to create any obstacles to the work of those workers who do not take part in a strike or who withdraw from it.

A strike should be proclaimed at least seven days prior to its commencement, with notification thereof to the director of the enterprise or factory.

394. The organisers of a strike must ensure, in co-operation with the management of the enterprise or factory, due protection of property for the duration of the strike, as well as uninterrupted operation of installations whose stoppage might involve hazards to human life and health or cause irreparable damage. The organisers of a strike should not restrict the manager's freedom to perform his duties in a manner adequate to the existing situation.

395. The law of 1982 on trade unions contains certain limitations and exclusions on the right to strike with respect to the content of demands, the specificity of the branch of activity or regarding the time element. Thus, the law bans political strikes, strikes resulting from disputes which are the simple sum of individual claims falling within the competence of Labour Courts, strikes concerning collective agreements or any other agreement before its period of notice or termination elapses, strikes in enterprises or factories located in regions which have been proclaimed disaster areas (see also para. 384).

The right to strike is not vested in civil servants, bank employees, employees of courts and prosecutors' offices, military units, establishments subject to ministers of defence and home affairs, etc., workers of enterprises producing, storing or supplying food, employees of the health service and others mentioned in the Law of 1982 on trade unions.

396. A strike may be preceded by a warning strike, the duration of which should be limited to the indispensable minimum and may not exceed two hours.

397. During a strike organised in accordance with legal provisions, workers preserve the right to social security allowances and other benefits due under the contract of employment. They do not retain the right to remuneration for the duration of the strike, but they may obtain a cash allowance from the trade union strike fund.

398. Participation in a properly organised strike is not considered an infringement of workers duties and has no adverse consequences for the participants; the same applies also to other forms of protest.

Anyone who leads a strike organised contrary to the rules laid down in the law of 1982 on trade unions is liable to penalty of imprisonment up to one year or a fine.

The organisation and conduct of or participation in a strike or in any other action of protest does not absolve the persons involved from legal responsibility for violation of the law, such as taking unlawful possession or use of property; or the use of force or unlawful threats to compel a third person to discontinue work; or hindering the director in the performance of his duties.

399. Since the law of 1982 on trade unions came into force, legalising the right to strike in Poland, there have been no formally proclaimed legal strikes, until the wave of unrest in May 1988. As the strikes of May 1988 are concerned, at the time of writing it is difficult to examine the formal aspects of their legality. Despite its legalisation, the strike is considered to be a particularly drastic means of pressure, causing harmful economic results which, in conditions of economic crisis in Poland, make strikes a particularly undesired measure. However, the trade unions admit the possibility of using this measure in particularly controversial social and economic situations. In May 1988 the All-Poland Alliance of Trade Unions (the OPZZ) announced its approval and support for any legally organised collective actions in support of justified workers' revindications.

Chapter XV. Workers' Self-Management

§1. GENERAL ASPECTS

400. The self-management system of state enterprises is one of the basic features emerging from the stormy period of the 1980s in Poland. The principles of that system are entirely original: this is not an imitation of the Yugoslav model, from which it differs greatly, mainly in the prevailing system of property, which is state property in Poland; nor is it similar to the Hungarian economic model. One must not look at Polish workers' self-management in a utopian way: it should be seen against the background of the social and economic crisis of the 1980s and of Polish conditions resulting from the socialist nature and planning principles of the state economy.

401. Poland had workers' self-management as long ago as 1956, the 'Polish October'. In 1956 workers' councils were called into being, but their significance was reduced in 1958 by their inclusion in the structure of what was called the 'Workers' Self-Government Conference', as one of the elements of the Conference, along with trade unions' workplace councils and Party executives. Although many in Poland expected much of the October 1956 social achievements, the erosion of the democratisation of political life in subsequent years had an undesirable influence also upon the further fate of self-management: the workers' councils lost, little by little, their importance and gradually disappeared, Workers' self-management came entirely under the tutelage of the trade unions, with general supervision performed by the Central Council of Trade Unions – a bureaucratic body which came under strong attack by workers in 1980. In a 1978 directive addressed to the organs of workers' self-government, the Central Council of Trade Unions recommended that the Chairmanship of each organ of workers' self-government be occupied by the first Secretary of the Party Executive and that the post of secretary of the self-governing body be held by the chairman of the trade union organisation. Workers' self-government became at that time merely a formal institution, deprived of its natural and authentic character.

402. In 1980 workers' demands for economic improvement and genuine representation were followed by demands for authentic workers' self-management. A draft of a law to this effect was negotiated between the government and the then trade unions in 1981 (Solidarity played a substantial role in these negotiations) and the law in the wording accepted by the trade unions was enacted by Parliament on 25 September 1981. The two laws enacted on that day: on state enterprises and on the self-management of state enterprises, were closely inter-connected.

403. Because of the implications of martial law the creation of self-management did not begin in earnest until 1983–1984. Moreover, the complicated situation in Polish trade unions in the first half of the 1980s also had a direct influence on the opportunities and the timing of establishing self-management. In 1987 there was workers' self-management in over 90 per cent of enterprises and factories, but in many cases not sufficiently active.

Both public opinion and the authorities of the state favour the development of workers' self-management, considering it to be a fundamental factor for the activation and psychological integration of the Polish people in matters of economic reform and for overcoming economic difficulties.

404. The problems of self-management and trade union activities in the workplace are closely inter-related. The field of activities of self-management, seen as the representation of the economic interests of employees in their roles as producers, interfere in many areas with trade union activities for the defence of workers' rights and interests. The two laws of 1982 on trade unions and that of 1981 on self-management were prepared in a hurry and under pressure; they have not established a proper delimitation of the respective competence of the two structures. This leads to difficult situations and an element of competition between them. No common pattern of relations between these two organisations in the workplace had been developed by 1987; relations still depend mainly on the strength of both organisations and on the wisdom and skill of their leaders. Strict cooperation in all matters being within the interests and competence of both organisations is recommended.

§2. GOALS OF WORKERS' SELF-MANAGEMENT

405. According to certain views held in Poland, the term 'self-management of workers of a state enterprise' does not duly express the essence of the situation. Article 33 of the law on state enterprises[1] reads thus: 'the director manages and represents the enterprise', while Art. 1 of the law on the workers' self-management in state enterprises[2] reads that: 'the staff participates in the management of a state enterprise'. Such an understanding of the employees' role in managing the enterprise is consistent with Art. 13 of the Constitution of the Polish People's Republic, providing that 'its staff take part in directing an enterprise'. Therefore the concern is rather with 'staff participation in enterprise management' than with a system of employee self-management, though it should be admitted that many staff functions have the character of self-management.

According to the law of 1981 self-management embraces decisions on major issues concerning the enterprise, presenting opinions, undertaking initiatives, putting forward motions and proposals and controlling operations of the enterprise.

The self-management organ carries out its tasks independently of the state administration, trade unions, and social political organisations.

1. See the Law of 25 September 1981 on state-owned enterprises (Journal of Laws No. 24, item 122).

2. See the Law of 25 September 1981 on staff self-management in state enterprises (Journal of Laws No. 24, item 123).

§3. STRUCTURE OF WORKERS' SELF-MANAGEMENT

A. Organs of self-management

406. The organs of workers' self-management are as follows:
1. the general meeting of workers of the enterprise,
2. the workers' council.
The self-management bodies constitute formal organs of the enterprise, according to Art. 31 of the Law of 25 September 1981 on state-owned enterprises, which lists the following organs of the enterprise:
1. the general meeting of workers,
2. the workers' council, and
3. the director of the enterprise.

B. General meeting of workers

407. The general meeting of workers constitutes a form of workers' direct participation in the running of the enterprise. Unless the statutes of self-management provide otherwise, the resolutions of the general meeting are valid if at least 50 per cent of the entire workforce are present at the meeting. Resolutions are adopted by a simple majority of votes cast.

The general meeting convenes a session at least twice a year. Following a written motion of at least one-fifth of employees the workers' council convenes a session within seven days. The meeting elects at each session, by ballot, the chairman of the session, his deputy and a secretary.

408. The prerogatives of the general meeting embrace:
– adopting the statutes of the enterprise, on the proposal of its director
– adopting resolutions on the division of that part of enterprise profits retained by the workforce
– the annual appraisal of the activities of the workers' council and of the director of the enterprise
– adopting long-term plans for the enterprise
– adopting self-management statutes on the proposal of the workers' council.
The general meeting has the right to express views on all matters pertaining to the enterprise.

C. Workers' council

1. Appointment of the workers' council

409. If not stipulated otherwise by the statutes, the workers' council is composed of fifteen members. It is elected by all workers of the enterprise on a secret ballot.

The term of a workers' council lasts for two years. The electorate may recall a member of the whole council before the term expires, after a motion signed by at least one-fifth of the electorate.

Every worker of the enterprise is vested with the right to vote; any worker may nominate candidates for the workers' council. Eligible for election are those workers who have worked at the enterprise for at least two years. However, the director of the enterprise, his deputies, the chief accountant, the legal adviser, managers and certain other persons are not eligible to stand. Members of the workers' council are limited to two terms of office.

2. Presidium of the workers' council

410. The workers' council elects, from among its members, a presidium, consisting of a chairman, one or more deputy chairmen and a secretary, for a period of two years. Workers holding leading positions in political organisations or in the trade union operating in the enterprise cannot be elected to the presidium of the workers' council.

3. Competence of the workers' council

411. The workers' councils possess decision-making prerogatives as well as a consultative and supervisory role. Their roles in decision-making include:
- adopting and amending the annual plan of the enterprise,
- approval of the annual report and of the balance sheet of the enterprise,
- passing resolutions on investments,
- granting consent for the conclusion of a contract establishing a joint-venture or a mixed-capital company,
- approval of the establishment or access to an association of enterprises,
- approval of decisions concerning merger or division of the enterprise,
- adopting decisions concerning enterprise-financed housing projects,
- adopting decisions concerning changes in enterprise operations,
- adopting decisions concerning divisions of that part of income remaining at the disposal of the enterprise into separate parts,
- acceptance of the sale of machinery and equipment no longer needed by the enterprise; acceptance of donations,
- making decisions concerning collective membership of the enterprise in social organisations,
- adopting decisions concerning associations for technical improvements and rationalisation,
- adopting on the proposal of the director of the internal rules of enterprise,
- adopting decisions concerning the organisation of an in-house referendum,
- election of its representatives to the council of the association of enterprises,

171

– adopting decisions concerning the appointment and dismissal of the enterprise director and of other managers, according to the Law of 25 September 1981 on state-owned enterprises (see para. 176).

412. The workers' council has the right to express opinions on all matters concerning the enterprise and its management. Appropriate bodies and institutions are obliged to consult the workers' council on matters concerning changes of decisions on the establishment and dissolution of the enterprise, the conclusion by the enterprise of long-term agreements and contracts with other economic organisations; proposals concerning conferment of orders and state distinctions; the director's decisions on allocation of accommodation. If the workers' council does not express its opinion within two weeks or other agreed time limit, it is taken to have no objections.

413. The workers' council has the right to put forward initiatives, motions and proposals on all matters pertaining to the enterprise, as well as to seek information from the director about the economic circumstances of the enterprise and about the activities of all organs of the enterprise; it also has the right to supervise all such activities. The director is obliged to inform the workers' council of his attitude to a proposed initiative or motion, to respond to requests immediately, or not later than within two weeks; and to make available all documents and materials necessary to carry out supervisory operations.

4. Operation of the workers' council

414. The workers' council convenes its sessions at least every three months. The presidium of the council should convene a session of the council on a written motion signed by at least one-fifth of council members.

If not stipulated otherwise resolutions/decisions adopted are valid when a quorum of at least 50 per cent of council members are present at a session; decisions are made by a simple majority of votes.

Decisions are voted by show of hands. An exception is voting on personnel matters, which are decided by ballot. A ballot may also be ordered on the motion of one member of the council. Detailed procedures for the operation of the workers' council and rules concerning the convening and holding sessions are specified in the statutes of self-management.

415. All activities of the members of the workers' council are voluntary and unpaid. A member has the right to retain his salary for any period of working time, during which he/she did not work because of fulfilling self-management functions.

416. The enterprise cannot terminate with notice the employment contract of a member of the workers' council during his term of office or during the subsequent year, unless the council gives its formal consent. This restriction does not affect situations justifying dismissal without notice.

§4. RELATIONS BETWEEN SELF-MANAGEMENT AND THE DIRECTOR OF AN ENTERPRISE

A. Competence of the director of the enterprise

417. The director of an enterprise manages the enterprise. The whole sphere of current management, including the organisation of activities and managing the work process, making decisions about the work of particular workers, giving orders etc., lies within the competence of the director. The director's management extends also to those spheres in which self-management bodies are vested with the right to decide, as a resolution passed by the self-management body constitutes only one stage in the process of decision-making in the enterprise. In the course of that process the director implements the resolutions and decisions of self-management bodies concerning the enterprise's operation.

The director of the enterprise takes part in sessions of the workers' council. If invited, he also attends sessions of the presidium of the workers' council.

B. Right of mutual suspending of decisions

418. The division of management functions between the director and the self-management organs required legal measures granted to both parties, to be applied in cases of malfeasance by the other party.

The workers' council may withhold implementation of the director's decision if it is:
1. incompatible with the resolution/decision passed by the workers' council or general self-management meeting,
2. if there was no consultation with the workers' council in matters where such consultation is required,
3. passed without the decision of the workers' council in matters where such decision is required,
4. incompatible with provisions of law.

The director of the enterprise is obliged to suspend implementation of a resolution/decision of the workers' council or of the general self-management meeting if this resolution or decision is incompatible with provisions of law. Incompatibility with law is one reason constituting grounds for suspension of the implementation of the resolution of a self-management organ. This results from the responsibility of the director for the effective operation of the enterprise.

A workers' council whose decision has been withheld has the right to submit to the director, within seven days, its objection to suspension. If, despite the submission of an objection, the director upholds his decision, the workers' council has the right to move for resolution of the dispute by specified disputes' proceedings (see para. 419).

C. Proceedings in litigious matters

419. Disputes between workers' council and the director of an enterprise are settled by an arbitration commission composed of a representative of the workers' council and a representative of the director and of a legally trained, invited arbitrator, who acts as the head of the commission. A dispute is considered to be resolved if both parties agree with the contents of the arbitration decision. If a dispute is not settled by arbitration, either party may submit the case to court for a final decision.

420. Each party (the director or the workers' council) has the right to institute legal proceedings in court against a decision of the other party if it seriously infringes social interests. This capacity has the character of a corrective measure in relation to the right to suspend implementation of a decision (see above para. 418), which is based on the criterion of incompatibility of the decision with law. The right to institute legal proceedings in court allows each party to veto the activities of the other on grounds of justification and purposefullness, if such activity also violates the general public interest.

Index

The numbers refer to paragraphs.

Index

Index

Index

WITHDRAWN
FROM STOCK

Europe's Hidden Potential

Europe's Hidden Potential

How the 'Old Continent' Could
Turn into a New Superpower

*Burkhard Schwenker
and Thomas Clark*

B L O O M S B U R Y
LONDON · NEW DELHI · NEW YORK · SYDNEY

First published in United Kingdom in 2013 by

Bloomsbury Publishing Plc
50 Bedford Square
London
WC1B 3DP
www.bloomsbury.com

Copyright © Burkhard Schwenker and Thomas Clark 2012

All rights reserved; no part of this publication may be reproduced, stored in a
retrieval system, or transmitted by any means, electronic, mechanical, photocopying
or otherwise, without the prior written permission of the Publisher.

No responsibility for loss caused to any individual or organisation acting
or refraining from action as a result of the material in this publication
can be accepted by Bloomsbury Publishing or the authors.

A CIP record for this book is available from the British Library.

ISBN: 9-781-4081-9227-6

7866048

Design by Fiona Pike, Pike Design, Winchester
Typeset by Hewer Text, Edinburgh
Printed and bound in Great Britain by CPI Group (UK) Ltd, Croydon CR0 4YY

CORK CITY
LIBRARY

Contents

'Every big historic development
started as utopia
and ended in reality.'

Richard Coudenhove-Kalergi
(1894–1972), founder of the
Pan-European Movement

Preface

This is a book about Europe and its potential. It is a potential that, in our opinion, has been widely overlooked and underrated.

Underrated? Have we been living on the moon lately? Or did we, for the purpose of keeping up a good narrative, just block out the fact that the continent of Europe has been stumbling from one crisis to the next, faced with a crumbling currency, overworked and dithering politicians, countries on the brink of bankruptcy, and millions of people worried about finding jobs and fed up with the bureaucracy and technicalities of the European Union – a union that seems as far away from its citizens as, well, the moon to the earth.

Yes, we are well aware of all these issues. And no, we did not want to write a book that reads like the pamphlet of two authors who have spent too much time in intellectual cloud-cuckoo-land. Instead, we are convinced that Europe will not only weather the current economic and political storms but also has the ability to grow far beyond its current state. And that, we believe, has indeed been widely overlooked – and underrated.

Sandwiched between the US – the sole superpower at the turn of the millennium – and China as the expected next superpower, Europe is hardly ever discussed as a potential leader of the twenty-first century. At best, it is seen as an able follower of trends set by others. At worst, it is regarded as a relic; a kind of vast open-air museum with a rich culture and good food, immersed in a glorious past, yet with limited prospects in the global economy of the future.

Some go even further and reject any general predictions on Europe's economic and political outlook, deeming it necessary to judge on a country-by-country basis. They point at the numerous languages and traditions in Europe, and the often different political systems and economic structures of its countries. In a nutshell, they prefer to focus on the divisive elements instead of the unifying ones.

Such a tendency is particularly widespread in Britain. When the British refer to Europe, they usually mean the mainland on the other side of the English Channel, as if they do not even see themselves as European. Such seeming isolationism, and the mindset that goes along with it, contradict any ambitions to create a concerted Europe.

To be fair, the United Kingdom is not the only member of the EU to devote most of its energy to setting limits for Europe, instead of helping expand its common cause and strengthening its identity. Elements of the 'island mentality' have spread to mainland countries as well. As a result, scepticism and frustration have dominated the 'European project' in recent years. No more concerted sense and sensibility; gone are the days when European activities conveyed even a whiff of euphoria to its citizens, as it did when the common currency was introduced – a currency that is currently at the centre of dispute and conflict.

As a result, there is a widespread feeling among the public today that the continuous efforts made since the end of the Second World War to further align and unify European nations and economies have reached a standstill. The mass media certainly contribute to this negative impression. Skimming through the press coverage since the sovereign-debt crisis started in 2009, one does not have to dig deep to find doomsday headlines.

'Disunited states of Europe' was the caption of the *Economist's* regular column on Europe, 'Charlemagne', in summer 2012 – a piece that stressed the increasing rift between Britain and the eurozone countries.[1] In the *New York Times*, famed economist and Nobel Prize winner Paul Krugman compared the recent development of the European Union and the euro with a classic Greek tragedy and devoted an extra-long column to the topic.[2] Gideon Rachman of the *Financial Times* pronounced in May 2010 'the death of the European dream'.[3] In France and Germany, the press was not all that uplifting either: the French daily newspaper *Le Monde* saw the European Monetary Union 'on the brink of a nervous breakdown' ('*au bord de la crise de nerfs*'),[4] while Germany's *Der Spiegel* simply titled it: 'Europe burns' ('*Europa brennt*').[5]

Given the recent negativity in the media, we felt even more compelled to write this book and share our vision of a Europe whose grand future is yet to come. We see such a positive approach as important, if only to consciously counter the tenor of the on-going debate about the 'old continent', in which a generally negative picture is threatening to gain the ascendancy. In economic and social contexts, we desperately need to spend more time talking about the opportunities, prospects and potential to which Europe opens the door.

However, the decision to devote this book to the continent's chances is less driven by a desire to go against the trend than by sheer conviction. We are simply convinced that Europe has the right set of skills for the upcoming challenges of an increasingly global economy. However we also believe that a unified approach is needed to fully deploy these skills. No single European country will be able to develop the power necessary to set the agenda, neither on an economic nor on a political level. Yet as a union of countries, Europe can do exactly that. It only needs to refocus on its bonding elements instead of actively deepening the ditches of separation. If we Europeans want to play a leading role in the globalized world of the future, our nations must pull together and grow together. There is simply no alternative.

Since the European idea first started with economic co-operation some 60 years ago and economic issues continue to be the driving force within EU policy, it seemed only logical to us to focus on business aspects in this book. We also believe that such an approach is not too narrow, considering that economic prosperity is the foundation for the development of so many other aspects of life.

This book will address not only Europe's future economic power as a whole but also its capability to develop a management style that can be exported globally as the best way of running companies in the future. European values and the characteristic attributes of European corporate management lay the foundation for this, while co-operation between political and business leaders creates its framework.

From the outset, we asked ourselves a simple question: is there something that typifies Europeans in the way they live and work; something that unites the European nations, despite their obvious diversities? Our discussions began during the time one of the authors wrote and published the German-language book *Europa führt!* ('Europe Leads!').[6] The fact that it was well received by its readers and sparked numerous interesting debates encouraged us to intensify as well as broaden our thoughts on the topic. The results are outlined in this book.

To us, the main criteria which define Europe at the beginning of the twenty-first century are its culture of craftsmanship and consensus. At first sight, this might not appear particularly remarkable or endearing of a region: craftsmanship sounds antiquated, consensus indecisive. Once you look deeper, however, you will quickly discover that both are tremendous assets. They clearly distinguish Europe from other regions of the world, including the US and China, and they are the foundation for a specific European management style.

This management style can be found in the Nordic countries as well as the Mediterranean ones. Its principles are applied in the Germanic and Francophone parts of the continent, in the Benelux and even in the new Central and Eastern European member states of the EU.

Long blamed for its unwillingness to outsource and its predilection for hire and fire, Europe has started to reap the benefits of its focus on people, products and technologies instead of capital markets. The financial and economic shock that culminated in the autumn of 2008 revealed the limits of the American management model with its far-too-strong bias towards financial matters. There is no doubt that American management methods have contributed much in the last several decades to better lead companies, and thus to the economy, bringing benefits to the workforce, the shareholders and the stakeholders. However, even the best model reaches its peak at some point. It is evident that the world is looking for an alternative. Europe can – and ought to – lead the way in this respect.

Many friends, colleagues and discussion partners have provided us with ideas and impetus for this book. While it is not possible to thank them all by name, we are very grateful to be blessed with such inspiring networks. Our editors, Thor Ekevall, a Brit with Swedish roots living in Wales and himself a passionate European, and Lisa Carden, have done a great job in speedily editing this book. We want to thank them – as well as our families, who have been very patient with us, as always.

Burkhard Schwenker and Thomas Clark, August 2012

Chapter 1

A period of transformation for global leadership

Before we discuss Europe's ability to become a global leader of the twenty-first century we should first pose certain questions: Is there a need for a new type of leadership? Do we currently have a situation where Europe could rise to the occasion and take on new responsibilities to better guide the way into the future?

The answer to both questions is yes. In fact, the timing is perfect. There is an increasing feeling among large parts of the world's population that things have to change. Many people are convinced that we simply cannot carry on behaving the way we have been in the last decades. They believe that we have to adjust our lifestyles in one way or another and that we need to change the course of doing business. Sometimes it seems that there is almost a longing for new ideas and principles to better handle our economy and set a political agenda, as the old means of doing things do not properly address the major challenges we meet today. Or, to put it bluntly, it is evident that the existing system has failed and is doomed to fail again if we do not alter and modernize it.

This widespread feeling has developed gradually in some respects, for example in terms of our attitude towards the environment. Some 30 years ago, calls for radically new measures in our attitude towards the climate and the use of natural resources were regularly discredited as the hysteria of a bunch of academics and scientists sitting in ivory towers. These days, it is the people who refuse to accept the alarming signals of concrete evidence who are seen as quixotic.

What really triggered the strong desire for change, however, were not so much environmental issues, but the shock of seeing how the world's financial and economic systems came to the brink of collapse within weeks. To most people, it is still puzzling how the insolvency of a comparatively small investment bank based in New York (Lehman Brothers) in September 2008 had such enormous implications for the daily lives of people in places as far away from each other as Bangkok, Berlin and Buenos Aires. The vast majority still does not know to this day what sub-prime certificates or credit-default swaps are or how they work. Actually, not too many self-proclaimed or supposed experts do either, once you go into detail. What the crisis has left with the public is the impression of a system out of control; an image of an economic framework thought to be rock-solid, almost falling apart merely because a tiny crack within the frame had appeared.

The majority of the blame for such an inadequate construction goes to the United States, as the power that set it up and dominated it. The US is also the country most heavily criticized for the way it treats the environment. And while we Europeans certainly should not point fingers at the other side of the Atlantic but rather ask ourselves why we have been so willing to participate in the new games of the financial markets, one thing should not be ignored by us: the inherent feeling in many parts of the world that it is no longer healthy for a sole superpower to dictate the rules of doing business on our globe. In this context, it is worth briefly recapitulating what has led to the crisis that shook the world.

Made in the US, felt everywhere

'The USA is responsible for the biggest global economic crisis' stated Bill Clinton in January 2009 at the World Economic Forum in Davos, referring to the worst economic downfall since 1929. The former

American president seems a particularly credible observer in this respect, because the roots of the crisis lead us back to the time when Clinton handed over the keys to the White House to his successor George W. Bush.

It was a time when the bubble of the New Economy had burst. In order to avoid a recession, the Federal Reserve swiftly slashed interest rates and flooded the market with cheap money. Given the importance of the American economy and the status of the dollar as the denomination for numerous globally traded goods, this had serious implications for other countries as well.

Yet the Fed did not bother all that much in this respect, reminding us of John Connally, Secretary of the Treasury in the Nixon administration, who rather bluntly told a delegation of Europeans complaining about his monetary policy: 'The dollar is our currency, but your problem.'[7]

A similar position, it seems to us, was taken by the Americans in 2001. We know this all too well, because the European Central Bank was under constant pressure at the time to take similarly drastic measures as the Fed. The ECB resisted the temptation. In the US, however, steps taken ostensibly to cure the effects of one bubble effectively prepared the ground for the next.

In the year 2001 alone, the interest rate (the federal funds rate to be precise) dropped from six to 1.75 per cent. Soon, standard interest rates on capital granted by banks were lower than inflation. In such an environment, it does not make economic sense to put money in savings accounts, as it effectively loses value. This was taken to heart not only by big players in the financial markets but also by ordinary people: they did what they were supposed to do in order to keep the economy going – they borrowed, consumed and invested.

Since most of them were hit badly by losses in the stock market after Internet and telecoms shares nosedived with a vengeance, they preferred to buy more tangible assets and focused on property. The real estate market became 'hot'. For the average American, buying and owning a house was driven by the notion that one became richer by the day by simply living in one's own four walls. However, many Americans did not qualify for traditional mortgages where private capital of 15 to 30 per cent of the purchase price was usually required to limit the risk. Yet in the first decade of the twenty-first century, such safety measures no longer mattered. The banks would lend money to almost anyone, irrespective of income and assets. A new category of mortgages emerged, which bankers internally dubbed 'Ninjas', meaning loans for people with no income, no job or assets.

Such easy-to-obtain money should have set off the alarm bells, yet hardly any criticism was voiced. Intriguingly, most of the warning signs did not come from the financial communities but other sectors. At the World Economic Forum in Davos, the CEO of Wal-Mart asked how it could be that his cashiers, whose income situation he knew with absolute precision, could be considering buying a second or even third property and were receiving all the assistance they needed from the banks. Nobody gave him a convincing answer.

The banks, giving handouts to the 'Ninjas', knew exactly why, of course. After all, the fact that they were willing to lend money to people with hardly any creditworthiness did not mean that they were also willing to take the risk of them not being able to pay back the mortgage at some point. Instead, they passed on the risk to others by bundling numerous mortgages and turning them into a new class of asset-backed securities. The actual procedures of the securitisation might have been complicated in all their detail, with so many different stages of bundling and re-bundling, as well as the dubious role of the rating agencies, whose trusted seals were required to turn the increasingly opaque 'pots of mortgages' into tradable securities. The result of all this financial wheeling and dealing, however, was simple: a regional issue with tangible assets (property in the US) became converted into a global issue with very intangible assets (securities traded globally). Yet this trading happened with utmost discretion, and only between financial institutions, 'off-market', as they call it, away from the transparency of stock markets and, thus, the public eye. Most financial institutions were willing to partake, allured by the high interest of these mortgage-backed securities, especially for those below the top ratings of Moody's, Standard & Poor's and Fitch, the so-called sub-prime certificates.

Lehman Brothers filed for bankruptcy protection on September 15, 2008, and the American International Group (AIG), then the biggest insurance company in the world, had to be bailed out by the US government with an $85 billion loan the next day, to prevent it from the same destiny as Lehman Brothers. The financial bombs planted so vigorously during the sub-prime frenzy exploded en masse and the implications were enormous. Driven by the fear of more bankruptcies of their peers, banks stopped lending to each other. This brought the financial flow almost to a standstill, a flow that is as equally important to the world's economy as blood circulating in the human body. Industries, which were heavily dependent on so-called structured financing, collapsed within weeks, as was the case with the shipping industry. Big corporations were not sure if they could pay their creditors and employees in due time, as the money market funds used for these purposes were emptied and deposits withdrawn. Some heads of state even felt compelled to explicitly guarantee their citizens that the money in their savings accounts was indeed safe, as Germany's Chancellor Angela Merkel did in a televised speech, together with her Minister of Finance at that time, Peer Steinbrück.

In the end, hundreds of billions of taxpayers' money was needed to keep the dominoes from toppling. The world was plunged into the worst economic crisis since the Great Depression some 80 years ago. There was no doubt that the roots of this crisis were in the US. Yet shouldn't Europe and its banks deserve their share of the blame, too? It is indeed true that some European banks, such as BNP Paribas, Credit Suisse, Deutsche Bank, HSBC and Credit Suisse, played an active part in the securitization of US mortgages, side by side with their (far more active) American peers. However, it was their US subsidiaries that steered these activities, and their involvement had less to do with their headquarters being in Europe but with their desire to act globally and, thus, take part in the games of the biggest of all financial markets. The majority of European banks, though, sat on the lower steps of the food pyramid and merely traded with sub-prime certificates. Often, they acted naively, lured by the high interest rates these apparently secure certificates promised; sometimes, they were victims of what seemed to be fraudulent behaviour.[8] Some European banks even made it a principle not to touch US mortgage securities, among them Banco Santander, whose Chairman Emilio Botín, when asked about his bank's exposure to sub-prime certificates, simply declared: 'We do not have those strange things.'[9] It is a pity that not many other European banks could say the same. Nonetheless, in the wheeling and dealing which led to the financial crisis, most European banks were followers rather than orchestrators. Thus, they clearly carry a different grade of responsibility than their US counterparts.

In continental Europe there were also no regulations in place that incentivized the reckless behaviour that led to the financial crisis. The situation is different, of course, when we look at the UK. There is no way of denying that the City of London was the cradle of some of the most lethal financial instruments, especially when it comes to credit default swaps (CDS). The unit that almost caused the collapse of AIG, for example, was based in London. Far away from its New York headquarters, the highly independent team of AIG Financial Products with a staff of less than 500 people put the jobs of more than 100,000 AIG employees at risk by freely issuing 'insurances' for bonds and securities. There was a reason why the team operated from London: the City simply offered them more freedom to create such insurances, even fictional ones, dubbed synthetic CDS. In a nutshell, there is no way to deny that some of the machinations, which laid the foundation to the financial crises, were conducted in the UK.

This might not come as a surprise, as the UK in general plays a rather special role within the European countries, an issue that we also discuss later in a different context (see Chapter 2). However, while we find that the UK's policies and economy were often more in line with the US than continental Europe during the last three decades, one also gets the impression that the willingness to curb the excesses of the financial markets are much stronger in Britain than in the United States. Some actions might be rather symbolic, such as stripping the former head of the Royal Bank of Scotland, Fred Goodwin, of his knighthood, or the combined public and political pressure, which led Goodwin's successor, Stephen Hester, as well as top executives at Barclays and Lloyds TSB to waive huge bonuses worth millions. Other actions, however, could have wider ramifications, such as a 50 per cent windfall tax[10] on bankers' bonuses, or considerations to make individual bankers more accountable by introducing a new criminal offence called corporate negligence.[11]

In other European countries, actions have already been taken. Ireland, for example, introduced a 90 per cent tax applied to bankers' bonuses – a reaction to the fact that nearly all of the Irish banks needed financial assistance from the state to survive. In Germany, the base salaries of members of the board from 'rescued' banks such as Commerzbank or Hypo Real Estate were capped at €500,000 at least until the banks had paid back a minimum of half the money they had received from the state. In general, a broad consensus was quickly formed within Europe that the so-called success based payments at financial institutions were unfair, as they let executives participate in (often short term) profits while no such thing happened when it came to subsequent huge losses.

As a result of such a clear market failure in these remunerations, European politicians pushed for stronger regulations. 'The bankers are partying like it's 1999, and it's 2009. Obviously, there's a need for stronger muscles and sharper teeth', said Anders Borg, finance minister of Sweden when he introduced a joint call of the EU to cap bank bonuses in Autumn 2009,[12] explaining that 'it won't be satisfactory for Europe to end up with broad principles and guidelines.'[13]

In contrast, the US authorities turned out to be rather mute and inactive when it came to punishing fraudulent behaviour[14] or reclaiming excessive bonuses[15] of executives who drove their banks into bankruptcy. This is quite surprising, as America traditionally tended to be strict about wrongdoings perceived in a reckless or even criminal context. In fact, some observers are outspokenly disappointed that President Obama did not leverage his massive political capital and huge popular support to bring the machinations of the financial industry visibly and forcefully to a halt after he came to power. The big question in our context is therefore: was the financial crisis just a chain of unfortunate, unintended coincidences with fatal effects, or was it the result of a systematic failure that clearly showed the limits and dangers of the American way of life and the long-famed American management model?

The American economy – from vibrant manufacturing to virtual monsters

Our modern economic system has much to thank the US for. This applies especially to Western Europe after 1945. When the Second World War came to an end, the United States had demonstrated the full extent of its strength. No other economy had been able to mobilize so many forces or deploy them so efficiently. Once the war was over, the United States decided not to pursue a policy of reparations and repercussions against the aggressor, Germany, but launched a massive reconstruction programme, which, at that time, was equally unusual and unique: the Marshall Plan. The plan was at the same time both a development aid and an effective way of transferring the American economic philosophy. The economic historian Christian Kleinschmidt is undoubtedly right to say that German companies would scarcely have been able to return to the global market in the wake of National Socialism if they had not aligned themselves with American management and production methods. High on the list of these methods were the technical processes and tools of modern production, advertising and sales promotion (later termed 'marketing') and the science of corporate organization. In this respect, the US has had a massive formative influence over other European economies as well (as it has had for countries in Asia and Latin America).

In those days, many ordinary people, as well as leaders, were very sceptical about competition, market economics and open markets. Even in Western Europe, a great number of decision-makers were by no means averse to the idea of cartels and price controls. The few opinion leaders outside America with truly liberal views needed the US as a reference point to cultivate their market-economy mindset and nurture an awareness of productivity issues and international competition. Today, these elements form the bedrock of our prosperity.

In the US itself, striving for productivity in an environment of free and, thus, strong competition led to an atmosphere of constant change. American businessmen were particularly savvy in adapting the ideas of the (European born) Industrial Revolution. First, in the so-called 'Gilded Age', when America's early industrial magnates emerged, they applied the principles of scale and scope to the extraction and refinement of commodities with much more vigour than in Europe or elsewhere in the

15

world: Andrew Carnegie with iron and steel, Henry Clay Frick with coal and coke, and John D. Rockefeller with oil. Second, when Americans perfected European inventions and turned them into mass products: Singer, the sewing machine; Remington, the typewriter; Bell, the telephone and Ford, the automobile. Over 15 million of Henry Ford's Model T were sold between 1908 and 1927; the vehicle became a huge catalyst in the conversion of a country dominated by farmers and agriculture into an industrialized nation. Even more interesting in our context is the massive impact Ford's assembly line production methods had. Ford's car factory in Dearborne, near Detroit, showed the way that most goods would become manufactured around the world in the twentieth century.

Thomas Edison reached an equally important milestone. The inventor of the light bulb and world record holder in patents (over 1,000) applied the methods of mass production to research. Hundreds of scientists calculated and experimented in Edison's laboratories in Menlo Park, New Jersey. They worked in teams and achieved groundbreaking results, not only in the field of electricity and telecommunications, but also for the motion picture industry and recorded music. Menlo Park was the birth of modern R&D as we know it. Edison, of course, also founded an iconic American company: General Electric (GE).

At the beginning of the twentieth century, the methods used in companies such as GE (institutional research), Ford (assembly line production), Standard Oil (enormous economies of scales) or Sears Roebuck (pioneer of the mail order business) had already paved the way for the US to become a dominating power in the global economy. At the end of the Second World War, the US could showcase an impressive industrial infrastructure with legions of skilled workers and thousands of products envied by the world. From household goods to canned food, from motorbikes to passenger planes, from denim jackets to moving images – the US economy produced it all. Very soon, new services around these products developed: fast food restaurants, drive-in cinemas, television networks, market research firms, and consultancies. It did not take long until the advertising wizards on Madison Avenue would earn vastly more than the steel managers in Pittsburgh. Setting up an ad agency required far less capital than a factory, yet the leverage effect of modern marketing was much higher than with physical goods, as were the fun factor and diversity dimensions. As a result, talent was enticed. In general, working in the service industry became more attractive than working in manufacturing, which showed the first signs of deterioration. However, the mix between services and products within the US economy was still healthy, certainly until the late 1960s. In fact, the US effectively served as a model reference for Europe well into the 1970s, despite the two oil crises during that decade which hit the US particularly strongly.

The situation started to change in the 1980s. This was a time when the US market became flooded with Asian products: consumer electronics, watches and, above all, cars from Japan and toys and plastic appliances from China. Shocked by the (seeming) superiority of their production methods, the US economy turned its back on classic manufacturing and focused its attention towards the service sector, such as marketing, consulting or headhunting, to name but a few. In one of the most promising sectors of the economy, information technology, the shift of preference from hardware to software also became more and more apparent. With the rise of the Internet, this tendency grew enormously. Suddenly, it was companies with virtual products and virtual ideas that dominated the headlines: a new economy was heralded. The announcement was muted when the huge speculative bubble burst, as we all know. At this time, it must have become apparent that the dominance of immaterial business (in the proper sense of the word) had become unhealthy.

'Now wait a minute', some of you might be saying. Surely these days, the biggest impact on how people around the world lead or change their lives still comes from US companies: Microsoft, eBay, Google, Apple, Facebook, Twitter? It is indeed true that the US economy continues to produce companies with outstanding concepts and business models. Silicon Valley remains the globe's cradle for start-ups with true transformational power; having said that, it also has to be made clear that its vibrancy and genius is not sufficient to cure the rest of the US economy.

It is an economy that has been dangerously dominated by a sector far more virtual than the world of IT will ever be: the financial services industry. If anyone questions its frightening speed to dominance, simply consider the following development: in the 1960s and 1970s, banks and insurance companies generated under 10 per cent of all corporate profits in the US. In the 1980s, the figure went up to 15 per cent. By 2007, it had climbed to a staggering 40 per cent. The activities of investment banks, hedge funds and private equity firms on Wall Street & Co. had become so lucrative that, in terms of profitability, it put everything else in the shade, even Google or Microsoft.

This was not possible with traditional banking services alone. It required the financial community to depart from its original mandate of keeping the economy liquid and to start creating a world of derivatives and 'structured products' so complicated and diverse that it could only be understood by insiders. Applying these financial products had strong implications for the rest of the economy and 'real' businesses, from public-listed corporations to leveraged buyouts.

Investment banks and bankers increasingly began to set the tone, the rest of the US economy following their siren song. Where the real economy had previously dominated, the ratio had, over time, been turned on its head. Broadly speaking, the way in which the US banks and insurance companies developed a life of their own and started trading with things such as asset-backed securities or credit default swaps (famously dubbed as 'weapons of mass destruction' by investment guru Warren Buffett[16]), is the reason why it sounds justified to claim that the US economy had indeed produced virtual monsters. With these monsters, the financial industry created a level of diversification and excessive trading that – as we now know with hindsight – spun completely out of control. 'Wall Street makes a bubble and gives it to the world' says the title of a chapter in *Predator Nation* by Charles Ferguson.[17] In the book, the author – who also made the Academy Award-winning documentary *Inside Job* – outlines numerous examples of irresponsible and even criminal behaviour of financial executives who remained unpunished. 'Finance has become America's dominant industry, while manufacturing, even for high technology industries, has nearly disappeared' observes Ferguson. He continues: 'The financial sector has become increasingly corrupt, with the widespread fraud that caused the housing bubble going completely unpunished.'

As Ferguson concludes however, the root of the problem goes deeper. It is a problem of attitude – the attitude drawn from and expected of a typical American manager.

The American management model – from export hit to obsolescence

We should not try to lay all the blame at the banks' doors. No responsible manager in the 'real' economy was ever forced to make decisions based more on the capital markets or on the quantitative notions, calculations or expectations of analysts than on their own strategies and convictions. Yet driven by the desire to maximize short-term profits, many American managers did exactly that. They increasingly avoided investing in industrial production, focusing instead on supposedly more lucrative business activities. The car manufacturer General Motors (GM) is a good example.

When you glance at GM's balance sheets around the turn of the millennium, you will quickly discover that the Detroit based company did not earn the majority of its profit by selling vehicles. It did so by offering mortgages and various consumer loans and managing the risk exposure of these activities.

In the proud stable of GM's marques, it was not Chevrolet, Buick, Cadillac or any other of its car brands that brought the highest profit margins, but a subsidiary called General Motors Acceptance Corporation (GMAC). Originally, GMAC's sole purpose was to help their customers to buy a car by granting them car loans. Over the years, however, it had increasingly become distanced from the original core business.

One might argue that this was a clever management decision, as GMAC's profits helped finance the struggling car business. Unfortunately, the truth seems to be rather that it helped the managers to divert attention from, and disguise, the core problem: that GM had lost its ability to build quality cars effectively enough that selling them would bring them sustainable income. The result of such a management strategy ended in bankruptcy. Most of the culprits responsible for this had retired when GM filed for Chapter 11 in June 2009. When they were in power, they based their decisions on short-term success, not long-term substance. This is a tendency in the style of American management that can be regularly observed. Today, we realize that overly keen endeavours to maximize quarterly profits bear great dangers. Quite often, these endeavours are driven by the concept of shareholder value.

Introduced by Alfred Rappaport in 1986,[18] this concept spread around the globe like wildfire and turned for many top managers into a doctrine. One of the best known and most widely respected protagonists of the philosophy was Jack Welch, long-term CEO of General Electric. Yet, in our post-crisis world, even he admits, 'On the face of it, shareholder value is the dumbest idea in the world. Shareholder value is a result, not a strategy (...). Your main constituencies are your employees, your customers and your products.'[19]

One should hold high such reflections, even at such a late stage. There is also much to learn from Welch's days as an active manager; he was a brilliant people person, irrespective of what one might think of his avidly promoted business management strategy, Six Sigma. However, his elevation to the 'gold standard of management' during his time at GE's helm during the 1980s and 1990s also had much to do with a portfolio strategy which knew no limits in terms of selling subsidiaries and buying new entities. In many respects one could argue that this was boldness at its best – 'Neutron Jack', as he was dubbed, had no regard for tradition. He only looked at performance. Nevertheless, in retrospect it seemed that, at some point, he overdid it. As GE Capital became more and more dominant for the corporation as a whole, some came to look at Edison's legacy more as a bank with interests in industrial companies than an industrial conglomerate with a finance arm. Irrespective of one's interpretation, even at GE – often regarded as the best managed American company – it became evident during the financial crisis of 2008 and 2009 just how dangerous an overexposure to finance could become: GE lost its triple-A rating and 78 per cent of its market value. The company was forced to cut its dividend for the first time in 71 years.

Jack Welch was long retired by then and his successor, Jeffrey Immelt, was still regarded as one of the best managers in the US. Yet the vulnerability of such a stronghold as GE indicated the limits of the 'American way of management.'

It was a management style that had dominated the global guidelines for leading a business. In fact, apart from the 1980s, when the Japanese management idea of the collective striving for continuous improvement (*kaizen*) briefly dominated, it seemed as if the American principles of running companies had become the only ones with global impact and influence since the Second World War.

There are a number of interrelated reasons for this:

■ America basically 'invented' management theory leading the way with the pioneer Peter Drucker (an Austrian who emigrated to the States), as well as the works of marketing experts such as Philip Kotler and strategists like Michael Porter. On a macro-economic level, luminaries such as Samuelson and Friedman were the ones who established schools of thought and shaped the course of discussions worldwide. Since the Nobel Prize for Economics was first awarded in 1969, 47 out of 61 scientists who have received the accolade had studied at US universities or institutes, nearly 80 per cent.

■ As a result, American universities have earned themselves a pre-eminent reputation worldwide. Big names, such as the Harvard Business School, the Sloan School of Management, Berkeley and Wharton have – rightly or wrongly – become synonymous with excellence in education. Either way, anyone with high aspirations makes sure to get their MBA from an American business school. Not until last year did a European school, the London Business School, make it to the top slot in the *Financial Times* rankings, alongside US rival Wharton. Continental European schools are more or less also-rans in these rankings. The few that do figure prominently, such as INSEAD, are themselves heavily influenced by American role models.

■ American universities very quickly developed an excellent tool with which to disseminate the American management philosophy: 'executive education.' There is no better way to go about this than to combine training for experienced managers with networking in international classes. European schools and universities were much too slow to leverage this tool for their own purposes, a few exceptions proving the rule. The fact that finding cash has always been an issue for American universities has undoubtedly played a part in the emergence of this pattern.

- Key international organizations such as the International Monetary Fund (IMF) and the World Bank, which influence the world's economies and hence the corporate sector, are based in the US. They are thus directly or indirectly influenced by US philosophy.
- The world's foremost rating agencies too are very obviously US-dominated. This is because the US Securities and Exchange Commission officially recognize only three agencies: Fitch, Moody's and Standard & Poor's.
- Global accounting practice uses principles formulated in the US, such as US GAAP. Even the European IFRS model that has since been developed borrows heavily from the American system.
- One last point: nearly all of the management tools and strategies that we have seen over the past 20 years are of American origin. Examples include the learning curve, portfolio strategies, diversification, reengineering, concentrating on core competencies, Porter's 'Five Forces' and shareholder value – not to mention practically all the tools of corporate finance. It is not insignificant that four of the world's five leading strategy-consulting firms are of American extraction. Roland Berger Strategy Consultants, a company with German and European roots and values, is the only exception.

There is another reason why American management philosophy dominates: many of us still admire the American way of doing business. If you ask consumers or businesspeople, as we do from time to time, which companies are truly global, they will probably mention an American company like Microsoft or Procter & Gamble, and not SAP or Unilever and certainly not the many medium-sized, family-owned continental European companies that are world leaders in their segments. We have to admit that American marketing and story telling have been excellent for many decades.

Considering these facts, there is no reason to be surprised at the dominance of the American management model over the last six decades.

Yet what exactly is it that typifies a US manager? Impressions culled from the work of the Globe Project[20] on leadership in the world's major regions suggest the following:

1. They have a short-term focus and a strong interest in fast results.
2. They prefer action to reflection and would rather attempt to solve problems by a combination of trial and error and case studies.
3. They place great trust in numbers and quantitative findings when making decisions.
4. They misunderstand management as a go-it-alone assignment rather than something that happens in co-operation with others.

Another characteristic of US managers is striving for an 'exit'. Take the example of Jim Kilts. After management positions at Kraft Foods and Philip Morris, he became CEO at the struggling cookie and cracker producer Nabisco in 1998. He made thousands of people redundant, managed a spectacular turnaround of the business within a very short period and then orchestrated a $15bn sale of the company to his former employer Philip Morris in 2000. His 'bonus' in the transaction: an estimated $100m. He then moved on to become Chairman and CEO of razor maker Gillette in 2001. Again, he did an excellent job of rejuvenating the business. And again, he actively pursued an 'exit' from the company by calling the CEO of Procter & Gamble. The result was a $57bn acquisition – and a reward for Kilts in the region of $165m.

Within the European business tradition, such pay cheques for a top manager might have seemed beyond any justification. In the US, it was perceived as the crowning achievement of an outstanding management career – and what applied to managers in the real economy applied even more to managers in the financial industry.

To summarize, we have seen an increasing focus on the short term and the implicit lack of attention to sustainability in the American management model. We have also identified the erosion of managers' willingness to critically review decision processes, at least as long as their personal wealth continues to accumulate.

With these observations, it is not difficult to see the factors that triggered and later drove the crisis. On top of this, there was also an almost religious belief in the findings of quantitative calculations, coupled with the received wisdom in the form of a backward-looking exercise seeking the patterns for success. What else, after all, are the case studies so enthusiastically produced by American business schools if not retrospective?

Yet with such a retrospective, it is now obvious that the American management model has reached its peak and needs to be revised. With utmost brutality, the financial crisis has revealed its weaknesses and pitched it heavily from the throne of undisputed superiority. It has become painfully obvious that the American management model is not able to deal successfully with the increasing complexities we find in the economy of the twenty-first century.

The question is, which other region can serve as a beacon to guide the way in the future? Which continent or country will serve managers, economists and even politicians as the role model for meeting the challenges of the twenty-first century? We bet that the immediate response of the majority would be Asia; and in particular, China.

Asia on my mind – the ascent of China, India and the 'Four Tigers'

When you look at the current economic development of China, India, Singapore, South Korea, Taiwan and Hong Kong, only one word comes to mind: amazing.

The pace of development in these countries is simply mind-boggling. South Korea is the world leader in high-speed Internet connection; its rollout of broadband and DSL services was much faster than in Europe or the States. Its biggest company, Samsung Group,[21] set a global record by investing over $40bn in just one year. India has become such a romping place for talented programmers and other IT experts that Germany decided to lure them in even at a time when unemployment was at a record high. Over the last years, Singapore and Shanghai have overtaken Rotterdam as the biggest port in the world (one by shipping tonnage, the other by cargo tonnage) and Hong Kong as a financial hub does not have to fear any comparisons with London or New York. Gone are the days when you would find the biggest flagship stores of Gucci, Prada or Channel in Paris or Los Angeles. Instead, you will see their logos in the most massive displays in Beijing, Shanghai and Hong Kong.

The enormous presence of Western luxury brands in the People's Republic is just one visible sign of change on the Chinese streets. Lanes long dominated by bicycles today are now solid lines of cars. China has become the biggest car market in the world, overtaking the US in 2009, and is currently the sales paradise for all global car manufacturers, from Volkswagen to Ford and Daimler. The production of vehicles in the country itself has increased more than eightfold between 2000 and 2011 (from 2.1 to 18.5 million),[22] catapulting China from ninth to the top spot in the list of the biggest car producers. For many, it is only a question of time until new domestic brands such as Chery, Geely and BYD Auto will flood the global market.

Similarly impressive figures could be quoted for many industries and sectors. China is well aware of its increasing prominence in the global arena and has taken strategic steps to secure and expand it. It tightly controls the allocation of rare earth metals, which are key ingredients for many new technologies in the economy of the twenty-first century – these range from batteries and plasma screens to hybrid engines and wind generators. Since China produces over 95 per cent of the world's supply of rare earth metals, this is no small issue. Long notorious for its pollution, China's new five-year-plan targets a massive expansion in 'green technologies'. The first results of this planning can already be observed.

What is truly astonishing is the enormous speed of transformation. Just five decades ago, the Chinese authorities were faced with the shambles of their economic policy. The agricultural collectivization led to chaos and famines; the attempt to industrialize the country with ideas such as melting iron with a mini blast furnace in every backyard, led to nowhere. China was a country that could look back to a period of 500 years of economic stagnation. The trigger for change was pressed no earlier than in 1978 when Deng Xiaoping started economic reforms. One stage after another, private ownership was reintroduced, entrepreneurship fostered and foreign investment introduced. By the end of the 1990s, the results of the reforms were firing on all cylinders.

In India, the period of liberalization did not start until after 1991. Before that, the subcontinent's economy was characterized by protectionism and strong regulation. In fact, trade barriers were so strong that it was virtually impossible to find any Western consumer brands in India in the 1980s, apart from tiny Cadbury snack bars sold in railway stations and on the streets, a rare exception granted to the British chocolate maker as a relic of British colonialism. Even Coca-Cola could not be bought in India until 1993.

While Chinese reforms were driven by Deng Xiaoping, it was the current Indian Prime Minister Manmohan Singh who effectively initiated economic change in his then role as finance minister. It is interesting to note that both had spent their lives as young adults in Europe; Deng Xiaoping as a pupil and factory worker in France (from 1920 – 1927), Singh as an outstanding student and researcher at Cambridge and Oxford Universities (1954 –1966). Their views on the economy and economic policy therefore had an inherent European angle.

India's growth rate in the last decade has been impressive, and the same can be applied to the so-called 'Tiger States': Taiwan, Singapore and South Korea (with Hong Kong being the fourth 'tiger'). Yet the most outstanding economic development, of course, has happened in China.

In 1978, China was the eleventh biggest economy in the world. With a population of about one billion at that time, the value of products and services produced was equal to that in the Netherlands where 16 million people live. In those days, Germany's economy was almost five times bigger and Japan outpaced China by a factor of 6.5. Today, China has overtaken both (Germany in 2007, Japan in 2010) and has become the second largest economy in the world. While there is still a considerable gap with the United States, most predict China will become the world's largest economy sometime between 2020 and 2030.[23]

Isn't it therefore self-evident that China will become the next world power and lead the way in all aspects, world politics, economic policy and management style? Well, it might. But history has shown that it is not always the seemingly obvious that turns into reality and that things don't always turn out as planned. Let us just look at the world powers over the last 500 years. The first leading nation in modern times was Spain. After Columbus sailed to America under a Spanish flag and founded a network of colonies, this boosted Spain's economy and it was regarded as the strongest economy during the sixteenth century. The resources from the other side of the Atlantic not only created enormous wealth in Iberia; it also helped to raise the Spanish status as a political and military power. When Phillip II's mighty and 'invincible' Spanish fleet, the Armada, was defeated in 1588 by the English under Elizabeth I, one might have predicted that England would replace Spain as the dominant force. However, things did not turn out that way. In fact, it was France that soon emerged as the new power. This came as a surprise, as France had been weakened by religious wars at the end of the sixteenth century that led to the eviction of thousands of Huguenots, many of them known to be diligent businessmen. However, the subsequent introduction of absolutism as a way to govern by the monarch and the implementation of the economic principles of mercantilism quickly turned France into a mighty stronghold, with the 'Sun King' Louis XIV as its best protagonist.

At the end of the eighteenth century, French dominance started to crumble and this time it was the Austrian Empire that came to be seen as the logical successor, due to its political and military strength and its leading role in culture and science, for example, as the cradle of modern medicine. Even after the end of the turmoil created by the French Revolution and the Napoleonic Wars, most political observers would have guessed that Austria would be the next dominant force, pointing at how Austria's Minister of State, Count Metternich, dictated the discussions about Europe's restoration at the Congress of Vienna in 1814/15.

Yet again, they would have been proved wrong, as the nineteenth century would become the English century. Steeled by the effects of the Industrial Revolution, England established an empire unseen before. From 1820 to 1870, England's economic output and growth was enormous, as was its global power.

CORK CITY LIBRARY

At the turn of the century, Germany was seen as the major challenger to such dominance. Strengthened by the effects of its unification into a true empire in 1871, the Germans set up a matrix for innovations, established chemistry and pharmacology as new industries and set new educational standards, both with excellent universities and the introduction of polytechnics. As we all know, Germany did not become the dominant power of the twentieth century, but the pre-eminent villain, having sparked and lost two world wars. Instead of Germany, it was the US that ascended the podium as the new major power in the Western world.

From an arguably very rapid time-travel trip through the powers-that-were we can draw one lesson: nothing is set in stone. The political situation in China combined with an increasing climate of confrontation with the West, particularly the US, means that the economic environment could alter quickly. We certainly hope that any kind of escalation can and will be prevented, as this would only lead to a backlash for everybody involved.

Yet, especially in a climate of conflicting interests, as we can currently observe between China and the US (one being the other's biggest creditor and manufacturer, the other its biggest consumer), the emergence of a third power could be exactly what is needed to ensure that the twenty-first century is going to become a century of prosperity for the world. This third power could well, we think, be Europe.

The vision for a new Triumvirate

This book is neither a swan song for the US economy nor is it meant to be a harbinger of doom for China's spectacular growth. On the contrary, we sincerely hope that the American economy is going to recover soon and sustainably. We also hope that the creation of new wealth in

China will continue with rapid speed and help bring about progress for human rights as well. What we do conclude, however, is that both powers could do with some guidance from a third party.

In the Roman Empire, Caesar twice formed an unofficial alliance with two other leaders, the so-called Triumvirates. He saw three parties on a par with one another as a good way for leadership exchange, as did many others later in history. A triangle allows constant circles of information and a flow of discussion, with minimal fear of deadlock when crucial decisions have to be made. In our context, the question is who could be the modern Triumvirate, leading the way to a prosperous twenty-first century?

As the reigning world power, the US seems an obvious choice and, despite the shock and obstacles created by the economic crisis, there is no doubt that the world can continue to learn much from the US. America still provides the most fertile ground for budding start-ups intending to break through globally. The country has also recognized that it needs to revamp its industrial production and invest more heavily in green technology. This awareness, combined with its large home market, might trigger a comeback in this respect.

It is also evident that China may be one of the driving forces for leadership in our century, as it has turned out to be the growth engine of the global economy in the first decade, at a time when consumerism as we know it in the West has just been conceived in a new domestic market of 1.3 billion people.

And who could be the third party? India? Brazil? Russia? Well, they all have much to offer and we have much to learn from them. They have also revealed promising growth lately. Yet in terms of what is required for a prosperous future, apart from growth, namely best practice in management, sustainability and co-operation between business and political leaders, one can argue a case for Europe.

The current transformation period opens a great window of opportunity for the 'old continent', but there needs to be a concerted effort by

European politicians and business leaders to seize it. The basis for this is awareness of what unifies Europeans and which strengths are unique to us.

Let's start with lesson one right here: the biggest economy in the world in terms of GDP is not the US or China. It is the European Union.[24]

Chapter 2

Europe's culture of skilled craftsmanship

If Europe wants to claim a leadership role in the world of international business in the twenty-first century, it first needs to identify what it has to offer. This has to be something that applies to all European economies. And it has to be something that distinguishes Europe from the economies of other regions.

This is not an easy task. The European Union in its present form is composed of 27 member states, has 23 official languages and more than 160 ethnic groups.[25] Within the EU, one can find various economic and social models, depending on different traditions and states of development. There are the Nordic countries with their strong welfare state model; the German-speaking countries with their social market approach; the more centralized economies embodied by the French model; the Southern European countries with rather nationally-oriented businesses such as Italy; the countries with a strong Anglo-American outlook such as the UK (and, to a lesser extent, the Republic of Ireland); and the Central and Eastern European members which have had to transform from a planned to a free-market model.

The EU's efforts to create an internal market might have started a process of convergence between these economic models. Yet the process certainly has not been completed and it appears that more people pay attention to the differences than to any common denominators. However, we do need a clear awareness of the elements that unify the European economies and make them stand out from the others.

Otherwise, Europe will neither be able to step out of the shadows of the American business model, nor create sufficient attention among the emerging Asian powers as a new role model from which to profit.

In this chapter, we want to scrutinize which elements unify the European economy and distinguish it from other leading powers in a positive and constructive way.

Learning from UEFA on the way to tackle a perception problem of European business

Leadership is closely linked to reputation. Europe's economy and its ongoing unification are often regarded as rigid and slow.[26] In an attempt to build up the degree of respectability it deserves, it is worth having a look at the world of sports.

The most popular and widespread sport in the world is football, or 'soccer' as the Americans call it (then again, they also decided to call the final of their domestic baseball season 'the World Series'). When you quiz people around the globe on which are the world's best soccer teams, you will hear similar answers, irrespective of where you ask. Rest assured that European clubs such as Barcelona, Chelsea, Manchester United, Inter Milan or Bayern Munich regularly feature on the list. It is also highly likely that people outside Europe will know exactly what you refer to when you utter words such as Arsenal, Ajax Amsterdam, Real Madrid, Benfica or Juventus. In a nutshell, football clubs from Europe are the best known and most admired in the world. One might argue that this is not all that surprising, as football has always been associated with and dominated by Europe. After all, it was invented here. Well, tell that to someone from Brazil or Argentina and you might be in for a surprise. In the history of the FIFA World Cup, three Latin American countries have won the cup almost as often as six European ones: nine versus ten times. On top of that, the unofficial crown of 'Best Football Player of All Time' usually goes to either a Brazilian (Pele) or an Argentinean (Maradona), depending on which school of goals you belong to. Finally, Brazil also has the best reputation when it comes to repeatedly churning out superb players. Yet it is still the European clubs that are better known than any others in the world and that have the reputation of being the best. Even South Americans acknowledge it.

The excellent standing of European football in the world has much to do with the efforts of the European Association of Football (UEFA), which has done a tremendous job in marketing it, especially with the introduction of the Champions League (which they did not even bother to call the *European* Champions League, implying that the best in Europe are the best in the world anyway). People around the world love to watch the Champions League, because it allows them to compare different styles: the English grappling with an Italian defence, Spanish dribbling magic against German discipline. At the same time, it is the best place to watch top-class football with its finest qualities. This notion unifies the European top clubs and lifts their reputation in the world.

When it comes to business, however, unfortunately the Europeans have not been as savvy in marketing or in presenting their skills to the global audience. Ask consumers which companies have a genuinely global reach and you will more than likely hear the name of an American company. Most people believe that Coca-Cola is the most globally recognized beverage company, given that the myth of the 'coca-colonization' of the world is widespread and well documented, even in movies such as Billy Wilder's *One, Two, Three* (1961) or the comedy *The Gods Must Be Crazy* (1981). Once you scrutinize available market research data, however, you will come to the conclusion that Red Bull has an even wider international exposure. The privately held energy drinks company is based in Austria and, hence, is a European company. The comparison between perception (usually in favour of US companies) and facts (often in favour of European ones) can be made in other sectors as well: General Electric is probably regarded as the industrial conglomerate with the biggest global presence when, in fact, it is Siemens. An educated guess might be that Disney or Time Warner is the media company with the highest revenue share outside its home market. In fact, it is the largely unsung media conglomerate Bertelsmann. And SAP is more global than Microsoft or IBM.[27]

The fact that Europe still lags behind the US when it comes to the *reputation* of its businesses is also evident when we look at the list of Best Global Brands. Released each year by the brand consultancy Interbrand, this is one of the most widely reported rankings related to companies and businesses. Looking at the 2011 rankings,[28] Europe can hardly claim any dominance. On the contrary, US firms occupy all of the top ten spots – the top three are Coca-Cola, IBM and Microsoft. The first European company on the list is German car brand Mercedes Benz in twelfth, followed by Finnish mobile phone brand Nokia (no. 14), German car brand BMW (no. 15), and French luxury fashion label Louis Vuitton (no. 16).

According to Interbrand, European enterprises are decently positioned, yet they certainly cannot claim superiority, at least over American corporations. Does that mean that European companies are just mediocre in the global arena, while European football clubs are the best in the world?

Well, let's dig a bit deeper. In evaluating the ranking of best brands, one should take into account that Interbrand belongs to Omnicon, the biggest advertising network in the world and that both are headquartered in New York. The fact that they are both US companies explains why Interbrand's method of evaluating global brands is in line with American marketing strategies. Interbrand is not to blame for that. In fact, the brand consultancy has been fairly transparent about its methodology, basic inflows can even be found on their website.[29] What it indicates, however, is that the (misleading) perception that US firms still dominate the global league of companies might just be one (overly marketed) puzzle piece in the big picture.

Europe's economic dominance in the league of global competition

Since this book attempts to lead us away from common (mis)perceptions, we searched for comparative studies that have a more comprehensive approach in evaluating global competitiveness. One excellent source is the World Economic Forum's Global Competitiveness Report (GCR).[30] Since the report is published each year, it serves as good radar to track development trends in competition.

Before the global financial downturn took hold, the US had reached the top position in this ranking (Report 2007/08). In the latest ranking (Report 2011/12), it had fallen to fifth position and the comments in the report weren't exactly favourable: 'The United States continues its decline for the third year in a row, falling one more place to fifth position', it states, adding: 'In addition to the macroeconomic vulnerabilities that continue to build, some aspects of the United States' institutional environment continue to raise concern among business leaders, particularly related to low public trust in politicians and concerns about government inefficiency.'

Judging from current headlines in the media about China and India increasingly dominating the global economy, one might presume that these two countries must have made big leaps forward during the last five years. They have not. China moved from position 30 to 26. India actually fell back six places, from 50 to 56. The other two members of

37

the so-called BRIC-States did not fare all that well either: in the latest ranking, Brazil ended up in position 53, Russia at 66.

The performance of Asia's 'Four Tigers' is more impressive. Singapore is currently ranked as the second-most competitive economy in the world. Hong Kong (11), Taiwan (13) and South Korea (24) all made it into the Top 25 in the list of 142 countries analysed. This result, however, is overshadowed by the dominance of European countries. Not only do they occupy the first and third positions, held by Switzerland and Sweden respectively, they are also by far the best represented countries in comparison to any other region, with seven European countries in the Top 10 and 11 in the Top 20. No fewer than 10 members of the European Union are among the most competitive; beyond Sweden, are Finland, Germany, the Netherlands, Denmark, the United Kingdom, Belgium, France and Austria.

This impressive track record should not make us Europeans become too self-confident, of course. Yet it is a reassuring indicator that we must have done something right in the last few years. Moreover, one should not forget that the European economies are the oldest developed countries, as industrialization started here. This means that we have been pretty good at constantly modernizing our existing businesses and infrastructure. Otherwise, it would not have been possible to be so well represented at the top of a global competition ranking at the beginning of the twenty-first century.

The World Economic Forum divides the countries examined into five groups, based on their stage of development. It builds its comparative analysis by measuring the grade of competition on 12 pillars, ranging from the legal and administrative frameworks, and the infrastructure of the economy, to the quality of education and the labour market, as well as the levels of innovation and business sophistication. Regarding the areas that seem, to us, particularly sensitive for a sustainable top ranking, the performance of Europe is even more impressive than in the overall ranking, as you can see in this table:

Table 1: WEF rankings, 2011/2012

Ranking	Nature (uniqueness) of competitive advantage	Capacity for innovation	Quality of local suppliers	'Intelligence and quality' of production processes
1	Japan	Japan	Switzerland	Japan
2	Switzerland	Switzerland	Austria	Switzerland
3	Denmark	Germany	Japan	Germany
4	Germany	Sweden	Germany	Sweden
5	United Kingdom	Finland	Sweden	Finland
6	Finland	Israel	Belgium	Netherlands
7	Italy	USA	Netherlands	Belgium
8	Israel	France	Australia	Austria
9	Belgium	Denmark	Canada	Denmark
10	Netherlands	Netherlands	France	Ireland
	USA (rank: 20)		USA (rank: 13)	USA (rank: 11)

Source: 'The Global Competitiveness Report 2011/2012', World Economic Forum[31]

The categories in this table are the bases to connect the major challenges of our time – climate change, scarce resources and demographic change – with growth. To us, the main elements necessary to successfully grow an economy in the twenty-first century are green technology, smart automation and intelligent production systems cleverly crossing machinery and equipment with high-end electronics and IT. This is the reason why industrial capabilities are so important to achieve sustainable growth in the future – and why Europe is in such a good position in this respect. While the manufacturing industries account for 18 per cent of GDP in Europe (in Germany, it is even 24 per cent), this share has fallen below 14 per cent in the US.

When it comes to the uniqueness of the competitive advantage (or nature, as the GCR calls it), European countries occupy eight of the top 10 slots, seven of them being members of the EU. In plain terms, this means that we Europeans are clearly the best at setting ourselves apart on the basis of our products and services. The high capacity for innovation signals that research and development are doing much better in these climes than many make us believe. Production too – or at least high-end production, is one of our strengths. European countries clearly dominate the ranks in the categories of 'quality of local suppliers' and 'intelligence and quality'. Another clearly appropriate source with which we can evaluate Europe's strength within the global economy is a long-term study conducted by Roland Berger Strategy Consultants, composed of an analysis of 3,000 large companies around

Table 2: Roland Berger 3,000 study

1998-2008	Europe	USA	Japan	BRIC
Origins of the top 3,000 (2008)	27.0%	38.2%	23.8%	11.1%
Sustainability	78.6%	76.3%	56.1%	66.3%
Revenue (2008)	34.1%	38.7%	15.2%	12.0%
Revenue growth (CAGR)	10.4%	9.3%	2.8%	28.8%
Profit (EBITDA) (2008)	41.6%	31.0%	10.6%	16.7%
Profit growth (CAGR)	13.1%	6.9%	7.5%	29.3%
Profitability (EBITDA/revenue in 2008)	19.8%	13.0%	11.4%	22.5%
Share of revenue outside home market (2008)	39.0%	29.0%	30.0%	20.0%

Source: Roland Berger Strategy Consultants' study of the world's 3,000 largest firms (2009)

the globe that are listed on stock markets (excluding companies in the finance industry). The study examined the growth, profitability and sustainability of these companies from 1998 to 2008. Its results can be summarized in Table 2 (opposite):

At first glance, it appears that the best performing companies are based in the BRIC countries. After all, this table reveals that large companies based in Brazil, Russia, India and China had the highest growth in terms of revenue and profitability, exceeding European countries by more than double. This can neither be denied nor neglected. Yet one should also not forget that these economies are much less mature than the ones in the 'Western world' and, thus, benefit from the typical statistically based effect. In other words, it is quite typical for younger companies to increase their key figures more markedly on a percentage basis than seasoned corporations. It remains to be seen to what extent China and the other BRIC countries can uphold such expansion in the future.

A rough idea of how difficult this is going to be can already be found in the 'Sustainability' section of Table 2. The percentage figures displayed in this rubric show, on a regional basis, how many of the companies that featured in the top 3,000 in 1998 still featured in this group at the end of the study in 2008. On the question of how many companies could stay at the top, the BRIC countries finished only in third place. The top position went to Europe, with 79 per cent of its large companies managing to stay in the global top 3,000 for the entire period. With such a performance, the Europeans left not only the Chinese or Indian corporations behind but also the biggest enterprises in America and Japan. Thus, top European companies remain successful longer than their rivals in other parts of the world.

Some might counter that the 'gold digging times' recently experienced by the BRIC countries will automatically create booms and busts, even for their biggest companies. Yet this type of reasoning

41

points to precisely the problem when you try to search for role models in the highest-ranking companies. The issue is that a 'gold digging atmosphere' tends to be a great period for adventurers but rarely for the crystallization of long-term leadership. For leadership, you simply need to have a certain degree of maturity. In the league of mature economic regions, however, Europe wins, in almost all categories:

- The largest European companies increased their revenues by an average of 10.4 per cent every year, much faster than their peers in North America (+9.3 per cent) and Japan (+2.8 per cent).
- The largest European companies also increased their profits at a substantially quicker rate; a growth rate of 13.1per cent is about 70-80 per cent higher than in North America (6.9 per cent) and Japan (7.5 per cent).
- During this period, European enterprises outpaced their US counterparts, as EBITDA margins climbed from 15.6 per cent to nearly 20 per cent, whereas the corresponding ratio in North America declined from 16.1 per cent to just 13 per cent.
- Europe's companies generate close to 40 per cent of their revenues outside their domestic market ('domestic' meaning Europe, not their national market). By contrast, American and Japanese ones have a far stronger focus on their home markets. This is even more applicable to the BRIC countries, which might be surprising to some.

After all, China is regarded as an export-driven economy. Yet it is the European economy that has created the true global players.

To round off the figures: 27 per cent of the world's 3,000 biggest companies have their headquarters in Europe. These 27 per cent represent 34 per cent of the total revenue and 42 per cent of the total profits reported in this league. We can therefore take pride in the fact that

Europe's companies grow faster than their international competitors, are more profitable, have a larger global footprint and maintain a more sustainable orientation.

A reshaped resurgence of a poorly reputed tradition as the defining point for Europe's future economy

In our opinion, the data from the World Economic Forum and Roland Berger Strategy Consulting provide a very compelling case for the current (and very good) state of the European economy in the global arena. The figures and findings assure us that in Europe we have a very solid foundation to build a case for a leadership role by Europe's economy. Nonetheless, we are also aware that the data provided is incomplete for our purposes. After all, important members of the European Union are not among the most competitive economies, such as Italy or Spain. Since countries such as Portugal and Greece are also missing, one can draw the conclusion that, so far, we have made a case for the Nordic and German-speaking countries as well as the Benelux states and, to a lesser extent, France and the UK.

If we want to authoritatively counter this claim, we have to come up with an authentic common denominator that defines the European economy as a whole. Ultimately, it comes down to finding the fabric that makes business culture – a fabric whose patterns can be presented to the world as the best way to move forward. While searching for this, we checked our experiences and went through our observations. One such observation had its roots at a construction site in the city where both authors have offices: Hamburg. Currently, Hamburg is building its version of the Sydney Opera House, the Elbe Philharmonic Hall.[32]

Observing the building-work progress has been fascinating, especially when huge cranes lifted up the enormous windows for the glass construction. Each window weighs over a ton, is several metres long and wide and shaped in a most unusual way, with a big hump in the middle. On a guided tour to the construction site,[33] one of us asked the guide which company manufactures them. We were told that the glass was shaped in Padua, by a firm called Sunglass.[34] Padua is about 1,300 kilometres away from Hamburg, so it seemed a bit of a palaver to ship the windows all the way from there, especially since glass of this shape and magnitude must be very difficult to transport. Couldn't they be made in a place much nearer? We were told that such industrial glass bending is an extremely rare craft and that Sunglass was one of the few companies, if not the only one, that could do it.

We had never heard of this firm and Internet and archive[35] research did not reveal much more than the fact that Sunglass existed. It seemed to be one of these hyper-specialized firms unknown even to a European business expert. A business correspondent based in Milan did not know the company either, yet he mentioned that there are quite a few such niche players in Italy, especially in the glass industry. He mentioned that he had recently met a spirited entrepreneur, Luigi Monti, who had climbed up the career ladder with jobs at Ferrero, L'Oreal, Danone and Fiat, only to end up running a struggling glassblowing workshop in Murano at the age of 39.[36] The young manager was drawn to the glassblowing skills of his old 'maestro' craftsmen who were following a craft practised for 800 years on a small island near Venice, world-famous for its glass products. Yet Monti despaired of the complete absence of modern management and saw this as the main factor why his and other firms in Murano were so badly hit by cheaper glass products from China or Morocco. Monti introduced cost calculations, expanded the product portfolio to also included pieces that fit better into a more contemporary style and increased and changed the marketing methods

– all this by keeping his craftsman motivated and willing to accept the changes as necessary to survive and prosper. The company is called Formia International. Since taking the helm, Monti has introduced a second brand, Vivarini.[37]

While the transformation of this boutique company is still ongoing and it is therefore too early to call it a success story, we should investigate at this point whether some bigger cases could be found to illustrate that Italy had successfully managed to modernize an ancient craft. As it happened, cases were easy to find. After all, the two biggest manufacturers of sunglasses in the world are both based in Italy. Number one is the Luxottica Group,[38] founded in 1961 in Agordo, north of Venice. Initially, the company only catered for orders of prescription frames from wholesalers, but soon it launched its own brands and, with a good mix of craftsmanship, technology, branding and marketing, helped to change consumers' traditional perceptions of glasses: from spectacles to 'eyewear'. In 1999, Luxottica bought the most famous sunglasses brand in the world, Ray-Ban, from US contact lenses maker Bausch & Lomb, who regarded the sunglasses business as not being lucrative enough. Today, Luxottica makes over $5bn in revenue and achieves an operating profit margin above 10 per cent. It has entered the Chinese market, owns hundreds of retail stores in the world and holds licences to produce sunglasses under such brands as Chanel, Tiffany, Versace, Paul Smith and Stella McCartney. The number two in the sunglasses market, Safilo Group,[39] was founded slightly earlier in 1934, also in northern Italy, 165 kilometres north of Venice in Pieve di Cadore. Everyone who has a pair of sunglasses from Armani, Hugo Boss, J. Lo., Yves Saint Laurent or Carrera, has bought a Safilo product.

Is it a coincidence that these two companies, both founded in the twentieth century, became global market leaders in the segment of an industry that has a centuries-old tradition? We think not. Instead, we see it as a case where a particular region's old crafts have been successfully transformed, resulting in the emergence of large flagship companies with global leadership status, even among highly- specialized niche players such as the glass treatment firm, Sunglass.

We intentionally wanted to start our case in a country which, these days, is thought of as one of Europe's weakest economies (Italy), and with a term at its core that is generally not associated with free market rules or forward looking attitudes – craftsmanship.

In a discourse on leadership for the twenty-first century, pointing to a culture of craftsmanship as a positive factor might seem somewhat odd at first. In fact, it will remind some of the time when Europe's economies were dominated by guilds. Today, these ancient 'interest groups' for craftsmen are often associated with protectionism, inflexibility and cronyism – lots of regulation, little invention. On the eve of the Industrial Revolution, guilds were criticized both by Adam Smith and Karl Marx: the former saw them as cause for insufficient competition and, thus, poor output and quality; the latter as oppressor, prohibiting diligent workers to be freed of their social ranks by the guilds' rigid structures.

These criticisms underlie the reason why guilds are held in such low regard today. It is indeed true that the end of the guild system was long overdue at the beginning of the nineteenth century. Yet taking a closer look, one can also detect that such a 'clustered' way of organizing skills has served the European economies quite well for centuries. When the first guilds emerged about a thousand years ago in different parts of our continent (called *métiers* in France, *guilds* in England and *Zünfte* in Germany), they actually fostered competence and competition instead of preventing them – and did so for a long time.

Historically, craftsmen organized in guilds brought good and bad results for the economy as a whole. What is interesting for the future are the signals that European businesses have started to embrace the positive elements of such a heritage and enrich it with modern management and strong service-oriented methods. As a result, Europe has developed what we call a 'modern culture of skilled craftsmanship'. The main criteria of this culture are:

- an awareness of the existing crafts of a region, including industrial skills and infrastructure;
- a vision and willingness to transform these crafts and skills to existing needs and adapt them to the challenges of a global economy;
- loyalty to their 'home base' without ignoring the benefits of international co-operation, global expansion and, above all, free trade;
- a keen interest in research and development and the constant improvement of productivity;
- a willingness to invest in the advancement of the existing workforce in exchange for continuity, loyalty and flexibility;
- a long-term approach to achieving economic success.

Not too long ago, some of these points would have been seen as old-fashioned and rather detrimental to a successful business strategy for the future. In the euphoria surrounding what is known as the knowledge society, we Europeans were mocked for years because our economies still included a substantial proportion of manufacturing. For management theorists and business strategists from the US, this was a clear sign of an anachronistic economic order. Today, our industrial strength draws envying glances and no self-proclaimed American post-industrialist laughs or jeers any more when a European politician says that 'a country without industries is a country without a future', as French Prime Minister Jean-Marc Ayrault did at his inaugural government declaration in 2012.[40] Moreover, the manufacturing infrastructure serves us as the basis to intelligently combine products and services to form new solutions. In the past, German company BASF simply sold pots of paint to car manufacturers. Today, it runs entire paint shops in the car plants of Mercedes Benz.

Both BASF and Mercedes Benz (or Daimler respectively) also illustrate another result of a culture of skilled craftsmanship: natural cluster building. Based in Ludwigshafen, BASF, the world's biggest chemical company, became the industrial standard-bearer in the Rhine-Main-Neckar conurbation – surrounded by myriad small and medium-sized service providers. With its headquarters in Stuttgart, the capital of Baden-Wuerttemberg, Daimler has remained loyal to its roots since Gottlieb Daimler and Carl Benz invented the internal combustion engine and the car some 125 years ago. By maintaining this loyalty, the carmaker has not only nurtured a legion of suppliers in the region but also enabled long-term and in-depth co-operation with educational institutions. The then CEO of Tata Motors, Carl-Peter Forster, stressed the importance of such relationships when we asked him at a meeting in Mumbai in November 2010 which regions of the world will dominate the automotive industry in the future. As an industry veteran who had worked for BMW in Munich and South Africa, he served as head of GM's German subsidiary Opel and, later, became head of the entire European operations of General Motors. These days he commutes between Mumbai and Oxford to supervise Tata's Indian car production, as well as its British subsidiaries Jaguar and Land Rover. Forster was the perfect authority to answer such a question, as he has deep insights into the American, European and Asian auto markets. He replied, 'One can manufacture a car almost anywhere in the world these days. The challenge is the engineering. The key is to make sure that you keep a good engineering base in your country.'

Forster makes an important point. The outsourcing theorists want us to believe that such high-end services can be set up just about anywhere in the world. This does not hold true in reality. Engineering services and engineers' creativity only flourish and grow in deeply rooted industrial clusters. This is because geographic proximity creates the best conditions in which trust, the cornerstone of close collaboration for research and development, can be built. As one of the top European car makers, Daimler always understood this lesson and acted accordingly, perhaps even more so after the failed merger with the Detroit-based Chrysler Group.

Engineers are a very important group among the skilled craftsmen of the twenty-first century. Some European companies continue to attract them without moving to a big town or vibrant metropolitan area – take two examples from Austria. Miba Group,[41] a leading supplier of engine bearings and so-called sintered (powder-made) components for cars, trains, ships and aircraft is based in Laakirchen, a town with fewer than 10,000 inhabitants. Managed from this small town in Upper Austria, Miba makes more than €300m in revenue, of which over 90 per cent is generated abroad. Upper Austria is also the Greiner Group's base, a global leader in the foam and synthetics industry (with expertise ranging from plastics packaging to the moulding of window frames). From its headquarters in Kremsmünster, with around 6,500 inhabitants, it directs over 100 production and sales sites around the globe.

Greiner Group's revenues are above €1bn. Both companies stick to their local roots without becoming parochial. This is typical of European companies that are best in class. They keep the expertise in research and development, quality assurance and high-end production at their headquarters or in close proximity (or at least a substantial part of these functions) and thereby create what we call a 'system head'. With such a 'system head', they can manage or maintain complex production systems throughout the globe, set up intelligent logistical systems or deliver new solutions that improve energy efficiency. When you look at the winners of the 'Best of European Business', an award organized annually since 2009 by Roland Berger Strategy Consultants, you will detect a system head structure quite regularly. You will also find many prime examples of Europe's culture of skilled craftsmanship.

Such a culture, however, is not just limited to Europe's most competitive countries. Take Spain and the Basque territory, for example, with their many 'hidden champions', such as Gamesa,[42] one of the biggest constructors of wind farm parks in the world, the ITP Group,[43] a leading manufacturer of gas turbines and aeronautical engines, or Panda Security,[44] a top-notch provider of antivirus and security software.

Such a culture is equally not only reserved for classical industrial manufacturing – take France and the dairy industry. It was companies such as Danone, Yoplait and Lactalis that turned yoghurts into high-end products, based on extensive R&D. Danone has even managed to sell its flagship products Actimel and Activia globally, despite the hitherto common belief that the milk and yoghurt market is almost necessarily regional. The French also proved that even formerly state-owned companies could become global leaders, with Veolia and Suez Environnement not only dominating but also basically inventing environmental services on a private business level.

You will find impressive companies that have managed to combine classic industrial expertise with ultra-modern technology offering new solutions everywhere in Europe. In Portugal, for example, a country that has recently been badly battered by its domestic situation, companies such as Vision box,[45] a leading provider of biometric and electronic security systems, and Surfacelab,[46] a maker of 'intelligent' surfaces that enable object communication via RFID, completely fit into this pattern, to name but two.

And it is in Italy, whose businesses are often criticized as being too national and, thus, narrow-minded in outlook, where you will also find numerous global champions, far beyond the glass industry. If you ever drive from Bergamo to the airport and wonder what is behind the bright red wall along the autostrada that stretches over a kilometre, it is a new science and industrial park which houses, among others, the research centre of the Brembo Group, the top class provider of braking systems for high-performance cars and motorcycles, whose customers range from Ferrari and Audi to Harley-Davidson and Ducati. Closely attached to the Brembo facility are laboratories of German carbon specialist SGL. Together, the two companies are working on new carbon ceramic brakes. Daimler's Mercedes Group is also involved in the project.

A culture of skilled craftsmanship versus a trading culture

Lego and Mattel are both highly successful toy companies. Yet there is a major contrast between them. While the Danish Lego Group still produces its characteristic plastic bricks at its headquarters in Billund, California-based Mattel has long ceded its own production and outsourced all its manufacturing. If you want to see how a Barbie plastic doll is made, you have to go to Asia.

The contrast is typical for the different mindsets and management philosophy on the two sides of the Atlantic. In her comparative study of American and European management styles, Ulrike Reisach, a professor at the University of Neu-Ulm, comes to the conclusion that the American management style is driven by a 'merchant culture'. It stands for efficiency, processes, speed and, consequently, high returns. This is in stark contrast to Europe's 'culture of skilled craftsmanship', which reflects a down-to-earth attitude, social integration, solid workmanship and a long-term outlook. This is a very illustrative comparison. However, we believe the term 'trading mentality' would be even more

51

accurate than 'merchant culture', not least in view of the financial crisis caused by the financial traders.

The differences between a culture of skilled craftsmanship and a trading culture also explain the differing goals of European and American managers. Reisach notes that power, growth, profit and – unavoidably – personal wealth play a predominant role in the US, whereas in Europe greater importance is attached to responsibility toward employees and the wider environment, continuity, and the desire to 'create something that lasts.'

In the American schools of management, such a desire is regarded as detrimental to professionalism and modern management. Lego's decision to keep manufacturing a seemingly straightforward product (plastic bricks) in a country with such high wages as Denmark would have been marked out as a warning example. It would have been regarded as a case where a management decision has been based on sentimentality not strategy. We cannot omit that the Lego Group did indeed go through deep trouble not too long ago; the Danish icon suffered huge losses in the years 2003 and 2004. High production costs were part of the problem. The company had to lay off several hundred people and closed a factory in Switzerland. With new product innovations and distribution ideas, Lego managed an impressive turnaround. However, even during its period of struggles, the family-owned group never considered completely folding production at its Danish headquarters, despite the fact that it owned two other sites for moulding the Lego bricks in Hungary and Mexico, countries with much lower salary standards than in Denmark.

With Mattel, the case is exactly the opposite. The American toy expert decided decades ago that it does not want to bother with production anymore. It simply does not see any particular strategic value in keeping this part of the 'value chain' in-house. Horst Brandstätter, owner of another renowned European toy manufacturer, Playmobil, remembers vividly when he first went to Mattel's headquarters in El Segundo, close to the Los Angeles airport. Invited by his peers from Mattel, he had a guided tour of the facilities. 'They showed me the floor where the marketing experts were located, the floor where distribution was handled, one floor for accounting, another for research and development', recalls Brandstätter, 'then I asked them: "and on which floor is manufacturing?" It did not exist.'

This was in the mid-1980s, at a time when Mattel had long started a kind of manufacturing 'hopping' strategy. First, it had moved production from the US to Taiwan, in 1967. When labour costs continued to increase in Taiwan, Mattel left in 1987 and let workers in China and Indonesia make Barbie & Co. Brandstätter did not want to follow such a path. Being a third-generation offspring of an entrepreneurial family with roots in a village close to Nuremberg, he felt both responsibility and gratitude towards the local workforce. Despite the conventional wisdom that toy making had no future in Europe due to cost constraints, he refused to outsource any production to Asia. Instead, he opened factories in Malta, the Czech Republic and Spain. In addition, he decided to invest heavily in the original production site in Germany, starting a €100m programme in 2005 to elevate Playmobil's facility in Dietenhofen to a state-of-the-art factory. For a company with annual revenues under €500m, this was an enormous investment. Moreover, Brandstätter had to set up a 'war chest' nurtured by the company's cash flow, as major banks refused to lend him money for the project, regarding it as too risky and economically unviable. Brandstätter's decision to go against the mainstream paid off, as a look at the last published balance sheet revealed. In the fiscal year 2010/2011 (ending in March 2011), the manufacturer of the Playmobil plastic figures reported an operating result of €110m on revenues of €530m. Net profit was €86m.[47] In comparison, Mattel managed an operating income of $1,041m on sales of $6.266bn. The net result was $769m, according to the 2011 Annual Report.[48]

To put these figures in perspective: the holding company owning Playmobil achieved a profit margin of 21 per cent on its operational business. Mattel, roughly 10 times bigger, had to content itself with 16.6 per cent. In the previous year, the gap was even wider with Playmobil having achieved a margin of 27.5 per cent and Mattel just 15.4 per cent. Numerous reasons might be responsible for the gap, but it indicates that the economic purpose of outsourcing has its limits.

Outsourcing manufacturing also has particular dangers, as Mattel experienced in the summer of 2007. When it became apparent that most of its toys that were produced in China had a toxic contamination, it had to start an enormous recall campaign.[49] This not only cost millions, it also badly damaged the company's reputation as makers of premium toys. Mattel's Chairman and CEO, Robert Eckert, is well aware of these implications, as one of his public comments suggests, 'If you'd asked me ten years ago, I'd have said our role is to earn a return on capital to make money. Today I've become evangelical about the fact that making money and doing good are complementary, not conflicting. It's a responsibility.'[50] Such lip service, however, did not make him or his colleagues on the board reconsider their general approach to production. It seems that relocating parts of the manufacturing back to the States was never an option. Instead the 'production portfolio' was spread wider 'to help avoid disruption', as the company stated, with principal manufacturing facilities now in China, Indonesia, Thailand, Malaysia and Mexico. The very different approaches of Mattel, Lego and Playmobil and Ulrike Reisach's general remarks on the different management cultures in the US and Europe, are supported by the findings of a transatlantic survey undertaken by Roland Berger Strategy Consulting conducted in 2009. More than 260 top executives in Europe and America participated in the survey. Two differences in their views on leadership and management stood out:

1. When asked whether personnel management is 'very important', 23 per cent of European executives said yes, compared to just 12 per cent of the American executives, who set significantly greater store by marketing and sales skills.
2. The same picture emerged in response to the question of whether 'social skills will become more important in future,' to which 22 per cent of Europeans said yes, compared to just 13 per cent of Americans. The latter attached primary importance to functional skills.

When reduced to the plainest terms possible, the differences between American and European views on leadership and management become abundantly clear. There is:

- the US trading culture vs. a European culture of skilled craftsmanship;
- the preference for profit and personal wealth vs. the European desire to create something of lasting value;
- the US shareholder returns and profit per share vs. the European long-term strategy;
- the US leadership model and personal aggrandizement vs. European management and social skills.

It took a massive financial and economic crisis to make US politicians and economists realize that they have stretched their culture of merchandising too far. 'We Americans must get back to the belief that we can produce something,' said former Federal Reserve Chairman Paul Volcker,[51] who chaired President Obama's Economic Recovery Advisory Board from 2009 to 2011 and was, thus, one of his closest advisors in the years after the financial crisis erupted.

It will be a cumbersome path back to such roots. Partly under the influence of American management philosophy, the US has run down its production capacity and neglected what remains. It has plotted a course for the knowledge society by building up services, especially in the financial sector. Today, it has become clear that this strategy was myopic and based on flawed assumptions.

In contrast, most European business people have never stopped their endeavours to lay the foundations for manufacturing. Thanks to the level of expertise built up and cultivated on the 'old continent', Europe's locations can stand up to competition, even from Far Eastern locations with low labour costs.

The differences between the American and European approach can even be observed in industries and companies who have decided to out-source manufacturing. Two vivid examples that illustrate this are the fashion retail giants GAP and Inditex. San Francisco-based GAP (which also owns the brands Banana Republic and Old Navy) has decided to source almost all of its fashion lines from Asia. Only 1.3 per cent of the clothes sold in GAP's stores are made in the United Sates. Spanish retailer Inditex, owner of the Zara stores, also did not want to bother with in-house textile production. However, the company made it a guiding principle that the clothes that they sold should be manufac-tured in the vicinity of the stores. This principle, combined with sophisticated logistics, enabled Zara to drastically reduce the time it takes until a newly designed collection can go to retail, from six to two weeks. What's even more interesting from our point of view is that Zara sparked the emergence of vibrant textile production in Spain – an industry that was thought to be long lost to Asia.

Europe's industrial skills and our ability to build up systems busi-nesses are important for another reason: they create potential for sustainable growth. Sustainability clearly requires the right conditions, especially regarding the financial markets, quite apart from all the issues we are currently debating in relation to education and integra-tion. It is also true that we can only achieve sustainable growth if we successfully tackle our biggest environmental problems, such as climate change. In other words, we must learn to translate our dealings with scarce resources into growth.

Americans still struggle to come to terms with this, as they have been used to an environment of abundance. In Europe, however, we are already well on the way. Green technology is emerging as a very definite driver of growth. Roland Berger Strategy Consultants believe that the global market for environmental technologies will soon be worth as much as $3.2 trillion[52] – more than the heavyweight markets for automotive engineering and engineered products. Europe's companies are excellently placed, commanding double-digit shares of virtually all market segments. And that is no coincidence: after all, everything that has to do with 'green tech' or the 'green transformation' is ultimately rooted in an intelligent combination of mechanical engineering, industrial systems engineering, electronics and technical services. This mix fits well with our skills profile, which is precisely why our high-end manufacturing base is so important. It gives us a positive perspective. Environmental technology is a classic example of how continental Europe's traditional 'culture of skilled craftsmanship' can be put to good use in the modern world – we will go in to more detail on this in Chapters 4 and 5.

International competition is predictably growing fiercer. Huge chunks of the economic stimulus programmes recently launched in the US, Japan and China have found their way into green technologies. In the production of solar panels, Chinese suppliers have forced both European and US pioneers to file for bankruptcy.[53] China has been accused of unfairly subsidizing its national players, causing the US Department of Commerce to impose high anti-dumping duties on Chinese solar-product imports.[54] Yet beyond rather standardized manufacturing procedures, Europe has kept its lead in the field of green technology.[55]

This lead is also exemplified in the most successful European companies as a whole, where the following criteria in terms of structure and management style can be extracted:

1. They have raised their productivity, while at the same time investing in growth, and have done so consistently over an extended period. In other words, they have not plotted the typical Anglo-American V graph (shrinking and then growing), but tackled both fronts simultaneously.

2. They pursue policies of differentiation. The top European companies consciously develop their systems business by intelligently combining products and services and beefing up those functions in which Europe has a competitive advantage: research and development, quality assurance, and high-end production.

3. They are more international than their American counterparts and their managers are more willing to visit even the remoter outposts of their empires. Almost every second top manager from Europe has lived and worked in the US; the reverse is true only for every fourth American boss.

4. They are more heavily decentralized than their American and Asian counterparts and entrust greater decision-making freedoms – regarding product adjustments, pricing, marketing and management issues – to local management teams.

5. They intelligently combine hard factors such as vertical integration and the cost position (i.e. the company's 'technical' ability to grow) with soft factors such as personal leadership, values, integrity and trust building (i.e. the company's human face and its willingness to grow).

These principles have served Europe's top corporations well. Today, some 23 of the world's 50 largest companies are headquartered in

Europe, while the number of American companies in this elite group has slipped from nearly half 10 years ago to just 16 today.

Whether you look at the top tier or at the overall competitive situation, Europe has certainly put itself in a good position for a leadership role by reviving its culture of craftsmanship and adjusting to the opportunities and challenges of the twenty-first century. Modern versions of skilled craftsmanship can be found everywhere in Europe, not only in the Nordic and Germanic countries, but also in France, Benelux, Central, Eastern and Southern Europe. There is, however, one member of the European Union that needs to be discussed separately: Britain.

The special case of the United Kingdom

Having mentioned earlier that Europe as a whole did well in preserving its industrial infrastructure while the contribution of the manufacturing sector has slipped below 13 per cent in the United States,[56] one should mention that the United Kingdom has scaled back its traditional production even more: its share in overall GDP is less than 10 per cent. Originally the global centre of almost all industrial production, it seems that Britain lost faith in its manufacturing abilities after the Second World War. Take the automotive industry as an example: once, British cars were regarded as industry leaders and in some categories, such as luxury limousines or sports cars, regular benchmark setters. Several decades ago, however, their quality became so poor that they lost any competitive edge. It required the help of competitors from abroad to rescue that situation. Jaguar and Land Rover, often loss makers under the reign of Ford, are now owned by Indian Tata Motors. Mini and Rolls-Royce belong to BMW, Bentley to the Volkswagen Group. It wouldn't really matter all that much who owned these

59

well-known brands, if they hadn't gone through such a long period of deterioration on the engineering and manufacturing sides.

It remains to be seen to what extent the new foreign owners can reinvigorate this situation, but it remains obvious that the working opportunities for talented automotive engineers in Britain have been on the low side lately. If it hadn't been for Formula 1, all automotive expertise might have left the country long ago. It is only thanks to people such as Frank Williams, Ron Dennis and, above all, Bernie Ecclestone, that some of the best minds in car engineering still work in the UK. Many Formula 1 racing teams have their headquarters in England, and it is in places like McLaren's futuristic lakeside research centre in Woking, Surrey that clever brains can develop and test their innovations.

However impressive this may be, it is not sufficient to create a viable industry with a serious economic impact. Numerous similar examples can be found and made in other industries, all coming to the same conclusion: Britain's industrial backbone is partly broken, partly fractured and very fragile.

Frustrated by the economic problems of the 1960s and 1970s, new stimulus programmes launched in the 1980s and 1990s focused increasingly on services. In its economic policy during these two decades, Britain rarely followed continental Europe but almost always followed the United States. In terms of its management style and strategies, British business leaders adopted best practice examples from the US, not Europe. This strong alignment is the reason why American management principles are often referred to as the Anglo-Saxon school.

Britain's clear association with the US was also very obvious in its policy towards the financial services industry – with the result that the UK was particularly badly hit by the financial crisis. As for the role it played in causing the crisis, some might argue that Britain's contribution was almost as high as America's. After all, the small unit of AIG responsible for credit-default-swaps (CDS) that brought the then biggest insurance company to the brink of bankruptcy was based in London. The British capital was also among the big financial centres around the world where hedge funds and private equity groups found the most favourable conditions in terms of low regulation and low taxes.

Today, Britain has become strongly aware that it needs to change course.

'For too long Britain's economy has been over-reliant on consumer debt and financial services', said Prime Minister David Cameron at the official launch of the Queen Elizabeth Engineering Prize at London's Science Museum on November 16, 2011, 'We want to rebalance the economy so that Britain makes things again – high-skilled, high-value manufacturing and engineering should be a central part of our long-term future.'[57] Cameron said almost the same in the Houses of Parliament[58] and the desire towards 'less city, more industry' seems to be shared by politicians across all parties in Britain. Many predict that it will be tremendously difficult for the UK to restructure its economy and build a new, sustainable foundation for itself. This may well be the case. Yet we have no doubt that the people of Britain are able to succeed in such an effort and rekindle their culture of skilled craftsmanship. After all, the British guilds were once regarded as some of the most accomplished, and Britain, of course, was the cradle of the Industrial Revolution. Furthermore, one just has to watch British TV programmes, movies or advertising spots to see how much creativity, humour and curiosity exists in this country. If just a part of this can be (re-)chan-nelled towards the creation of modern versions of craftsmanship, Britain will succeed.

One precondition, however, is necessary. Britain must embrace the European idea. Given that Britain had been a standalone world power for such a long time, with its empire stretching to all parts of the world, it is perhaps understandable why the UK has struggled for so long to closely align itself with other members of the European Union and is perceived as today's biggest blocker of further integration within the EU.[59] Based on sentiments and politics, this situation might drag on for a while and at some point even end in a blow up. However, from an economic point of view, this has to come to an end. The reason is pure necessity: British companies need a home turf that goes beyond their national boundaries if they want to successfully compete against the rising Asian powers. The solution for this lies not within the Commonwealth but rather within Britain's biggest trading partner, the European Union. The need to link arms on the 'old continent', of course, does not only apply to Britain but also to all European countries, even the bigger ones. Neither Spain, France, nor Germany will be able to take a leadership role on their own in the global economy of the twenty-first century. It requires a concerted effort, a European effort. Now this is what we call a prime example of a culture of skilled craftsmanship, on a pan-European level.

Asia – torn between a trading culture and a culture of craftsmanship

It is one thing to distinguish Europe's business mindset with the one prevalent in the United States, the leading economy of the twentieth century. Yet it does not address the question as to what extent Europe also has an edge over Asia in terms of its skilled craftsmanship. You may be sceptical at first. After all, it is well known that the Far East became the undisputed 'factory of the world' in the first decade of the twenty-first century, led by Taiwan, Indonesia, and, above all, China. At the same time, India established itself as a global leader in software development, thanks to an ever-soaring number of talented programmers.

Looking back, one can also see that the Far East has a long tradition of impressive craftsmanship and inventive power. The Chinese invented the compass. Indians discovered how cotton and cashmere wool could be woven into textiles and they introduced the button to the world. And without the dexterity of Asians to turn the protein fibre of a worm's cocoon into a shiny fabric, silk could not have turned into a luxury item with global appeal. While it was the German Johannes Gutenberg who had built the first printing press, the roots of printing as such are on Chinese soil, as is the case with papermaking. As the inventor of dynamite, the Swede Alfred Nobel is often referred to as the father of explosives, yet the very first chemical explosive, gunpowder, goes back to China. And, of course, there is the ongoing dispute regarding the extent that spaghetti-making was influenced by Marco Polo bringing noodles from his expedition to China to his hometown of Venice (Italians tend to have a very strong opinion on this one).

With its historic track record and a current industrial output that brings not only textiles and toys to the world but also the most sought-after high-tech gadgets, ranging from plasma screens to laptops and smart phones, one is tempted to conclude that Asia is certainly not behind Europe in terms of skilled craftsmanship. Rather the contrary, it seems to have overtaken the 'old continent'. We agree that Asian countries have managed an impressive even astonishing development over the last decades. Yet we also believe that it is too early to make an authoritative judgment if, and to what extent, a sustainable culture of skilled craftsmanship has developed over this period. The industrialization of the region is simply too young to make a call. While the Industrial Revolution had started to transform Europe more than two hundred years ago, the Asian economies remained virtually unchanged until after the Second World War: they were deeply ingrained in agriculture.

In countries such as China and India, it took regulatory decisions by the respective authorities to intentionally open up their markets to trigger a profound economic metamorphosis. Once these decisions were taken (1979 in China and 1991 in India, as mentioned earlier), a shift towards capitalism emerged which brought these countries closer to both the US culture of trade as well as the European culture of craftsmanship. Today, the world is impressed by the breathtaking speed with which these countries are being transformed, particularly China. Due to modern technology, a huge internal market and centralized decision-making, the Chinese economy seems to have taken little more than a few decades to reach the same stage that took Europe centuries to accomplish. In terms of construction and luxury on display, China and some other Asian economies have even outpaced Europe on many fronts. All this cannot be disputed. However, we should not ignore that these are the fruits of 'gold digging times' based on an enormous backlog of demand.

During a meeting in his Shanghai office in the autumn of 2010, Paul Gao, CEO of Chery Quantum, a new automotive company in the making, explained the recent car frenzy as follows: 'For Chinese people of my generation, owning a car is a status symbol. A sign that they have moved away from the lifestyle of the old China of our parents where the sense of personal freedom was limited to as far one could get by bicycle. You pedalled for an hour and that brought you to the suburb of the city you lived in, but that was all. Buying a car means: now I can go anywhere.' Gao agreed that this feeling among Chinese people in the early twenty-first century has a striking similarity to the American way of life in the twentieth century. In both cases, the car serves as a 'symbol of freedom'. The difference, of course, is that the introduction of automotive vehicles in the US marked the beginning of the 'carbon economy' while we are now close to its end. As a consequence, Gao sees the current sentiment in China as a 'temporary phenomenon' with very limited duration. His children, he explained, are being 'brought up with much greater awareness towards environmental challenges'.

Mastering these environmental challenges will play a decisive role in determining to what extent Asia is able to build a sustainable culture of skilled craftsmanship. So far, the industrialization in China and other Asian countries has been nourished by cheap labour and a very production-friendly milieu with comparatively little regard for the environment or people's well-being. At the same time, some new industrial players in the regions have been rather slapdash in their treatment of people's and other companies' intellectual property. Both are typical effects of economic 'gold digging times'. These times will not last forever.

What has distinguished the European economy in the last several years is its ability to massively overhaul its industrial infrastructure, making its culture of skilled craftsmanship fit for the twenty-first century. It is a century that will most likely see the post-carbon period of industrialization. At the moment, Europe is best prepared for the new challenges to come; the continent is clearly the world leader in green technology. Europe's advantage is that it can build on its age-old industrial expertise while developing new innovations. Take the automotive industry as an example. Asked whether he thinks that China will soon overtake Europe as the leading car producing region thanks to its aggressive push towards electronic vehicles, Gao replied, 'If an e-car were just a battery on four wheels, this might be the case, because we're all starting from scratch in terms of battery research and management. But the Chinese automotive industry still has 75 years of experience to make up for when it comes to the mechanical parts of a car.' This explains why he has chosen a strategic path for his new car company (a joint-venture of the Chinese car maker Chery Automobile and the Israel Corporation set up in 2007) is to focus on consumer needs and not on building up engineering and production assets. Gao freely admits that he would love to outsource the whole engineering and production of the new vehicle in the planning stage if that were possible and concentrate on his vision 'to control the whole brand experience'.

Now this sounds very much like an archetype of the American business culture. It might therefore not come as a surprise that Gao uses a

US-based company as the role model for his plans: Apple. Obviously, we do not want to extrapolate the opinion of just one modern executive to the whole Chinese economy. Many other players might lean more towards the European approach. Yet his statement is an anecdotal indication that China and the other Asian economies are at a crossroads and haven't decided yet whether they want to march down the American path of a culture of trade or follow the European way of skilled craftsmanship.

In this respect, it seems appropriate to turn to another European asset where it is easy to draw a clear line for China: this is the continent's culture of consensus.

Chapter 3

Europe's culture of consensus

From a purely economic point of view, the path to the future is clear: Europe's nations need to come together and be a united front in order to claim a leadership position in the global economy of the twenty-first century, as no single European country will be strong enough on its own to face the competitive power of the rising Asian nations, not even the 'export champion', Germany. Europe's economies have already benefited greatly from the creation of an internal market within the European Union but we need to continue our efforts to cultivate a truly barrier-free 'home turf', offering our high-potential companies the economies of scale necessary to stay in, or rise to, the global top league.

As we have already established, a culture of craftsmanship is deeply ingrained within Europe and this culture could act as a binding agent stretching all over the continent, bonding economies as different as Finland and Portugal, Poland and Italy. However, is this culture of craftsmanship sufficient as a foundation for a common European business culture? It seems that we are at a stage where most European managers and citizens still regard themselves, first and foremost, as belonging to a single nation within Europe and often focus more on the differences than the similarities to other EU states. In short, the question is: if and to what extent do we need a 'European feeling' to fully realize the continent's potential?

We believe we do need this 'European feeling' – for the simple reason that in order to establish Europe as a role model for conducting business, and to successfully export its principles to other parts of the world, we must rely on people acting as ambassadors for Europe: people who spread the 'European way' as a promising path. Yet these 'ambassadors at large' will only be convincing when they have a strong sense of European identity They can only make an impact if it is not just an elitist phenomenon. We need thousands – ideally millions – of such ambassadors.

The concept of Europe – from dynastic thinking about peace efforts to economic credo

There are many reasons regarding how and why someone can become a European with true conviction. People who have lived, studied or worked in different countries of the EU tend to feel more European because they have had the opportunity to personally discover the benefits of diversity under a common umbrella. Being exposed to the European institutions also follows the legacy of Henri Saint-Simon who put these institutions at the 'nucleus of crystallization for European integration'.[60] Well, let's put it this way: if a person regularly encounters the bureaucracy of Brussels, Strasbourg or Luxembourg or even works for the European Commission, European Council, European Parliament or European Court, he or she is presumably more likely to develop a European spirit. However, a leading 'multi' European lifestyle or working for an EU institution is a result of the European idea rather than the reason for its existence. If we want to find the roots of the concept of Europe, we have to dig deeper. It is therefore worth going back to the days before the political and economic project of Europe was started in the 1950s.

In the decades and centuries preceding the construction of the EU, the main group of people who had a pan-European sentiment belonged to the aristocracy and the ruling royal families. The Habsburgs serve as a good example. Thanks to their successful marriage policy – whereby strategic political alliances were forged or reinforced – they managed to rule (for various periods of time) over countries as different as Austria, Hungary, Spain (at the peak of its power), the Netherlands (including most part of what is today Belgium), Bohemia, Slovenia and Slovakia as well as parts of Italy, Germany, Poland and Romania. By separating the Habsburgs into a Spanish line and an Austrian line we can better understand which member of the dynasty reined where and why, but it somehow disguises how well the family nourished its network all over the continent. For the Habsburgs, the concept of Europe was a family affair.

The House of Saxe-Coburg-Gotha illustrates the extent to which such dynastic thinking led to the creation of an impressive pan-European fortress. With its origins in the small town of Coburg (today part of the State of Bavaria in Germany), the family managed to place its offspring so well in the mighty European monarchies that they were represented on almost a dozen of Europe's thrones at the end of the nineteenth century, ranging from Britain and Belgium, Norway and Denmark to Germany and Russia. Looking at photographs taken in Coburg in 1894 during the engagement ceremony of Tsar Nicholas II to Princess Alexandra of Hesse-Darmstadt, one cannot fail to notice the resemblance to group photographs of today's Heads of States at European Council summits. In one picture, the aging Queen Victoria is seated in front, standing behind her is the young Wilhelm II, Emperor of Germany which became united when Victoria was 52 years old.[61] Victoria was Wilhelm's grandmother and, thus, she was always happy to consult him on family and political matters. Of course it helped that Wilhelm was her favourite grandchild. Victoria herself had benefited greatly from the advice of another trusted family member. In the early days of her reign, she often took advice from her uncle, King Leopold I of Belgium. Kaiser Wilhelm adored Queen Victoria, but he was not all that fond of his British uncle Edward (who later became King Edward VII) or his cousin George (later George V) who were also present at the 'family gathering' in Coburg in 1894. However, he cultivated a close correspondence with one of his Russian cousins, Tsar Nicholas II.

Considering the family's ties all over Europe, it is easy to imagine why and how they had developed a kind of 'European feeling'. They had learned how to deal with Europe's different traditions and languages, and thus benefited strongly from its rich diversity. These 'family ties' also contributed to the establishment of common grounds on the continent.

With the rise of modern nation states, however, their hitherto pan-European sentiments became increasingly overshadowed by nationalism. One by one they each found it impossible to reconcile a European and national feeling. Eventually they had all either opted voluntarily for the latter, or were forced to do so. The result was that 20 years after the picturesque pan-European family reunion in Coburg, Wilhelm found himself engaged in a painful and bloody war with his cousins George and Nicholas.

The First World War was a time that saw the elimination of the European spirit. In a way, it was simply wiped out by the propagated nationalism for the masses. Looking back, it is quite obvious why this was so easy to achieve and why it happened so quickly. The 'European feeling' was too elitist. Since it was intentionally reserved for a very limited number of people – the members of the ruling dynasties – it could never penetrate into large parts of the population. As a consequence, it could not be sustained against new concepts that had serious mass appeal: nationalism and national identity.

Many scholars, philosophers and journalists saw the dangers of nationalism early on – and suggested countering them with European initiatives. Among them were French sociologist Henri de Saint-Simon,

French poet and novelist Victor Hugo, German philosopher Konstantin Frantz, Austrian novelist and activist Bertha von Suttner and Austrian diplomat and politician Richard Coudenhove-Kalergi. Saint-Simon, with fellow Frenchman and historian, Augustin Thierry, regarded the policy of restoration, agreed at the Viennese Congress of 1814/15 after the Napoleonic Wars, as the seed for conflict and war and countered it with a plan for an integrated Europe, including the creation of a European Parliament. Later on, the concept of a more strongly associated or even unified Europe was often taken up and presented at peace conferences, such as the one in Paris in 1849 where Victor Hugo presided over the 2,000 attendees and predicted in his now often quoted speech: 'A day will come when you France, you Russia, you Italy, you England, you Germany, you all, nations of the continent, without losing your distinct qualities and your glorious individuality, will be merged closely within a superior unit and you will form the European brotherhood.' At this event, Hugo also coined the term 'United States of Europe'. More than 40 years later, at the Peace Congress in Berne in 1892, Bertha von Suttner filed a petition to found a Confederation of Europe. 'Europe is one', was a popular phrase of the Austrian Baroness who later became a Nobel Peace Prize laureate.

These spiritual pioneers of Europe had noble motives, good intentions and strong ideas. In fact, the structural concepts drawn by Saint-Simon and Augustin Thierry of 1814 have a striking resemblance to EU institutions today.

The problem at the time was, however, that their ideas were not implemented (and this might explain why history has put many of them into the realm of utopians and romantics). In their lifetime, most scholars had to concede defeat in the battles for their European ideas against the prevailing national sentiments, just as the high aristocracy had to.

Even after the end of the First World War, the time was not ripe for European integration. When Count Richard Coudenhove-Kalergi and

Archduke Otto von Habsburg started the Pan-European Movement in 1926, they realized that they had to penetrate their mission widely. They even founded 'pressure groups' to influence politicians around Europe to take up their ideas of a Pan-European Union – in vain. It would take another 20 years and another bloody war to convince Europe's national powers that commencing a process of integration would not be against their interest but would be for the benefit of all.

This change of mind might have been triggered by the shock of the Second World War and the strong desire to avert another military conflict in Europe over the long term. Yet the steps towards achieving this intention were predominantly taken on an economic level.

Turning to economic policy as the driving force for building the European dynasty was both clever and extremely far-sighted – for two reasons. First, the economic targets chosen by the new European institutions – growth, job creation, education – are exactly the issues that preoccupy most ordinary people. In short, they help to truly penetrate the European idea. As long as European initiatives successfully boost programmes and initiatives that help achieve these targets, we have a way of attracting the attention of the European population in a positive way and fostering a kind of European patriotism. Second, the concept of centralized nation states that had dominated the political landscape in Europe in the nineteenth and twentieth century appears more and more outdated when we look at the challenges lying ahead in the global economy of the twenty-first century. Solving large-scale breaches of intellectual property rights with China is better handled as a European mandate than dealt with by separate national delegations, as are trade disputes with the United States. In a period of amplified mobility driven by cyber networks and cloud computing, the EU member states need to raise their levels of co-ordination – not only on external issues, but also internal ones. If they want to avoid large corporations basing their investment decisions for establishing or relocating factories and offices on subsidy-fishing and tax exemption poker, they need to make a concerted effort.

In the context of this book, it is important to bear in mind to what extent economic matters and business affairs have already contributed to the integration of Europe. It is the topics and initiatives that often seem technical or even dull from the outset that have led us to a European Union and a common currency. These are truly tremendous achievements.

Economic changes lead to new political structures and new concepts of identity

Few people will dispute the accomplishments of the European Union in terms of having brought peace and prosperity to the continent over the last several decades. Yet critics might argue that we are still far away from a widespread European feeling of belonging among the continent's population. They might point at the lack of a common language, 'cultural conflicts' and stereotypical prejudices evident in the enormous struggles with the euro, and the failure to adopt a European Constitution. They might thereby conclude that we simply lack the necessary ingredients to create a real European identity. Admittedly, we still have a long way to go before we can claim a genuinely integrated, or even a unified, Europe. Nevertheless, we see it as a safe bet that the integration process is going to continue. There might be a temporary standstill or occasional setback in certain areas and periods. Yet, on the grand scale, a strong political Europe is irresistible.

Why? It is irresistible because the current economic changes in the world clearly demand it. As previously mentioned, Europe's nation states appear to have gradually become phased-out models in terms of their size and structure. Their initial mission as the main instruments for managing and directing people's lives does not work all that well any more, when you look at it from an economic point of view. Some of the issues they currently handle would be better left to the regional authorities, who are closer to their constituents. Others need to be shifted to a higher level, such as the European institutions, to become successful policies. In order to make this happen, the national powers will have to hand over more parts of their power and sovereignty – which poses the question: Are they prepared to do so?

The answer is 'yes'. The willingness to relinquish sovereignty on a national level was the precondition for European integration at the outset. It paved the way for Europe as a political project and the birth of the EU. This shift is not yet completed. National politicians might not be particularly keen to cede more power, but they have realized (at least the responsible ones) that further passing of competence and jurisdiction from a national to a European level is beneficial and, to an extent, even necessary to ensure a prosperous future on our continent.

It is a future where Marshall McLuhan's vision of a 'global village' briefly becomes a reality, where the opportunities to access information and education will accelerate profoundly, where the way we work and compete is going to be driven by a degree of flexibility and mobility never experienced before. Yet are political changes and even identity building driven by economic developments? They are. Economic developments led to the emergence of modern nation states – and it is economic developments that will cause their demise.

Let's take a step back to examine why and how national identities have developed and we will see what lessons we can learn regarding the emergence of a European identity. In the pre-industrialized era, which was dominated by agricultural economies, the concept of nations did not exist, at least not as permanent institutions. They were not required, because the economy had very rigid structures and the sense of belonging was determined by status and local loyalties. What life could be or bring was largely preset by birth. The options to take a different path in life were extremely low, as was the ability to travel. All this changed with the Industrial Revolution. The new methods of production tore down traditional workplaces. New means of transport such as trains, steam boats and, later, the automobile, combined with massive construction efforts to build tracks, canals and more solid roads gave people the ability to travel to an extent never experienced before. There was a sense of excitement, but also of being lost. To fill this vacuum, new structures to organizing life were required, giving people guidance and a new sense of belonging. It was these circumstances that prompted national movements and the rise of modern nation states in the nineteenth century. The political and administrative structures of these states helped in mastering the enormous economic transformations: the law was codified, education and certificates became more standardized, and the right balance between investment security and safe and sheltered labour sought.

Following the British-Czech philosopher and social anthropologist Ernest Gellner, the economic metamorphosis of the Industrial Revolution did not halt at organizational changes. It also led to a shift in people's self-image as members of a certain community. In the past, they had considered themselves, first and foremost, to belong to their local community. When they became uprooted during the Industrial Revolution, they lost this focal point. As a consequence, they looked for new meaning and found it in their role as citizens of the newly created nation states, where a 'codified culture' with shared values was provided to them. National identities were born.

In Gellner's theory, these identities only emerged because industrial society required them to. Thus, could it be that today's economic challenges require the formation of a European identity that will emerge almost automatically, as long as we push the right buttons in our economic policy and business principles?

75

There are indeed some interesting analogies here. On an economic level, we are in a very similar situation to the early days of the Industrial Revolution: we ride on a massive wave of economic change. At the time the Industrial Revolution, it was James Watt's patent of the steam engine in 1769 that served as the catalyst for this wave. In today's Information Revolution, it has been the World Wide Web, developed by the Brit Tim Berners-Lee and the Belgian Robert Cailliau in 1990. In the eighteenth century, Watt's invention profoundly altered the way people produced goods, yet the political and ideological ramifications only became evident much later. The Information Revolution has already brought enormous changes to the way we work, but it is still nation states that dominate politics. This, however, is not surprising, because we know from the days of the Industrial Revolution that there is going to be a time lag until we can see the full impact of our revolution on a political level. In the past, the industrialization of a certain region served as a harbinger of its upcoming unification with other regions into a nation state. Tomorrow, we might well see that the phenomena of the so-called post-modern economy leads us to a unified Europe.

It would be interesting to know if Gellner, who was a member of the school of critical rationalism, would have accepted such an 'extension' of his theory to a European level, especially since the economist and philosopher had a truly European biography: born in Paris to a German-speaking couple from Bohemia, Gellner was brought up in Prague and outside London. He went to Oxford during the Second World War and taught at Cambridge and the London School of Economics until he returned to the Czech capital towards the end of his life. Is it really possible to develop a European identity today as was done some 150 years ago on a national level?

At first sight, it appears as if the creation of a national identity was much easier, because people were mentally prepared for it. Looking back, it seems as if the people of all those tiny German principalities were just waiting to finally be turned into citizens of a national German Empire (created in 1871), and that the unification of the inhabitants of the Italian peninsula (in 1861) was inevitable from a cultural point of view, not an economic one. After all, they spoke the same language, which means that they could quickly understand each other – a huge difference to today's European Union with its many languages.

It is true that a common language helps to integrate people, but it is by no means the only or most important factor. The huge economic disparities between Lombardy in northern Italy and Campania in its south have brought a big rift between the inhabitants of Milan and Naples, despite the fact that they have shared the same language for centuries. At the same time, the Milanese cut their ties with the inhabitants of Bolzano, irrespective of the fact that German is still predominantly spoken in the capital of Southern Tyrol. In fact, many apparent language disputes in Europe have economic disparities at their core, for instance Dutch-speaking Flanders and French-speaking Wallonia or regional use of idioms in Spanish – Catalan, Basque or Galician. As long as people can see the (economic) benefits, they can quickly adapt, even on a linguistic level. The best example is Switzerland where German, French and Italian have been official languages since the country's existence in its present form in 1848.[62] Admittedly, the number of languages spoken within the European Union (now 23) is much higher, making it virtually impossible to learn and speak all of them. Yet Europe's language variety is small in comparison to India, where more than 1,500 languages are officially recognized and nobody claims that the subcontinent cannot develop its own identity due to this language variety. We should also keep in mind that even China has quite a diverse range of languages, so while a person living in Hong Kong speaking Cantonese might get by trying to read and speak Mandarin, he or she would not be able to communicate in *Shanghainese*, the local idiom spoken in Shanghai. In short, the Asian powers on the rise also have to deal with multiple languages across their territories. To our benefit, the Internet has contributed a great deal to the establishment of English as the lingua franca in Europe – and this will help to speed integration.

We believe that the more politicians and business people manage to develop truly compelling answers to the new economic challenges on a European level, the more we will see a genuine and widespread European identity emerge on the continent. Populists like to counter that it is only economists who see it this way and that it is only an elite group that can reap the benefits delivered by integration. The vast majority of 'ordinary' people, they argue, have a very different view: to them, the economic deeds of Europe are complicated, distant, extrinsic, unfair and, as a consequence, objectionable.

Well, such claims are misguided. While certain developments such as lobbyism or the bureaucracy and privileges within the European institutions undeniably alienate many 'ordinary people' (and rightly so), they clearly share the view that, bottom line, the assets of the European integration significantly outweigh the drawbacks. This is evident in an opinion poll regularly conducted by the European Commission since 1983. The question posed is: 'Taking everything into consideration, would you say that (your country) has on balance benefited or not from being a member of the European Community (Common Market)?' With the exception of the United Kingdom and, to a lesser extent, Greece, Hungary and Austria, the majority of the interviewed people in all EU member states have answered this question with 'yes' and ticked 'benefited'. In 10 countries, the positive quorum even reached a two-thirds majority, witnessed in regions as different as the Benelux countries (the Netherlands, Belgium and Luxembourg), the Baltic Republics (Lithuania and Estonia). In Ireland, Luxembourg, Poland, Slovakia and Denmark more than 70 per cent saw benefits.

Table 3: European Commission poll results

Country	Benefited	Not benefited	Don't know
Austria	44%	46%	10%
Belgium	68%	29%	3%
Bulgaria	46%	30%	24%
Cyprus	48%	46%	6%
Czech Republic	54%	39%	7%
Denmark	70%	23%	7%
Estonia	68%	24%	8%
Finland	61%	33%	6%
France	52%	38%	10%
Germany	48%	42%	10%
Greece	47%	50%	3%
Hungary	40%	49%	11%
Ireland	78%	12%	10%
Italy	43%	41%	16%
Latvia	47%	47%	6%
Lithuania	67%	20%	13%
Luxembourg	73%	20%	7%
Malta	59%	25%	16%
Poland	73%	18%	9%
Portugal	51%	37%	12%
Romania	61%	27%	12%
Slovakia	72%	22%	6%
Slovenia	53%	42%	5%
Spain	59%	30%	11%
Sweden	53%	34%	13%
The Netherlands	67%	26%	7%
United Kingdom	35%	54%	11%
EU average	52%	37%	11%

Source: European Commission, Standard Eurobarometer 75, May 2011[63]

The results indicate that 'ordinary' people are absolutely aware that the European Union has served its people well. Contrary to some opinions voiced, they also fully understand that the EU is not about dispensing the same cake differently, but that it helps to make the cake bigger – to the benefit of all.

True consensus instead of false inspiration

It is one thing to acknowledge the benefits of the European Union, but it is a completely different thing to feel attached to it. In this respect, the European project has scored few points so far. When 25,000 individuals in the member states were asked about their personal feelings towards the European Union in a Eurobarometer poll in 2005, 'enthusiasm' was ranked among six attributes to choose from. 'Indifference' was chosen three times as often as 'enthusiasm'. It's no wonder that the EU stopped asking this question in subsequent polls. The result seems to epitomize the core problem of the EU: while it is recognized to be useful, it does not inspire. It is perceived as technical, complicated, detached, tedious and bureaucratic.

Also complex, but much more exciting than the current story of Europe, are the current changes in China. We might disapprove of China's totalitarian regime and its violation of human rights, yet anyone who has visited China recently cannot fail to be impressed by the breath-taking speed and extent of its economic transformation. Take one example, in 1995 Shanghai did not have a single metro line. Just 15 years later, it champions the longest network in the world: 11 lines, 434 kilometres long, carry two billion passengers per year.

China organized both the Beijing Olympic Games 2008 and the World Expo in Shanghai (2010) with such pomp and grandeur that the message they wanted to convey was clear: we are a new superpower on the rise. In terms of the ongoing economic development, spectacular stadiums, bombastic exhibition halls and impeccably choreographed performances are just the tip of the iceberg. Away from the limelight, the Chinese are constantly building new highways with dozens of lanes, new high-speed trains and even whole cities – in a manner never before seen in history. For the 'factory of the world', nothing seems impossible. As a result, the Chinese economy has regularly sported two-digit growth rates per annum in the last several years. The great success stories and awe-inspiring images of China spark everyone's imagination. In China, things really get done.

In comparison to this galvanizing Asian 'galaxy', the European ecosystem presents a rather sober picture of an old continent in a stagnant state. It seems that, in the EU, things more often get discussed than actually done. Proposals are often dissected to a point where every original idea is hopelessly diluted and all enthusiasm completely wiped out. Europe's dominant attitude, it appears, is dithering.

On a factual level, we know that this conclusion is unfair and incorrect. Once we thoroughly examine the track record of the EU, we discover quickly what tremendous achievements have been made. And when we recall the enormous progress European companies have made in improving their global competitiveness (Chapter 2), we are reminded that young Europeans do not need to move to China or another BRIC country to find an inspiring business environment. They have it right on their doorsteps.

So why is it, then, that we and the EU's officials often find it so difficult to put Europe's achievements of the last decades into absorbing stories and powerful images? The answer is simple: the structures and machinations of the European institutions are not made for storytelling. They are made for consensus seeking. This explains why its decisions constantly and consciously gravitate toward the greatest common denominator.

Moreover, successes have often to be talked down. After all, one member making too many waves of success could all too easily rock the boat of consensus. Such an environment of caution and clauses leaves little room for legends and heroes. Instead, it leads to obscurity and disinterest. In any case, solutions reached by consensus are seldom the fruit of emotional enthusiasm. They tend to be the outcome of long, drawn-out negotiations. Frequently, they are peppered with exceptions and escape clauses. Exhaustion rather than elation is the predominant sentiment when a solution is reached. To summarize, achievements reached by profound consensus can rarely be transformed into box-office hits for the public.

One might argue that this applies to every decision-making process, certainly among democratic societies. The difference, however, is its degree. In national politics, the heads of governments or states usually have a certain leverage to put their feet down when things get out of hand. It is granted to them by the constitution or *realpolitik*. On a European level, there is no such power concentration. There is no president who also has the power to act as commander-in-chief. There is no front-runner who can form their own government after winning an election. And there is no prime minister who can reshuffle the cabinet when they are displeased with it. On an EU level, each person who sits at the negotiating table has to live with the others gathered there as well, whether they like it or not. And the negotiators usually have to talk for as long as it takes to reach a compromise that is carried by everyone at that table. This, of course, is just the first stage. Once a decision has been made, it often needs to be approved by other European institutions. Frequently, it requires ratification on a national level. Sometimes, it calls for execution on a regional level. At each step, one deals with people who draw their loyalties, or 'political capital', from separate sources; one meets people who speak different languages. In a nutshell, the complexity on the way to compromise is enormous. Given the people and parties involved, it is no wonder that many documents produced on an EU level end up being almost unreadable. And no wonder that, for the vast majority of people, political decision-making on a European level is a mystery wrapped in an enigma.

Ask yourself: do you really know what the European Council does? Are you familiar which powers are vested in the European Parliament? Could you name even a third of the existing Directorates General in the European Commission and explain their mandate? Given the complications of competence, we can quickly draw a long list with very basic questions, such as when is the European Court authorized to decide a matter? And when can the European Court of Auditors intervene?

Rest assured, working in such an environment is not the most rewarding thing if you look for day-to-day work completion and job satisfaction. Considering how entangled the EU's structure is, it is also surprising that anything ever gets done. Yet the amazing thing is, it works. Contrary to some international organizations who have indeed drifted into endless 'talking shops', the EU has managed to build its house steadily, step-by-step.

The reason for this outcome is precisely Europe's strong culture of consensus. It is a culture born out of the conviction that co-operation is more important than the care for one's ego – a culture that puts problem-solving over principle-seeking. This has not always been the case. In fact, it used to be the opposite. For centuries, Europe's history was laden with battles over principles and sieges laid to satisfy egos. Europeans were quick to use weapons against each other and it did not take much for nations to go to war. With the emergence of modern nation states and nationalism, the confrontational course between the peoples of Europe became even worse. Early propagators of the European idea, such as Victor Hugo or Berta von Suttner, saw the dangers early and warned that such a course could only lead to catastrophe. Yet most Europeans believed in the cleansing effects of military confrontation and saw war as a legitimate means to achieve superiority. It took the shock of the Second World War to alter this mentality. Finally, they realized that it was not principled confrontations they ought to aim for, but the principles of consensus seeking.

It was this change of mentality that laid the foundations for European integration. Without a strong determination to listen and talk to each other over and over again in order to reach agreement, the political and economic project of Europe could never have been started – and we could have never come this far. In a way, the culture of consensus is the cornerstone upon which the common European house is built.

This is unique in the world, certainly in its quality and density. Convinced Europeans no longer despair about the complexities of consensus-seeking in a multi-cultural group. Instead, they have become inspired by the diversity that comes along with it. They tend to acknowledge that it is – more often than not – worth ceding some ground in a certain situation, as the other parties might do the same at some point later. Europe's ability to productively 'wrestle' until a solid result is achieved, its conviction to put co-operation over ego and its respect for the accomplishments of others involved are enormously important qualities both in politics and business and in our ever-increasing globalized world more so than ever.

However, there is a downside. The achievements of long-wrought consensus are a hard sell, particularly as they run detrimental to the requirements of the media. Driven by a headline culture, scoops and little space to explain complex details, most mass media are out for news that is easy to convey. They need pictures of shining heroes, sound bites of villains, black-and-white stories with clearly distinguishable positions that polarize audiences.

Europe's culture of consensus delivers none of these things. This is why the media often get so frustrated with the European project. They just do not know how to put it into newsflashes and fifty-line stories.

During the long debate about the necessary framework for the euro in times of a huge economic crisis, most media outlets struggled greatly to convey the changes discussed and adopted in a reader-friendly way – and understandably so, the issues are complex. The issues at stake might be enormous, but even big figures in the billions became inflated so quickly that they almost lost their meaning to the average reader. The frustration with the technicalities of each issue explains the longing for a 'human touch', a conflict or even conspiracy, ideally in the classic Shakespearian sense. This is the way most media boiled down the European summit on the 28–29 June, 2012, to the long night when Germany's Chancellor Angela Merkel 'lost' to Italy's Prime Minister Mario Monti. The timing was perfect as it was the same night that the German squad lost against the Italian 'squadra azzurri' in the European Football Championship, allowing journalists to write about a double-whammy against the Germans, caused by two Italian 'Super Marios': while the German soccer team was defeated by two goals scored by Mario Balotelli, Merkel was defeated on the negotiating table by Mario Monti. Most Italian media wrote about Monti winning against Merkel, most German media about Merkel having been betrayed. In reality, of course, it was nothing more than a very hard fought political compromise: the European 'rescue fund', ESM, should receive the mandate to financially support not only to member states in the eurozone but also their banks (an issue vividly pleaded for by Monti to cut the vicious cycle of his country's becoming more and more indebted by rescuing their national banks). Yet this mandate could only come to fruition once a European or eurozone-wide bank union with strong supervisory powers had been established (an issue stipulated by Merkel to agree to Monti's claim, who had secured the support of Spain and France before and during the negotiations). In a nutshell, it was a compromise that appeared good for Europe and the euro. It also appeared that both 'major players' knew this exactly and, thus, did not encourage – not even in the slightest way – stories about victory or betrayal. Merkel even accepted an invitation by Monti to travel to Rome just a week after the summit in Brussels and the two appeared together in front of the press to put a halt to further rumours of a serious rift between them. Yet the media still focused exactly on the supposed split by interpreting negative 'body language'. Were the stories about conflict fabricated? Well, not as such, but they were clearly inflated. Yet it is black and white that stirs the greatest public attention, not shades of grey (at least not in this context). Shakespeare wasn't the only one who knew how to play that game when he wrote his plays. The press is well aware of this fact, too.

The mass media's need for catchy sound bites is another reason that some reporters appeared almost grateful when the euro sceptic MEP Nigel Farage insulted EU President Herman van Rompuy in the European Parliament in February 2010, accusing him of having 'the charisma of a damp rag and the appearance of a low-grade bank clerk'.[64] Finally, a clear-cut story; news that everybody understands. Farage loudly reminded his colleagues that van Rompuy earned a salary higher than US President Obama, although he had not even been elected by the people and was an obscure figure to the vast majority of them. He finished his tirade with the words, 'Who are you? I'd never heard of you. Nobody in Europe had ever heard of you.' The *Irish Times* called Farage's comment 'schoolyard stuff', yet saw it as an indication that van Rompuy has 'some way to go before asserting his personality and will on the European stage'.[65]

Since he is the first permanent president of the European Council, and hence, in a way the EU's first president, it is arguable that some people had hoped he would be more inspiring and publicly engaging. Some might worry how badly he could fare in comparison to the first president of the US, the legendary George Washington. Yet van Rompuy knows that his mission is not to become a public legend, but to help foster agreement between the EU heads of state. This is no mean feat, especially in times of the urgently required and never-planned-for bail out packages for some Euro countries. It requires a balancing act of delicate diplomacy and hands-on action and the level of success is much higher when he stays in the background than bathes in the limelight.

Does this mean that Europe is doomed to stay celebrity- and passion-free? No, it just means that it has its priorities right. First, you need to build a house that can hold everybody, and only then should you throw a housewarming party. Party-lovers might criticize the slow motion of the construction work and become impatient, but we had better make sure that it is set on solid ground before we start popping any corks.

Celebrating unification before it is won can be very dangerous, as the history of the US shows. The Founding Fathers of the United States, such as Benjamin Franklin, George Washington, John Adams and Thomas Jefferson, did a superb job of presenting documents such as the Declaration of Independence and the US Constitution as beacons for unity and freedom. Unfortunately, its foundation was flawed because the most controversial issue between the states – slavery – was not resolved. The Constitutional Convention of 1787 called for the regulation and eventual abolishment of slavery, but at the same time allowed certain states exemptions that paved the way for continued 'imports' of slaves. It was a flawed compromise. Since a real consensus on this key issue had not been achieved, tensions between the states grew stronger over the decades and finally culminated in the bloody Civil War (1861 – 1865). On top of that, President Lincoln was assassinated just as the war ended.

Some argue that high emotions and hopes initially caused the heated environment in the US – an environment in which war was seen as the only solution. Some also argue that the real foundations for the United States were not properly laid down before slavery was finally abolished

87

and the spirit of freedom could, at least formally, spread within the country – a country then severely bloodied by a military conflict which had left more than 600,000 dead.

On its way to integration, Europe is trying everything to avoid a similar destiny. As a consequence, it refrains from celebratory propaganda. The risk is simply too high that expectations raised by such propaganda cannot be fulfilled. In such a case, the mood can quickly turn sour, resulting in conflict and insurmountable confrontation.

The price for such a strategy is having to sit at the round-table of consensus before an agreement can be announced and settling for seemingly unspectacular outcomes. So far, Europe's path to unity has not been flanked by great leaders who inspire fierce passion and pathos. It has been driven by diligent negotiators achieving broad agreement by their willingness to compromise. This seems like a small price to pay if it has helped avoid segregation and military conflict.

The different approaches taken by North America and Europe on their way to integration and unity reminds us of an anecdote: a Westerner and an Indian talk about true love. The Indian is accused that in his society, marriages are planned, negotiated and arranged instead of being left to people's free will and the true emotions of the couples. He admits that this is true, but counters that it often leads to more solid relationships than in the Western world where everybody longs for 'love at first sight' and relationships that mirror the Hollywood movies. To illustrate his case, he draws the analogy of a stove. In Western relationships, the flame is at its highest level at the beginning. Under such conditions, the only positive thing that can happen in the future is keeping the flame at this level. Unfortunately, it often goes down over time, leading to disappointment. In Indian relationships, it begins with the attempt to spark the flame. At best, it ignites, yet only at a very low level. However, there is room for the flame to burn brighter and this could happen if everybody is prepared to make an effort. Since the level of satisfaction in human beings usually depends on making progress, ask yourself which tactic is more promising in the long term if keeping and fostering the relationship is the target. European integration has started on a low flame, but the flame has become bigger over the decades, because everybody involved worked really hard at nourishing it. There were no giant leaps at the outset. It was a step-by-step tactic driven by the hope that we could end up making three steps forward and two steps back – and not the other way round. So far, we have succeeded. This was merely possible because everybody involved adopted a strong culture of consensus.

In many respects, we have already reached a stage where we can better present the results of our efforts to grow together. A process that had started with the formation of the European Coal and Steel Community in 1951, followed by the European Economic Community and the European Atomic Energy Community, created by the Treaties of Rome in 1957, has become less technical with the merger of the three into the European Community in 1967 and its transformation into a European Union by the Treaty of Maastricht in 1993.

How dangerous it can be to push forward too quickly in the unification process is evident in the current disputes about the rescue packages of countries belonging to the eurozone. The introduction of the euro was an enormous step towards the integration of Europe and it is by far its biggest visible symbol. However, in Europe's euphoria to introduce it, the responsible powers (intentionally) neglected to reach complete consensus in all aspects that a common currency touches. Today, more than 10 years after the start of the European Monetary Union, the member states struggle hard to overcome these shortcomings. We are confident that they will ultimately manage. Yet it should teach us a lesson that first, we need solid and complete consensus on all levels.

Obviously, convinced Europeans are keen to see the days when Europe is able to present itself as more unified to the world. In theory, it would boost the European feeling of belonging if people saw athletes perform under the European banner in international competitions instead of their current national flags. However, right now any such suggestion would be counter-productive, because it would only cause alienation and protest. We are not ready for such a change. It might well be that we never will, but it is not all that important for our cause. People from London, Cardiff, Edinburgh and Belfast all belong to the United Kingdom, yet in international football tournaments or the Commonwealth Games they compete against each other under the English, Welsh, Scottish and Northern Irish flags. This does not mean that they do not consider themselves as British, especially since there are many other big sports events, including the Olympics, where they compete side by side under the same flag, the Union Jack.

In fact, in the globalized economy of the twenty-first century, it is beneficial to have a society where people develop identities on different levels and degrees. As long as we stay in our specific country in Europe, it is just natural that our national identity will dominate. However, once we leave Europe, we become more aware of our European identity. It starts when we arrive at the airport in the foreign destination: all EU citizens have passports of the same colour and format. And it continues at the currency exchange office, where the common currency is depicted by the European flag, normally right up at the top of the list of currencies.

In various polls commissioned by the European Commission between 1990 and 2006, tens of thousands of citizens of the EU's member states were asked if they ever thought of themselves as not only belonging to their nation, but if they also consider themselves as Europeans.[66] More than half of them said that this happened to them 'often' or 'sometimes'. Considering how many grandparents and great-grandparents of these people had inflicted death and devastation on each other on the battlefields, this is an amazingly strong 'European feeling'. From this point of view, Europe's achievements over the last 60 years do not appear slow and bureaucratic at all, but truly inspiring.

We mentioned earlier that enthusiasm was ranked lowest on the European Union's list of attributes but we should also mention the strongest feeling related to it: hope. This was named by more than 40 per cent of the people asked.

Chapter 4

The European way of management

In the previous two chapters, we identified two criteria that all Europeans have in common: a culture of craftsmanship and a culture of consensus.

Until relatively recently, these attitudes were regularly criticized by the ruling (mostly American) management gurus and the Anglo-Saxon media for inhibiting competition and business performance in a modern economy. Preserving skilled craftsmanship was charged with being a backward looking, outdated culture one that was unable to outsource the industrial production to cheaper places. Steadfastly seeking broad consensus apparently led to long periods of inactivity, slow decision-making and a lack of leadership.

As we know today, these criticisms were not justified. On the contrary, after the worldwide economic earthquake, triggered by a meltdown of the financial markets, the need for and the advantages of a modern type of industrialization (which clearly requires a culture of skilled craftsmanship as its foundation) became evident and generally accepted – not only in continental Europe but also in the US and UK. Looking forward, we predict that our European culture of consensus seeking will also become accepted as an ever more important asset during a period when the way we communicate and deal with each other is radically changing, no longer predominantly dependent on the mass media but allowing intensive interaction through the new tools of networked communication.

We are convinced that Europeans could use their culture of

craftsmanship and consensus as the two pillars to build a new leading powerhouse. The reasons are obvious: they enable you to deal with complexity, one of the most important qualities in the globalized economy of the twenty-first century. Even in times of tension and distress, most Europeans still appreciate and cherish the positive side of diversity. On top of that, they have evidence that listening to each other and taking various opinions on board does not have to lead to slow reactions and standstills, but can provide particularly solid results – results which are shared and, thus, convincingly carried out by many.

In this chapter we want to translate the assets and attitudes that are typical for European citizens into guidelines for business people. In other words, from the mentality that dominates our continent we will extract some principles for structuring, running and leading a business in today's complicated fast-moving global economy.

In our attempt to draft a European way of management, we do not have to start from scratch or limit ourselves to theory. Many of Europe's enterprises have already taken the recommendations outlined in this chapter on board. Our most successful companies espouse a long-term focus, particularly with regard to employment, preferring short-time work to wanton hiring and firing. They seek to keep their businesses deeply rooted in society. They champion a broader understanding of corporate performance and nourish a credible corporate culture. They are also more interested in interdisciplinary teamwork than individual egos.

These European flagship companies can serve as good examples and benchmarks for others, not only in Europe but also in other parts of the world. In fact, we would be most delighted if the guiding principles of this chapter provide impetus to business leaders from countries and cultures outside the continent of Europe, because we certainly do not want to exclude others or suggest that they cannot manage in this manner because they are not European. Our intention is in fact, the opposite. We want to make a contribution to a best-in-class leadership with suggestions that can be adapted universally from China, all the way to India and Brazil. Ideally, the lessons we draw from Europe will have worldwide appeal.

We also want to stress once again at this point that we do not want to thumb our noses at America with the proclamation of a superior European way. We know exactly what the European economies owe the United States and we are convinced that we will continue to learn much from the US. What we hope for, though, is a more balanced approach to learning and taking from each other. Hopefully, our thesis will encourage new and productive debates with the other side of the Atlantic on the right approach to shaping and reshaping the principles of doing business.

In general, we see the following paradigm shift in management strategy for the global economy of the twenty-first century:

- When trends are no longer reliable, numbers are of limited use as a decision aid. A final tweak to optimize the cost of capital in the shareholder value model, for example, may bring more analytical elegance, but it won't add an iota of reliability.
- When figures are no longer reliable, we must free ourselves from the notion that we have to quantify each and every plan or investment down to the last cent. Being business savvy and having a good feel for technology, products and customers are more important.
- When the business environment changes as fast as it does these days, short-term action may be necessary to quickly manoeuvre through the challenges, yet it still needs a clear and stable vision to provide orientation for the long term.
- When the people in our companies feel increasingly unsettled by increasing complexity, values and well-crafted management skills become especially important.

In our opinion, Europe's culture of craftmanship and consensus is particularly well positioned to cope with these challenges. A European way of management ought to be reflected on five different levels:

1. a new approach to corporate strategy
2. a corporate structure based on decentralization
3. a strong commitment to profitable growth
4. a system of strong checks and balances at the top
5. a corporate culture based on long-term values

Let us have a look at these five levels in detail to see which guiding principles can be extracted.

A new approach to corporate strategy

Until the end of the twentieth century, top managers and their consultants operated on a fairly standardized procedure in developing a corporate strategy. They started with a period of intensive research, aimed at finding trends and developments in the company's industry as well as its environment. The material was accumulated, analysed and then turned into various market forecasts. Based on these forecasts, the company defined a strategy. The board adopted the recommendations made in the 'strategy book' and then based its major investment plans, as well as its revenue and profit targets, on this strategy. An approved strategy usually covered a period of 10 years, while medium-term planning covered five years.

Under this framework, the focus of a corporate strategy was always on a target. The main purpose of strategy-making was to clearly define a destination the company ought to reach in the future. Once the target

95

was defined, such as a revenue figure, a market share, a growth rate or a profitability margin, it was all about mapping out the path to these as precisely as possible.

In finding the right strategy for a company, chief strategy officers and consultants regularly applied sophisticated mathematical models developed by American economists. Take, for example, all the various 'economic value added' or 'discounted cash flow' methods. They were used to assess the risk to a corporation's specific asset (by applying the so-called beta coefficient) and to stipulate a business unit's required rate of return (with capital asset pricing models – CAPM). Such formula-driven instruments provoked the notion among CEOs that every planning exercise and investment appraisal can be calculated almost to the last cent. It also provided them with a sense of security in their role as leaders. In all good conscience, CEOs and board members felt that they could tell their employees: this is where we want to go and this is what we can achieve. Management could set up organizational charts that remained valid for quite some time.

As we all know, the financial crisis wiped out any sentiment of stability and controllability. Within a few weeks, hundreds of pages of long-term planning and defined strategic targets were abruptly turned into waste paper. A crisis of such magnitude went beyond any worst-case scenario calculated on those pages. The crisis was not factored into the strategy at all.

If business leaders want to learn from this experience, they have to change their approach to strategy. Some might argue that the crisis was an extreme occasion that occurs only once or twice in a century (we hope so too) and, thus, can never be factored into any strategy planning. Fair enough. But the issue goes much deeper. As we can already see today, and will continue to see to a much larger extent in the future, the business environment in which most industries operate has started to change so rapidly that we are about to lose the parameters required for our strategic calculations. After all, every formula needs sufficient historical data, mixed with reliable forecasts, in order to give us useful guidance for the way forward. Portfolio analysis, for example, is useful only when growth rates are strong and stable. Today, this is the exception rather than the rule. Volatility has become so great and trends chop and change so quickly that these days quantitative forecasting models rarely work. Within just a few years, biotechnology, nanotechnology, optical systems and information technology have completely changed our business environment, radically affecting both processes and products. Additionally, the prices for natural resources are exposed to so many speculative factors that it has become impossible to even define a reliable range to quantify the cost.

It is also increasingly rare to find long-term trends following recognized patterns, even in cases where production or services are shifted 10,000 miles away. Take one example; due to the ever-decreasing cost of long-distance telecommunications, it was thought that increasing numbers of Western companies would transfer their call-centre operations to places with cheap labour, such as India. The trend seemed to be substantiated by investments like language-accent training to ensure that customers would not even realize that they were speaking to somebody who was thousands of miles away and who didn't even work for the company but was employed by a specialist for business process outsourcing (BPO). Just at the time when we felt sure that this had become a long-term trend, we started to see the first companies bringing their call centre operations back home – after they had discovered that the proximity to other corporate functions is important after all. European companies that have 'in-sourced' their call-centre activities from India include British utility firm Powergen (a subsidiary of German energy company Eon), Spanish bank Santander and the Royal Bank of Scotland. In the US, Delta Airlines did the same.

Let's take another example: for years, we have seen a shift in textile mass production to the Far East and we have been told that, from a business perspective, fashion factories can no longer be sustained in the Western world. Suddenly, however, textile companies were 'off-shoring' their production from Asia to Europe, because they realized that fashion trends change so fast that flexibility and speed in releasing new collections are more important than cost benefits.

Whether it is the sudden reversal of trends or a complete shift in research and operations due to new technology developed at mind-boggling speed, all of these factors take away the puzzle pieces strategists need to construct a picture clear enough to set a strategic target with long-term validity. This applies not only to companies working in industries that are known to shift very quickly, such as IT or biotechnology, but also to enterprises operating in the so-called 'old industries'.

Take automobile production. At first sight, you might regard setting a strategic target to 'sell X million cars by 2020' as a sound idea. After all, we have observed a great deal of consolidation in the automobile industry and building cars is – apart from rare exceptions such as custom-made sports cars or high-end luxury limousines – a business driven by scale, i.e. high volumes. Given the many current initiatives in e-cars, it might also seem sensible to strategically aim for a certain market share as a producer of electronic vehicles. Once you dig into the materials, however, you will quickly discover that such strategy-making could soon lead in the wrong direction. In a world of mega-cities packed with a new generation of environmentally conscious consumers, the whole concept of individual transportation as hitherto known could be challenged, not only by a few do-gooders but by hundreds of millions of ordinary people. Maybe the 'one person/family-one car' mentality will become passé, as the majority of people resolve that it no longer makes sense to (exclusively) own an item that, on average, is used only three per cent of its lifetime (research has shown that a car is already the most underutilized of all consumer goods). As a consequence, consumers might look for other ways towards the mobility provided by cars. The increasing emergence and popularity of car sharing and online car hire services somehow suggests this. Depending on how much significance you put on these services as indicators of change, you might conclude that offering new solutions to meet this desire is actually a much better strategy for a car company than expanding production to make it into the top-three manufacturers. It also could turn out that e-cars will never reach the expected break-through and remain a niche phenomenon while fuel cells take off. Maybe it will be a specific hybrid system that leads the way to a new generation of mobility engineering. Or maybe the key to the vehicle of the future lies not so much in engine development, but rather in material technology with the advance of ultra-light carbon fibre.

We do not know which scenario is going to become reality. This example, however, raises a much broader issue: if the future of an industry that has developed so steadily so far and has remained faithful to the internal-combustion engine for over 100 years appears imponderable, what is the point of trying to set a long-term strategic target anymore for any company or industry?

Indeed. In an economy exposed to so many variables, we simply need a different approach to strategy-making: we should no longer see strategy as an outcome, but as a process. In other words, it is no longer the end (e.g. setting the new strategic target for 2020) that is so crucial, but the means that help us manoeuvre towards a promising future, even if we do not know the destination it will lead us to.

In the scientific discussion, the question of whether corporate strategy should focus on the outcome or the process is not new. In business, however, the reality is that almost all companies have subscribed to the result-oriented approach. The reason for this is simple: focusing on a target has a strict, rigorous ring to it. It intuitively makes sense. It gives you a plan, a number to gun for and, hence, a (supposedly) objective basis for decisions. It is also fairly straightforward to communicate. It allows the CEO to confidently and convincingly proclaim both to his workforce and the outside world that this is where the company wants to end up.

Traditionally, Europeans have always had a certain mistrust towards such an approach. They inherently know that business reality is more multi-faceted than a results-oriented corporate strategy. Beyond this, they have developed a strong dislike for self-proclaimed business leaders who attempt to single-handedly show the workforce where to go or why they have to be left behind. There are several famous examples of European CEOs who have failed miserably because they publicly carried their personal vision for the company like a Catholic bishop holding the golden chalice at a High Mass procession.

The former CEO of Daimler, Jürgen Schrempp, is such a case. Triggered by his conviction that Mercedes Benz could only continue to prosper in the future by becoming a piece of a bigger 'Welt-AG' ('World-Plc') which manufactures passenger cars of all types and brands around the globe, he orchestrated a merger with Detroit-based Chrysler and bought a stake in Japan's Mitsubishi. Unfortunately, his strategy to expand to North America and Asia by acquisition turned into a disaster, not least because Mercedes engineers in Germany refused to share their knowledge.[67] In the end, Schrempp's successor Dieter Zetsche had to reverse the whole strategic adventure and returned Daimler to its roots.

Jean-Marie Messier felt compelled to totally transform Vivendi shortly after he took the helm at the French conglomerate, and regarded it as a clever strategy to sell or spin off the traditional water business as well as the waste management, energy and construction units and acquire US-based Seagram Universal with its music and film operations. For some reason, he thought it would be possible to run a Hollywood studio from

Paris, and he was never shy in presenting his vision of Vivendi as a huge integrated media and telecommunications company, offering movies, music, games and books and using the rich media content to beef up its own mobile phone unit.

But before his 'mastermind' ideas became reality, he was kicked out. The same happened to Thomas Middelhoff when he went too far in his attempt to spin Bertelsmann from a decentralized media conglomerate with strong operational growth into a centrally controlled company driven by mergers and acquisitions and portfolio management. It is not a coincidence that all three top managers – Schrempp, Messier and Middelhoff – felt strongly drawn to the US and US-style management. After all, they saw themselves as media-savvy dealmakers in the best tradition of American business leadership. In the end, they had to learn the hard way: that running a company with strong European roots is not about sound bites and wheeling and dealing, but about achieving operational excellence by *collaboration*.

In order to meet the challenges of tomorrow's ever changing global economy, the CEO of the future does not have to be a shiny self-promoter but needs to be a thorough manager. The Canadian academic Henry Mintzberg and his colleague Jonathan Gosling had already spotted the dangers of too much leadership-focus among CEOs in 2003. 'Most of us have become so enamoured of leadership that management has been pushed into the background. Nobody aspires to being a good manager any more; everybody wants to be a great leader', they wrote in a paper published in the *Harvard Business Review*[68] and warned, 'Just as management without leadership encourages an uninspired style that deadens activities, leadership without management encourages a disconnected style that promotes hubris. And we all know the destructive power of hubris in organizations. So let's get back to plain old management.'

This also applies to the CEO's role as 'chief strategist'. In order to enable a company to swiftly react to sudden shifts in trends or technological development, it is important to set up a 'cockpit' that monitors and displays many different signals, even quite weak ones. It is equally important to have good people who can bring these into context. In such a strategy process, scenario planning needs to become a regular feature of strategy development – not the kind of best-case/worst-case analyses which essentially just reflect different assumptions about the same sets of figures, but genuine alternative pictures of the future. Only bold sketches of what lies ahead can help us anticipate and prepare for unexpected developments. Painting alternative pictures of the future also enables us to communicate in a way that does not rely solely on growth forecasts and projected profits – and in a way that can captivate people's imagination.

In retrospect, it is often easy to see why certain scenarios became reality. Today, no one will be all that surprised to hear that the new networked office consumes much more paper than an office in the days when we did not have PCs with word processing facilities, email and Internet access. In the 1980s, however, most people in the paper and pulp industry were utterly convinced that the amount of paper used in offices would significantly go down. Many feared the future of a paperless office. Back then, it required the ability to put the sociology and habits of human beings into a balanced context with new digital technology to develop a credible scenario where the amount of paper in an office using PCs would actually rise.

Another example of underestimating ultimate requirements and the need for a different kind of strategic thinking is the collapse of the shipping industry in 2008/09. Deeply shocked by the unprecedented slump in chartered tonnage, the majority of weathered industry veterans were convinced that there was only one strategy for the future: discharging vessels. There were certain fleets built up during the boom years that would never be used again. Yet what about a scenario where vessels would curb speed by half during their voyages in order to reduce fuel consumption and, thus, cost? Wouldn't that mean we would require the same number of ships to transport just half the amount of goods than we did before the crisis? It would. And, in fact, this is exactly what happened.

Scenario planning is much more work than its linear antecedent. It involves a large number of active parties and, thus, forges a link between strategic planning and operational management. From the outset, it gives people a feel for the issue of uncertainty and fosters a common understanding of how the future might look.

In a way, one can compare the different tools and tasks required in yesterday's and tomorrow's strategy-making with different types of nautical navigation. In the past, strategic planning happened in an environment where the whole world with its different destinations and available sea routes was fairly well mapped out. Developing a good corporate strategy was like equipping an ocean liner for a cruise. Today, however, destinations and routes constantly shift. It is no longer possible to pick a thoroughly tested route, pre-program its course and then limit yourself to a few checks and balances. The crew has to be constantly on alert, ready to react to a plethora of eventualities, as the way forward resembles more an unknown expedition than a familiar cruise. In a sense, today's business leaders find themselves in a situation similar to the famous explorers who left for long discovery journeys at the beginning of the modern world.

Today's modern information technology makes it much easier to get a handle on unexpected events by processing the flood of data into various scenarios. Social media might also serve as useful tools, as they have the ability to involve large target groups in the process of opinion building. They can provide a rapid testing ground for the scenarios formulated. Our experience shows that it is now possible to develop robust, cogent scenarios within three to four weeks. That leaves more time to think about which milestones might trigger the relevance of a new or different scenario. This is important, as there is one thing even modern scenario planning cannot do: it cannot decide for you when to back which vision of the future.

This is where the strength of Europe's culture of consensus and skilled craftsmanship comes to the fore. When complexity causes uncertainty among a company's workforce, solid, hands-on management skills and compelling values are essential. European companies do not need a CEO who pretends that he always knows which direction the company will go or where it ought to end up, for fear that he would otherwise lose authority, cause confusion or create a climate of helplessness. If the right structures are in place, there will be enough people with sufficient experience around who can help in finding the right path as the company moves along. These people are used in complex situations. They have heard of the necessity to closely align a corporate strategy with economic and global political contexts. And they know when it is better to discuss things thoroughly before taking any action and when it is required to speed up the decision-making process and move swiftly. In short, Europe delivers a solid grounding for a new approach to corporate strategy.

In the new European way of management, corporate strategy is no longer about developing omniscient strategies with long-term targets. Instead, it is about setting up wide-ranging trend and technology monitors and organizing the strategy-making process based on these signals and the company's long-term values. Franz Fehrenbach, CEO of Bosch from 2003-2012, said that, during the crisis and especially in the period that followed, he moved to 'managing the company based on a handful of principles rather than just the numbers'.[69]

In tomorrow's fast-moving economic environment, such an approach is going to be the basis for success. It requires a shift of how we define and develop corporate strategy. In this shift, Europe is especially equipped to lead the way.

Decentralization as key to a responsible workforce

When we consider the best corporate structure for the future, focusing on one point in particular will help improve management practice: more decentralization. Conceptually, it is not difficult to choose between 'centralize' or 'decentralize', because the benefits of decentralized organizations are plain to see and can be summarized in four principal arguments.

1. Better knowledge of the market: market knowledge, including knowledge of political and regulatory matters (which are becoming increasingly important), is greatest where direct contact with the customer exists and where business is done.
2. More innovation: decentralized structures encourage creativity because they cultivate entrepreneurial freedom. This predictably leads to healthy competition for the best and most responsive ideas.
3. Greater flexibility: the smaller, leaner and more independent units become, the faster and more flexibly they can adapt to changing market conditions or new strategic solutions, such as joint ventures or regional mergers.
4. Greater motivation: decentralized management mobilizes the workforce because entrepreneurial responsibility frees up latent potential. At the end of the day, personal profit and loss accounts mean more than responsibility for abstract key performance indicators.

Since the advantages of a decentralized corporate structure are apparently so evident, how is it that we have seen so many efforts within big international companies to centralize management?

One reason is the constant allegation that implementing and upholding a decentralized organization is too expensive. By its very nature, a decentralized structure multiplies administrative tasks. While this is not always a bad thing as such, it is regularly and loudly criticized as automatically leading to bureaucracy and inefficiency. In this respect, a corporation with a decentralized structure is confronted with similar criticisms as the European Union.

Regularly, CEOs feel compelled to react to criticism (usually sparked by analysts and spread by the media) for having an inefficient structure by streamlining their company's organization and bundling decision-making at their headquarters. Especially when times get harder we can detect repeated waves of centralization: managers hope this will help them exploit economies of scale and make their companies become more cost-efficient. Often, this hope comes at a high price. It rarely leads to long-term success.

We should also regard decentralization with some scepticism, however, as the danger of a bloated bureaucracy indeed increases. The challenge is, therefore, to combine the benefits of a decentralized organization with the cost benefits of centralized structures. This goal can be achieved, above all, by systematically evaluating every task. What functions are vital to the business and must, at all costs, be given decision-making freedom to keep customers satisfied by staying responsive to their needs in a timely fashion? And what other functions can rigorously be bundled together in production or service centres? Essentially, decentralizing responsibility means nothing more than preferring to solve a problem by the smallest and lowest business unit capable of solving it.

Here again, we can draw an analogy with the EU. In order to evaluate what should be handled in Brussels and what should be left to national governments or regional bodies, Europe has subscribed to the principle of subsidiarity. This means that, in general, every issue ought to be left to the lowest and least centralized unit – the local authority. Only in such cases where it is impossible or too inefficient for an issue to be handled by the local powers moves the competence up – first to a regional, then to national and, lastly, to a European level. Predictably, the interpretation of what can be handled where, and with which degree of efficiency, causes many arguments in specific instances. However, as such, the principle stands.

Business leaders have the advantage that the application of the principle of subsidiarity within their company is, to a lesser extent, driven by political considerations than by sheer business logic. This involves 'decomposing' a complex optimization problem, to use a mathematical term. The result? Better solutions can be reached faster and less expensively. The method works well, provided that the overall problem is broken down properly. Headquarters is tasked with tailoring the right regional cut, guided by principles that will facilitate optimization on the ground. On a technical level, modern communication and management systems help them to evaluate specific cases and provide accountable answers. Enterprise resource planning (ERP) programs can support every conceivable combination of performance indicators at short notice. Web-based benchmarking systems significantly improve the learning curve. And powerful knowledge management systems can effectively transfer acquired knowledge to all points throughout the company.

However, all this technical wizardry only creates the conditions for decentralized management. Far more important is the management culture. Decentralized management is only possible if local or regional executives enjoy the trust of their superiors. Too much control makes processes and systems excessively complex.

From outside, granting others sufficient freedom to take real responsibility sounds like a relatively easy task of leadership. In reality, it is one of the hardest skills to master. In today's notion of top business people as action- and power-driven figures, the ability to let go is all too often misinterpreted as laziness. Listening and following advice can often be misconstrued as being indecisive and more weak than wise.

Under these circumstances, it is understandable why CEOs find it so difficult to hold on to a decentralized structure, particularly in tough times when critical voices and calls for leaders with punch-through power become loudest. Firmly and unwaveringly resisting these calls requires a steadfast character from a CEO and a deeply-rooted company culture based on decentralization.

In the end, it will pay off. Take the example of media company Bertelsmann and the way it weathered the recent depression. As Europe's biggest operator of TV and radio stations and also Europe's biggest magazine publisher, Bertelsmann's business is, to a large extent, dependent on advertising markets. Since the first cost that companies tend to cut is usually on the marketing side when facing economic straits, leading to drastically reduced advertising expenditures; Bertelsmann was quickly and badly hit after the outbreak of the financial crisis in autumn 2008. In 2009, the media company had to report a deficit of more than 300 million euros for the first six months of the year. Bertelsmann seemed poised to end the year with a loss. It would have been the first annual loss ever recorded, and for a company that had been trading for 174 years at that time, a particularly unsettling premiere. The pressure on its then CEO, Hartmut Ostrowski, must have been enormous. After only 18 months in the job the media mocked him, particularly because he had announced very ambitious growth targets for the company before the crisis broke but it appeared that he was not even able to hold on to existing revenues. Ostrowski was portrayed as dry, heavy-handed and uninspiring. In a nutshell, he was the wrong man for the world of media. In this situation, his personal desire must have been to take the reins more tightly and increase his executive powers to prove to the public what he could do as the central commander. Ostrowski refrained from such temptation. Instead, he trusted that Bertelsmann's culture of decentralization was the best way to go forward, even during the worst economic crisis in 70 years. Following the tradition of the hundreds of former managing directors at Bertelsmann, Ostrowski thought each unit should be granted the leverage to run their units as if they were their own enterprises; he called upon them to come up with suggestions to save money. Since many units had already gone through cost-cutting programs in order to solve the structural problems of the media industry, one might think that many of them replied that squeezing out more savings would be impossible. But that's not what happened. On the contrary: 2,500 recommendations for individual saving measures were made. First calculations suggested that executing them would bring Bertelsmann annual savings of €900m. In the end, it took out almost one billion in costs[70] – enormous for a company with revenues of €15.4bn at that time. The individual saving measures ranged from using cheaper paper for magazines or books to save material costs to less investment in original programming or film and series acquisitions. Each managing director had to decide him or herself how far he or she could go without risking the very foundations of their business unit. Cutting jobs was almost always regarded as the last resort and, in the end, less than four per cent of the total workforce (of over 100,000 people) had to go. As an act of solidarity, the managing directors and the board voluntarily agreed to reductions in their remuneration, leading to salary cuts of up to 50 per cent for the top earners. The results of all these efforts were that Bertelsmann managed to end the year with a small profit instead of the dreaded first-time loss. On top of that, even in a year as tough as 2009, the company managed to reduce its debts, and decided to invest – a total of €660m. For the managing directors responsible, thriving from extreme cost-cutting measures, while at the same time investing, was not a contradiction in terms but an entrepreneurial necessity – a measure required if they were to stay strong in their competitive fields.

To us, the way Bertelsmann weathered the storm of the economic crisis is a good illustration of how a decentralized structure based on trust and tradition works as a management principle, even in the most extreme business environment. There are numerous other European companies that have taken decentralization to heart. Spanish Telefónica is such a case. In its transformation from a national telephone operator into an international powerhouse of telecommunications, its decentralized structure turned out to be pivotal. To this day, the managing directors running the various country operations – Telefónica is active in six European countries and 16 American countries – can act very independently. Madrid decided to stick to tasks that are evidently better left to headquarters, such as corporate strategy (including mergers and acquisitions into new terrains), research and innovation. In other words, they followed the classic 'system-head' functions we mentioned in Chapter 2.

In its efforts to best implement a decentralized structure, Telefónica constantly looks for managers with a strong entrepreneurial spirit and curiosity. For a company with specific national roots, openness to other cultures is quintessential for sustainable success in the international arena. This includes efforts to elevate people from different nations and continents to top positions.

The Japanese economy set the international benchmark in the 1980s. Since then, its companies have dropped back sharply and this has to a large extent to do with its top positions being mostly reserved for Japanese, who, when posted around the world, tended to live in enclaves and were reluctant to embrace the cultures of the countries they lived in. Beyond this, nearly all decisions – even on a local level – were still made at headquarters in Japan.

With such a mindset, you can never be really close to local markets. This, however, is an imperative for international success in the twenty-first century, as the world is becoming ever more heavily regionalized. Regional identities and cultures are acquiring sharper contours, rather than assimilating, as classical theories would have us believe. With few exceptions (such as Apple's iPod) 'world products' that were supposed to generate demand around the globe have been unable to gain a foothold. The world is not flat – i.e. one-dimensional – after all. As the BRIC economies, for example, grow in strength, their cultures too are growing in stature, such that these regions can also influence the rules of the game. Ever better and more powerful information systems may be able to put the information you need at your fingertips, but if those fingertips actually have to travel to the head office, they are simply too far removed from the source to be able to interpret them correctly. Based on the experience within their own continent, European companies have come to learn this lesson. This even applies to corporations from France and Britain, the two European countries with arguably the strongest historical tendency towards centralization, mirrored by their political structures.

In the United Kingdom, Serco Group[71] – once mocked by *The Guardian* as 'probably the biggest company you've never heard of' – started a tremendous success story with a management style driven by decentralization. Specializing in all types of government services, it has a truly global presence today with a workforce of 70,000 people within all sorts of countries and cultures. Last year, it was voted Britain's second most admired company.

In France, family-controlled Groupe Mulliez[72] has shown what tremendous success management, based on entrepreneurship given to staff on the local level can lead to. Funded by Gérard Mulliez in 1955 when he opened a small self-service shop in Roubaix, a French village on the Belgian border, the group is now active in over a dozen

111

countries. In its main business alone, retail giant Auchan, Groupe Mulliez employs 175,000 people around the world who work in over 1,000 supermarkets and over 2,000 small shops, from Russia to Morocco to China. Its various business units – from retail to car repairs and DIY shops – are allowed to operate independently. The holding limits its activities to new investments and upholding the company culture. Participation in the business success is part of the culture, as more than 10 per cent of Groupe Mulliez is owned by the employees.

It is encouraging to see that more and more European companies subscribe to the principle of decentralization. Until 2008, Spanish wind farm expert Gamesa[73] followed a heavily centralized management style. At that point, the company realized that such an organizational structure was neither suitable nor sustainable for its intended international growth. It completely restructured itself and left decisional power to regional managers in the US, China, India and Brazil. The change of philosophy paid off. Today, Gamesa generates more of its revenues outside Europe than on the continent.

When the two French utility companies Suez and Gaz de France merged in 2008, board members of the newly formed GDF Suez had to decide whether they would want to follow the central command nursed by Gaz de France or rather the decentralized structure of Suez. They opted for the latter, despite the fact that the French state is the major shareholder.

And in Britain, Associated British Foods, the construction and engineering giant Balfour Beatty, as well as IT and automation specialist Invensys, are all prime examples of multi-billion companies with tens of thousands of employees which have adopted a decentralized management style.

The awareness that the ever-increasing global complexities require decentralization is one of the key strengths of the European management style. One pivotal reason why Europe's companies have improved their international competitiveness lately is that they are better able to handle diversity – which is also why they already have more decentralized structures than their competitors in the US, India, China and, above all, Japan.

A strong commitment to profitable growth

If you run a company that draws its strengths from a culture of craftsmanship and consensus, as many European enterprises do, can you then go out and credibly claim that maximizing the company's value is your paramount dictum as a manager? You can. In fact, you ought to.

On the face of it, the notions of 'skilled craftsmanship' and 'shareholder value' sound like a clash of terminology and culture, not least because shareholder value has come to epitomize exclusive, short-term profit-seeking – to the elation of the capital markets and the benefit of capital backers, but at the expense of the workforce and the common good. This might indeed be the case if you consider the core meaning of shareholder value to be an obsession with share price development. The way we look at a manager's prime task of raising the value of a company, however, has nothing to do with a CEO becoming a slave to the moods of the market. Instead, we base it on the fundamental tenet of its worth evaluation.

For an owner of a company (or its shares), one who is not driven by a fast exit for 'a quick buck' but by the wish for steady returns of one's investment, shareholder value has to be measured in terms of the future cash inflows that one can expect from the company. The 'currency' used consistently in this context is free cash flow. This is the volume of finance available: money that can be paid out in dividends or invested in new strategic projects. Thus, it is the amount of free cash flow that determines the true value of the company, not the share price at an arbitrary moment of a given day. We are aware that the shareholder value theory assumes that functioning capital markets always reflect the 'fair' share price based on free cash flow. Yet we are also aware that the theory does not work in practice.

In order to increase this free cash flow, it is not enough to let a company grow. It has to grow profitably. In other words, a company needs to increase its revenues (usually thanks to new technologies, new markets or better products) while, at the same time, cutting costs, for example by benefiting from economies of scale or factor costs.

Looking at maximizing the shareholder value from this perspective, it should become clear that there is no contradiction regarding sustainable business development with a long-term view. We gladly and openly subscribe to Milton Friedman's famous *bon mot* that 'the business of business is business'.[74] Yet this only holds true if we succeed in combining a fundamental profit-seeking stance with Europe's culture of consensus and skilled craftsmanship. This leads us to value-based management that is far removed from the buzz term 'shareholder value', which has become the one-sided interpretation of the financial community.

Having outlined our approach to value creation with its core on traditional entrepreneurship and operational excellence, we still need guidelines for how to best deal with the world of finance. The reason is simple: the development of our key 'currency' – free cash flow – is not only stipulated by a company's business performance as such, but also by the cost of capital. Value can only be added when a company earns more than the cost of servicing its debt and equity capital. Seen from this angle, it becomes clear that a CEO and his team also have to put their management efforts into lowering the cost of capital. They can achieve this by better cash management, negotiating more favourable financing terms or improving the structure of loans and bonds.

For a long time, many European companies and their managers have been criticized for not being open enough to financial innovations that provide new sources of funding and, thus, faster growth. To a certain extent, this was a fair criticism. Since many continental European countries had been used to bank-based systems instead of the market-based systems that had become dominant in the Anglo-American world, tapping into capital sources outside the infrastructure of the banking houses was long seen as rather dubious or too laborious by European managers, particularly those running small or medium-sized companies. Broadly speaking, it took Europe a while to warm to the key players of modern financing, such as investment banks, private equity firms, hedge funds, sovereign wealth funds, venture capital and rating agencies. There is no doubt that these players have brought greater transparency, dynamism and performance to the management's offices – things we ought to be grateful for. However, as we have already outlined in Chapter 1, their contributions became overshadowed at some point.

In the first decade of the twenty-first century, financial markets simply became too important, allowing financial considerations to become the predominant factor. The indiscriminate belief in the ability of capital markets to take the lead, together with excessive yield expectations, became part of the problem, as had gross oversimplification – driven by the quantitative spreadsheets favoured by analysts and rating agencies. All of this ultimately led to the failure of the American management model. This is why some of Europe's managers can now reap the benefits of their reluctance to follow every trend and dictum set by the finance world. For managers, the litmus test for welcoming or rejecting a specific relationship with the financial community should depend on the outcome of just one question: does it support my aim of achieving profitable growth?

If managers follow this recommendation, they will automatically strive to restrain the abusive powers of the markets. Given how fast and concerted the well-connected global financial community acts, this is certainly not an easy task. Nonetheless, we already see signs that it is possible. When some European companies discovered that the principles applied by the three dominant rating agencies to grant their quality seals were no longer in sync with their own entrepreneurial convictions, they decided to do without ratings for their bonds and they still found enough capital to prosper. The mechanical and plant engineering group Dürr is one example of such an approach.[75] Other companies realized that the loud demands of financial analysts to come up with absolute figures as guidance for future targets could not be reconciled by the ever-increasing complexities of business reality, and they acted accordingly. A study published by financial service provider BNY Mellon in October 2010 reveals that more and more firms are now communicating target corridors and qualitative estimates of business development rather than specific numbers.

Porsche serves as an excellent example to illustrate what it means to run a company on the dictum of profitable growth and what can happen once this path is left in an effort to outsmart the financial community. When Wendelin Wiedeking became CEO of the Stuttgart-based maker of luxury vehicles in 1993, the company was in the midst of restructuring and on the brink of bankruptcy. With both wit and obsession for detail, Wiedeking brought Porsche not only back to profit but also managed to transform the small sports car maker into the most profitable automotive manufacturer in the world.[76] Wiedeking broke rules and caused a stir whenever necessary: he brought in a team of Japanese engineers to show the proud German workforce how to truly efficiently build vehicles. Yet he also understood the need to motivate employees by staying loyal to them and giving out rewards to people who followed his passion for operational excellence. Boosted by enormous self-confidence after his astonishing success in the first decade, Wiedeking looked for new challenges and, together with his CFO, found them in the financial markets. When Porsche refused to report quarterly figures, despite being obliged to by the rules of the Deutsche Börse where the company was listed,[77] it was still regarded as part of a management spirit driven by profitable growth with a long-term view. After all, as Porche's management point out quite reasonably, a company selling less than 100,000 cars per year with very few models, and in a very high price segment, faces fluctuating quarterly sales, which, as a consequence, are more often than not an obstruction instead of an indicator of Porsche's performance.

Things changed when Wiedeking started his mission to take over Europe's biggest car maker, Volkswagen Group. For the media, the story made great headlines and allowed them to draw the biblical parallel of David versus Goliath. Porsche quickly became the largest shareholder of VW. When the company revealed that it had secretly accumulated a massive amount of share options to further increase its stake, it basically wiped out almost all free-floating shares. This forced Anglo-American hedge funds, which had 'shortened' Volkswagen shares, in their conviction that they would lose value, to desperately buy them at enormously high prices in order to meet their obligations. Many people might have felt a certain level of satisfaction at the news: a medium-sized company in continental Europe had beaten the mighty American hedge funds at their own game. It was also mind-boggling that Porsche could report higher profits than revenues in its fiscal year of 2007/08. However, the vast majority of the profits were no longer made by selling cars, but by the tremendous increase in the value of Porsche's Volkswagen shares and options. On the cash flow side, these profits were completely irrelevant. They were merely book profits. What was very real, however, were the enormous debts Porsche had piled up in order to acquire the majority of Volkswagen. Porsche's story ended rather differently than in the Old Testament: instead of Porsche taking over VW Group, it was Volkswagen that swallowed the sports car maker.

In the end, Porsche's prize for playing the games of the financial community had cost the company its independence.

This case should be a reminder to European managers that, basically, it hardly ever pays off to play financial games, however smartly you think you can play them. If you want long-term management success, it is better to stick to the principles of profitable growth. In this respect, managers should also remain realistic regarding what they can achieve on an operational level and refrain from dreaming up grand plans that are beyond their capabilities. This is particularly important in their dealings with capital markets. If you want to follow the European way of management, you must communicate both honestly and modestly with the financial community, but this communication must also be based on the following considerations:

- Expected (and targeted) returns should always take account of returns that have been realized in the long term. Over the last 30 years, the world economy grew around three per cent annually. A recent study by Charles Schwab[78] shows that industrial corporations could achieve returns on capital between four per cent and seven per cent since 1970, depending on the segment and inflationary pressure. On the biggest major stock exchanges, the best average return on investments was nine per cent per year. Predictably, it is possible to earn over the odds, but common sense makes it clear that you should not expect it.
- We will not be able to change the disclosure rules or the requirements of quarterly reporting. Yet the accounting principles of some commercial codes in continental Europe can still serve as a useful complement to IFRS reporting in the sense that their main anchor is the principle of prudence.
- Reporting and communication should always centre on a strategy and vision that encompasses technologies, products and resources – in the best tradition of shareholder value. Ideally, communication should take

the form of scenarios that convey the company's convictions, how it sees the future, where it sees development potential and what it targets as milestones.

- Strategic convictions belong on the boss's desk, which means that CEOs should no longer leave communicating with the capital markets to the CFOs.

We are profoundly aware that following these guidelines is not an easy task. It remains to be seen whether analysts and other capital market players can indeed be won over by strategic convictions, rather than numbers and quantitative targets. However, by being confident and persevering in this approach (not to be confused with being vain and arrogant), managers have the best chance to regain entrepreneurial freedom. And it is exactly this freedom that they need for their path to profitable growth.

A system of strong checks and balances at the top

Good management requires effective monitoring – for one simple reason: even top managers need a corrective mechanism. This conviction is reflected in the legislation of numerous countries around the world. However, there is large variation regarding the question of who should double-check important business decisions, to what extent and in what way.

In terms of regular control within the company, there are traditionally two different approaches. The first model calls for meetings where non-executive directors sit with executive directors at the same table. The controlling figures jointly discuss strategy with the figures holding operational power. They adopt decisions with one voice, as members of

119

one body – the single Board of Directors. The second model is a stark contrast to the first, as the non-executive directors have no involvement in the initial decision-making process. Key decisions are taken only by executive directors (at the board of management) and then handed over to the non-executive directors for approval (at the supervisory board). Under such a structure, no individual is allowed to vote on both boards at the same time. And no individual can hold both Chairman and CEO positions, which is often the case in the one-tier board structure.

The two-tier board is mandatory for public limited companies in a number of continental European countries, while the one-tier board has been common in the UK and, as a consequence, many other Anglo-American countries, including the United States. In 1972, the European Commission suggested that the two-tier board should become the standard structure within Europe. In the Commission's draft directive (known as the 5th Directive on company law), worker representation on the supervisory board was also proposed.

We think that the proposal was a move in the right direction because the two-tier board caters much better for effective control as it structurally sets a distance between the operational and the controlling levels. Especially in the light of a growing complexity of the global economy, it can only be a good thing to put proposed strategies and key decisions through two readings. However, due to strong resistance from Britain, the directive never became European law. A revised version proposed in 1983 called for national legislators of the member states to establish the two-tier board at least as an option. This amended version, though, was rejected, too. It took the EU until 2001 to finally adopt a European Company Statute. After 30 years of negotiations (yes, in certain cases the European culture of consensus can take quite some time until compromise is reached), companies in each corner of Europe can finally chose between a one- and a two-tier board when they register as an 'SE' (*Societas Europaea* which means 'European Company'). A majority of the more than 800 public corporations that have registered have set up a two-tier board. Yet this has more to do with the fact that most of them come from Germany and the Czech Republic, two European countries that have strongly subscribed to a separation between management and the supervisory board.

Looking at the (still pertaining) company laws at a national level, one can find a plethora of ways of structuring company boards in Europe and, thus, of organizing suitable checks and balances concerning management decisions. France is already convinced of the benefits of a two-tier system, Poland made the establishment of a separate supervisory board mandatory, and many other Eastern European countries introduced it as an option, such as Bulgaria, Romania and Slovenia, to name but a few. Since the reform of its company law in 2003, Italy also allows its companies to set up a two-tier board, yet there is also the possibility to choose between the Anglo-Saxon model of a one-tier board or to stick to the classic Italian company structure with its rather specific organization. Sweden also has a rather idiosyncratic system, one which comes closer to a one-tier board but makes the representation of employees within the controlling board of directors mandatory.

So where does all this leave us in terms of extracting a European way of controlling management decisions? We can see that three principles have become increasingly apparent:

1. an unwillingness to let the person in charge of the operational management also take a lead role in the controlling procedures;
2. a strong determination to appoint non-executive directors with sufficient experience and independence to seriously and thoroughly control the management board;
3. an openness to not only let representatives of the shareholders take controlling mandates towards the top management, but also the workforce.

At first glance, it seems clear that a CEO should not be able to influence the procedures meant to control his own work. This is less obvious when you look at the reality of the company board in the past. Even with the much stricter two-tier board model, there are numerous cases that indicate that the internal controlling procedures were not taken all that seriously. Formally, the two-tier board model calls the shareholders of a company to appoint the members of the supervisory board at the annual general meeting. It is then the supervisory board that appoints the management board. In practice, however, it has often been the CEO who nominated the candidates for the supervisory board. In short: he decided who was going to control him. This all too often resulted in a club of buddies instead of a body of controllers. This habit, while still not extinguished, has been strongly reduced in European top companies over the last 10 years.

The one-tier board gives even more leverage to the CEO to manipulate the way in which important management decisions are questioned – or not. The danger is particularly high when he is chairing the meetings. In the US, this is still standard procedure. According to a study published in August 2010 by Conference Board,[79] a respected American think tank, the positions of Chairman and CEO being held by the same person was found in three quarters of the US companies examined. In the States, not having the double title of 'Chairman & CEO' is quite often regarded as a sign of weakness for the top executive running a company. When the shareholders of the Disney Corporation took the chairmanship from Michael Eisner in 2004, reducing his function to solely being CEO after 20 years of holding both titles, it was regarded as the beginning of the end to his tenure. A year later, Eisner stepped down.

In the American management culture, combining the role of Chairman and CEO is a logical consequence of the conviction that a company needs one leader who provides a single vision and mission. In Europe, such a concentration of power is seen with great scepticism – not only in continental Europe but also even in Britain. This is evident by the fact that British companies have made a considerable effort over the last 20 years to separate the roles of Chairman and CEO. Looking at the issue was triggered in the early 1990s by the financial scandal surrounding the late media tycoon, Robert Maxwell, who was found to have fraudulently exploited the pension fund of the Mirror Group by hundreds of millions of pounds. Shocked about how uncontrolled Maxwell was and how easily he could rip huge financial black holes in the stock-listed company, the government appointed a committee to come up with recommendations to prevent such abuse in the future. The result was a groundbreaking Code of Best Practice (Cadbury Report, 1992) that unmistakably pointed out the dangers of leaving the roles of Chairman and CEO to one person. At that time, this was common in Britain and many members of the 'old boys club' reacted with bewilderment. Nevertheless, the recommendations made such a strong impact that company control could no longer be regarded as a business club exercise. As a result, the number of publicly listed companies in the UK granting a double role to the top manager has been reduced to about 15 per cent, while it is still between 70 and 80 per cent in the United States. This is yet another sign that Britain has actually become more European in its management principles than might appear on the surface.

The enormous accumulation of power in one person that is so typical for American corporations is based on the rationale that it makes for simpler management and clearer communication, both inside and outside the company. In isolated cases, that may indeed be true. On the whole, however, it embodies precisely the risks inherent in the American model: leadership instead of management and simplification instead of balanced reflection.

The widespread conviction in the States that a manager in charge needs sufficient manoeuvring space to act freely is a reflection of the political system. The US is known to champion the first past the post principle: whoever gets the most votes effectively gets them all and ultimately gets to say how things are done, at least temporarily. Such a 'winner takes it all' attitude that systematically ignores minority votes, irrespective of how close they came behind the majority, gives the winning politician much more leverage to push through his political program than he would ever have in a representative democracy, where even the victor must seek to establish consensus among other parties in order to govern – at least as long as he or she did not win an absolute majority of the votes, which is rarely the case these days.

Some political theorists and management schools in the States might argue that a high degree of undisturbed decision-making to the 'chief commander' results in more efficiency and accountability. Unfortunately, experience shows that it actually leads to greater fostering of egos. Keen to set a new 'era', people in power are bound to take resolute even radical decisions to set themselves apart from their predecessors and visibly start a new course. Admittedly, this is more exciting than executing boring compromises based on hard-wrought consensus. In the long term, however, it leads to a zigzag course, more prone to boom and bust, and sparks polarization and tensions.

Given that the UK has also subscribed to the 'first past the post' principle in politics and arguable allows the British Prime Minister even more freedom than the US President, it is somewhat astounding that Britain has resolutely taken a path to curb the power of its top executives. This is, of course, a path that is highly welcome in our opinion. Europeans have come to understand that even the most gifted and inspiring manager needs regular and institutionalized control if he or she wants to be of long-term benefit to the company. The bottom line is that continuity should be much more cherished than celebrity CEOs.

The second and third principles typical of the European way of securing strong and effective checks and balances concern, and are concentrated on, the people who are chosen to exercise the controlling mandate. In order to secure effective internal control, the supervisors need to have an in-depth understanding of the implications that key decisions proposed by the top management can have on the company. And they need sufficient distance from the very people they ought to control. In short, they need to be independent.

By and large, the best European companies have made significant efforts in the last few years to improve the quality of their supervisory boards or non-executive directors respectively. European CEOs have come to understand that experienced supervisors scrutinizing their decisions and proposals from different angles and perspectives ultimately actually help them to become better managers. It also increases the likelihood that the company is navigated soundly into the future. The basis for such a reflection is, of course, our deeply rooted culture of debate and consensus.

We believe that the companies in the BRIC countries, as well as the ones in the Tiger States, could draw from the experience of European boards in this respect. To be fair, it should be mentioned that American companies have also increased activity to make sure that the number of truly independent directors on their boards goes up. They are, however, still very reluctant to follow an idea that has become more and more established in Europe: letting representatives of a company's workforce take part in the controlling procedures. From a purely ownership perspective, it does indeed sound a bit strange that not only representatives of the shareholders but also of the workforce should supervise the management board. Given that a CEO is at the top in the chain of command and can theoretically give instructions to any employee concerning day-to-day operations, it appears almost impossible to let the very same people he can instruct control his strategy and key decisions. After all, how can you supervise your own boss? Moreover, letting people with no ownership rights have a say in which direction a company should move seems to dilute the share-holder value principle.

Once you start reflecting on the idea, however, it becomes obvious why such an approach can lead to better checks and balances. The simple reason is that a top manager wishing to successfully execute his or her ideas needs to win both the trust and approval of the owners of the capital of a company as well as the very people whose work will turn them into reality. Some might counter that employees simply lack the education and experience to authoritatively judge important management decisions and strategies and, as a result, will constantly harp on about preserving or even expanding workers' rights, or obstructing any necessary measures, irrespective of the overall economic conditions, and regardless of the competitive environment. There is no doubt that, overall, it might take a workers' representative a bit longer to acquire the skills needed at a supervisory board than, let's say, a seasoned businessman or businesswoman who has once run a company himself or herself.

However, experience shows that employees can quickly grow into the task and are both willing and able to see the overall picture, as long as they feel that cultivating a long-term relationship with them is the overriding intention of the top executives and not 'hire' and 'fire'. From a management point of view, the benefits to be reaped from letting employees into the supervisory board are tremendous, because it makes it so much easier to carry a decision through once it has been ratified. It cannot be a coincidence that the European countries with the longest tradition of worker co-determination are the ones which have best expanded their global competitive lead lately: the Nordic and Germanic countries, as well as Luxembourg and the Netherlands.

To this day, the majority of EU members have already made co-determination on the board mandatory with regard to companies of a certain size – those employing over 500 people. Having said that, co-determination is not yet a principle that has gained full acceptance within

Europe. The UK and, to a lesser extent Ireland, are rather dubious about it. Some Southern European countries (Spain, Portugal, Greece, Malta and Cyprus, to be precise) as well as the three Baltic republics have refrained from making it a mandatory part of the checks and balances in place. We also do not wish to omit that a strongly institutionalized worker co-determination process can lead to abuse and misconduct, as was the case at Volkswagen Group where lavish company trips 'all inclusive' (yes really *all* inclusive, even escort services) were taken as a means to buy their consent for key decisions. At the same time, however, it is the famous automotive executive, Ferdinand Piech, who does not tire of mentioning that the support of the workers' representative was decisive in enabling him to prevent the Volkswagen Group from going bankrupt shortly after he took the role of CEO in 1993. Piech – who was not in the least involved in a series of bribery scandals, nor did even know about them – took the benefits of worker co-determination, including their representation on the supervisory board, seriously and kept its virtues in high regard, both during his tenure as CEO from 1993–2002, as well as today as Chairman of the supervisory board. Considering that Piech is a member of the super-wealthy Porsche family and, thus, a prime example of a born capitalist, this praise for co-determination is truly an accolade.

One last thing ought to be mentioned with regard to a strong balance between power and control at top management level: while the EU has abstained from making the two-tier board the standard structure for Europe's companies, it has still recognized that exercising independent judgment as a non-executive director can be tricky when you discuss things only in the presence of the CEO and other executive directors. As a consequence, the European Parliament, in a resolution published on 10 March, 2009 stressed, 'that non-executive board members should consider carefully the possibility of having meetings without executive board members being present.'

We strongly agree.

Live the values you preach

Good management needs values and principles. Since the financial crisis unfolded, it has become a truism to say that CEOs need to focus more on values. But paying lip service to ethical principles is not enough. Management based on values only really works if the defined values are truly internalized. This is precisely where personal leadership comes into play. Only leaders who clearly and unmistakably live out the values they preach can make up for the lost security in the ever-changing global economy of the twenty-first century. They can inspire trust, integrity, authenticity and respect, but also courage and responsibility.

What is important is a set of values that everybody who is involved in a company's operations can relate to. A manager who is committed to profitable growth, in line with Europe's principles of craftsmanship and consensus, will automatically build a bridge from his company's shareholders to other important stakeholders, such as the workforce or the community. The reason is simple: in the European way of management, there is a fundamental belief that a company's value cannot be elevated without nurturing the trust and motivation of its staff, certainly not in the long term. After all, it requires the creative ideas of employees to drive the engine of profitable growth. And the more employees feel that the owners of a company and their trusted managers are prepared to share success in the good days and do their utmost to protect their jobs during the bad ones, the more they are willing and able to devote full energy and a committed *esprit* to their jobs. In a nutshell, Europe's management is based on building relationships with the workforce instead of creating an atmosphere of fear or quick fortune-making. Achieving profitable growth also forms the basis on which taxes can be paid – and paying a fair share of taxes is always the best way to prove commitment to a community or a state. One thing, however, should be crystal clear: building bridges and keeping them steady will never be free from conflict. This is where moral courage comes into play. Courage is not only required when it comes to major issues like corruption, but also in day-to-day management. If managers want to maintain a strong and healthy corporate culture, they should never get tired of asking themselves at the end of each day: was my behaviour determined by the values I preach? Even when a promotion is at stake? Even when executing corporate values runs detrimentally to my material benefit? The answers to these questions will govern whether you are a person who sticks to your principles or whether you quickly throw them overboard when times get tough. In terms of our values, management by opportunism is a no go. If you want to lead your company to long-term success, you must adopt an unequivocal stance and a clear, uncompromising commitment to honesty and reliability.

Management rooted in clear-cut values can also not be substituted by organizational structures such as a 'values office' or 'propaganda' spread through glossy internal communications. Values quite simply have to be practised from the top-down by a combination of role models and transparency, even in times when something goes wrong or was shaken through conflict.

We are, of course, well aware that writing about values can quickly sound like hypocrisy, especially when it comes to behaviour in business, where everything seems ultimately subordinated to the grand goal of profit maximization. Agreed, as long as corporate values are not personally internalized in a professional situation, they will always sound a bit shallow. A few paragraphs in a book will not make critical readers believe that many European companies already have a sound approach towards values – and we do not expect such confidence in advance.

However, there is one thing we want to stress: we are absolutely convinced that Europe's approach to values is one of the most crucial factors for its ability to take a leadership role in the global economy of the twenty-first century.

Five convictions and a basic principle

To summarize, the European way of management is defined by the following five convictions:

1. The best strategy to lead a corporation into a prosperous future is to equip it with the right tools to spot trends and new developments early on and to train employees to understand and interpret them. The regular stream of information obtained in such a manner helps to responsively manoeuvre the company in the right direction. The traditional method of setting five- or ten-year strategic targets from the outset and then executing the strategy no longer works in the ever-changing global economy.

2. The best way to structure a company is to follow the principles of decentralization, which means that responsibility should be left to the smallest units able to deal with a task. As long as employees 'in the field' can handle new or changing customer demands within their unit, they should be allowed to act independently. The same applies to new ideas and innovations. Centralized units or headquarters should only step in when their help is requested or evidently needed. Their role is not to restrict freedom and flexibility but to help employees 'in the field' to better meet their responsibilities – by enabling them with service-centre functions and by motivating them.

3. The best way to secure a company's future is to permanently strive for profitable growth and outperform competitors on a long-term

basis in the most important 'currency' – free cash flow. Modern European managers do not follow a kind of romantic notion that a culture of skilled craftsmanship does not require growth. Since the cash performance of a company also depends on the cost of capital, they are interested in good and productive relations with both financial institutions and capital markets. Yet they are also not willing to become slaves of the finance world and submit to their limited definition of 'shareholder value'. Shareholder value as such is never a strategic target but rather the result of a good strategy.

4. The best way to ensure permanent high quality executive leadership is to set up a controlling body composed of people who have enough expertise and independence to scrutinize and question key decisions made by the CEO and his or her team. In order to look at these decisions from different angles, it is helpful to bring in supervisors with a variety of backgrounds. In order to make sure that key decisions can be executed smoothly and effectively, it is advisable to let workers' representatives have a say, too, on a supervisory level. One person should never hold the roles of CEO and Chairman. Companies should also opt for a two-tier board structure.

5. Establishing and nurturing a corporate culture with long-term values is the foundation for good leadership, strong management and a company's success. This ensures that every stakeholder in a company can relate to the set of values – from the shareholders to the workforce, from the customers to the community – centuries-old 'ever-green' values such as integrity, honesty and reliability have to be the main pillars in the value catalogue. Managers need to uphold these values by serving as credible role models and clever bridge-builders. They need sufficient courage to mediate between the stake-holding parties and, if unavoidable, face conflict.

Irrespective of how easy or difficult you find it to relate to each of these convictions, it should be obvious that all of them have one thing in common: they are driven by a strong belief in teamwork. Predictably, no business culture in the world would neglect that the success of a company always depends on the concerted effort of the many people involved.

However, what makes Europe different is the degree of its belief in teamwork. Ask yourself: has the American management model of the last decade distinguished itself with high regard for teamwork and mutual respect for each party involved? To us, it appears that the dominant force was rather the notion of a 'CEO superhero' – a single person who is able to 'clean up' or rescue a company by almost single-handedly implementing a new strategy and setting radical measures to execute it. The course of US corporations, it seems, was more determined by elite groups from the financial markets and their interests than the workforce or community.

Ask yourself: do the rising Asian companies stand out for their particular high regard for individual employees? Are they known for community building and respect for the environment?

Japanese corporations might be renowned for their strong emphasis on team effort but, at the same time, their management culture does not award its operational teams with a high level of freedom. In Japan, teamwork has more to do with employees at the 'bottom' executing the decisions made at the very top instead of granting teams enough responsibility to find new solutions and ways of operating. This is arguably the reason why Japanese companies have performed so excellently when it comes to the structured work of industrialized production typical of 'the old days', yet it began to struggle when more and more industries called for a more flexible and intuitive way of doing things, putting the focus on the process, not the structure.

Obviously, European companies have many faults as well. It is impossible to come up with an example of a company on the old continent that can serve as a role model for implementing the five convictions – for the very simple reason that there is always a gap between the ideal world of theory and the rough soil of reality. Nevertheless, Europe's culture of skilled craftsmanship and consensus is the most credible evidence that teamwork is held in high regard and taken very seriously. Good craftsmen distinguish themselves through respect and reliance on each other's work. And consensus, of course, can only emerge when you have a group of people with different opinions. All this leads to a type of teamwork where individual responsibility and reflection is not forfeited, but rather the contrary: it is a process where responsible and reflective individuals are willing to work on a joint solution that is better than each individual one. Worried about the insecurities that lie ahead in the fast-moving global economy of the twenty-first century, we tend to think that managers who can execute their vision with a vengeance can best manoeuvre a corporation to future success. It is the impression that 'radical times' demand leaders willing to risk radical approaches. And in order to pursue such an approach, they need sufficient 'absolute' power.

Traditionally, the people who are granted such power are very interesting characters. Often inspiring, regularly eccentric, almost always able to charm, cajole or instil fear, they are noticed and respected wherever they go. They are a perfect sell to the media. In actuality no single person can have the right answers for the plethora of challenges a company has to deal with in an environment of global competition. Modest and intelligent leaders know that, too. Only CEOs with all too big egos do not.

Scared by its history, most Europeans of the last three generations have become extremely suspicious of 'strong leaders' – and rightly so. Considering that about half the names among the 100 largest economic entities on this globe do not refer to states but to corporations, it should be clear just what is at stake when CEOs are given too much power. In an article published in the *Harvard Business Review*, Peter Drucker emphasized that effective executives 'think and say "We", not "I", and reminded CEOs to 'always consider your organization's needs and opportunities before your own.' Austrian-born Drucker, of course, is one of the fathers of management theory; his books have had a tremendous impact on American management principles and he has been extensively consulted by some of the most well-known US corporations with some of the most famous CEOs. In this context, it is obvious that there is no black or white, right or wrong when we talk about management principles on both sides of the Atlantic. In fact, quite a few of the principles described in this chapter overlap with the ideas of best practice that were originally propagated in the US.

This gives us hope that the European way of management will not be misinterpreted as exclusively superior, but as a bridge-builder – between the US and China, Brazil and India, and between many other economies in the world.

Chapter 5

A plea for new European initiatives

We need a Europe that is economically and politically potent for our companies to exploit the full strengths of the European management style. European companies need large domestic markets in order to excel in the competition against their American and Asian counterparts in the long term. Only then can they develop the strength to become sustainable global leaders. This concerns our sales markets, but also our resource base, our technological capabilities and – most importantly – our attitude towards Europe.

European integration started on an economic level and, to this day, issues such as trade, competition and market regulation are still at the very heart of the European Union. Considering the significance of the state of the economy for our standard of living and the importance of the workplace for people's well-being, this is clearly justified. In an era of ever increasing global competition, this applies even more so.

However, neither a set of European management principles nor Europe's culture of craftsmanship and consensus, as such, will equip the EU with the necessary tools to visibly lead the global economy of the twenty-first century. They serve as important cornerstones for our continent, but it remains to be seen to what extent we are able to build a true powerhouse upon them.

If the leaders of the EU member states want to seize the moment, they have to continue the efforts taken by their predecessors over the last 60 years and advance or even complete the European house. Yet one thing must be crystal-clear: Europe can only live up to its potential if it is willing to act and present itself as a real union.

This does not mean that we have to attempt to level out the diversity that makes our continent so special. India and China – frequently mooted to be the rising powers of the new century – also have enormous cultural contrasts and language barriers within their respective regions. The difference, of course, is that both China and India are countries in a classic sense, while the European Union is not. There have been many discussions and debates about the extent to which the creation of a 'United States of Europe' is feasible and/or desirable. Some people argue that this can never be, at least not in a way that resembles the United States of America. Sceptics refer to the failure to adopt a European Constitution and the signs of retreat from the Schengen Treaty to have open frontiers within the EU as evidence that Europe has already overstretched its integration attempts and, thus, its 'building efforts'. The years-long discussions concerning the extent to which heavily-indebted members of the European Monetary Union can and should be assisted have prompted critics and the media to question the future of the euro, and even to paint dark scenarios of the European Union falling apart altogether.

Clearly, there have been enormous challenges for the EU recently and we certainly do not want to diminish their magnitude. Moreover, we cannot ignore the fact that the European project could indeed come to a standstill or shift into reverse – no one can predict the future. Yet we still do not subscribe to the negative sentiments towards further European integration. The bottom line for us is that the economic rationale around the requirement of a common European market will prevail. This rationale will ultimately lead us to grow together.

Despite our optimism, currently talks about a 'United States of Europe' are thought to be badly timed. The European project as it stands today is still very much a work-in-progress. As a consequence, proclaiming a grand vision is not helpful at this point. We should rather focus our efforts on strengthening the existing structure and filling in any missing parts that are needed to achieve true integration. Once we take enough initiatives to improve currently blurred or inconsistent elements within the regulatory framework or implement new ideas for issues that hitherto have remained unaddressed, we have the best chance to reach the path of success. After all, it is the emergence of (seemingly) minor details that will provide clarity for the big picture.

We recognize that the European institutions are already working hard to clear existing obstacles to further integration in some arenas. In others, we believe that fresh impetus is needed. What Europe needs now are new initiatives that inspire and mobilize its citizens; projects that spark enthusiasm for European unity on a broad level. We see potential to build such lighthouses in a number of areas.

European professional cards as a means of boosting mobility

One of the pillars of the European Union is the promise to allow people to move freely between and work in every member state without restriction. People who make use of this and live and work in different countries within the Union often become the best ambassadors of the European idea, as they have personally had the benefit of experiencing different cultures and languages without having to deal with bureaucratic hassles and restrictions.

Unfortunately, not many have capitalized on this chance to widen their horizons so far. In 2001, the European Union found that EU citizens 'have about half the mobility rate of US citizens'. In the last decade of the twentieth century, only 4.4 per cent of inhabitants had moved to another member state.[80] Even within their own country, Europeans seem to have been reluctant to leave the place where they were born and brought up. In 2000, the American economist Alan Krueger, who served as chief economist at the United States Department of Labor in the mid-1990s, published a working paper[81] in which he compared labour movement in America and Europe. He found that 'internal region-to-region migration rates are more than twice as high in the US as in many European countries'. Krueger took 1987 as the reference point for his research. In this year, he states, '2.8 per cent of Americans moved between state boundaries, but only 1.1 per cent of Germans, 1.1 per cent of Britons and 0.5 per cent of Italians moved across regions within their respective countries.'

There are numerous other studies looking into this issue. They arrive at different numbers, yet their message is always the same: Europeans do not like to move. Critics often see this as evidence for a truly 'old continent', populated by timid and narrow-minded people who lack the pioneering spirit required to successfully face the challenges of a fast-moving global economy. We do not believe such an assertion. In our opinion, mobility – like so many things – is not a question of mentality, but of encouragement. In this respect, the European Commission catered for a major boost to movement in 1987 – with the introduction of the Erasmus Programme.[82] It paves an easy way for European university students to study or work in another EU country for a period of three to 12 months. Since then, over two million students have taken this opportunity; quite often Erasmus has opened the doors for them to experience a different language and different culture firsthand. For many it has had lasting effects as it encouraged them to be not only able but also willing to pursue a career away from home. Matthias Parey of the University of Essex and University College London and Fabian Waldinger of Warwick and the London School of Economics conducted a study on the impact of the Erasmus scheme.[83] They recorded the data from German university students from five cohorts, graduating between 1989 and 2005, to analyse how studying abroad affects labour market mobility later in life. 'We find that studying abroad significantly increases the likelihood of working abroad after obtaining their university degree', they concluded. 'Graduates who have studied abroad are about 15 percentage points more likely to work abroad after graduation.'

Today, highly skilled young academics represent by far the biggest demographic group of people who move from one EU member state to another. The 'generation gap' in terms of mobility is also evident when you look at two surveys published by Eurobarometer. In 2005, EU citizens of all age groups were asked whether they were prepared to move to another country if they could not find work at home. Less than a third (31 per cent) said they would take such a step.[84] In January 2011, the Gallup institute asked 30,000 Europeans aged 15 to 35 whether they were willing or would like to work in another European country – and the result was quite different: more than half of them (53 per cent) ticked 'yes'.[85]

People who are keen to take the opportunity to move to another EU country are not only an enormous integrative factor for the European idea, they are also very important for growth and prosperity for the future. International companies, as well as certain industry sectors as a whole (IT, tourism, marketing), want to recruit people with cosmopolitan backgrounds and outlooks. On top of that, we see an increasing disparity in jobs and talent among the EU states. While countries such as Spain or Greece struggle with very high unemployment rates among young people, others such as Denmark, Sweden, Germany and the Netherlands face a shortage of skilled labour. The greater the mobility of the European workforce, the greater the chances to level out the disparity.

Obviously, this is going to be a huge challenge. Language barriers have to be overcome and local authorities have to make sure that we avoid 'ghettoization' or 'shadow societies', phenomena that Europe experienced in the 1960s and 1970s with the influx of so-called 'guest' workers. This time, we need to make sure that people who arrive from a different EU state are not regarded as 'guests', but that they are provided with an environment where they can gradually feel at home.

One major precondition has to be fulfilled in order to achieve this: we have to ensure that EU citizens can use their skills and pursue their professions in every part of the Union. Young European citizens have been brought up with the notion that an unrestricted free movement of labour is one of the main pillars of the EU and they have come to cherish this freedom highly. If we do not want to massively disappoint them, we have to make sure that each European citizen can experience this freedom on a personal level, if and when he or she wishes to do so, without obstacles.

And this is where the problem lies: currently, there are still too many obstacles, ranging from infuriating bureaucracy to mandatory additional tests and training periods, all too often detached from reality. If you calculate the number of regulated professions in the 27 member states of the European Union, you end up with over 4,800 – an incredibly high number.[86] Even if you try to condense the many titles and definitions of these professions into approximately similar job profiles, you remain stuck with 800 different categories. Phew!

Trying to harmonize the provisions needed to pursue a profession in the various member states has been one of the most frustrating and futile efforts in the early history of European integration, which is not all that surprising given how well-protected professional services are by their interest groups on a national level (which, incidentally, is the case pretty much all over the world).

It took 17 years for agreement to be reached regarding how to co-ordinate the training of architects so that their diplomas would be automatically recognized in each member state. Such a long period of negotiation was pushing it, even within the realm of our culture of consensus. Thus, the European Commission took an alternative approach and called for a general system of recognition in 1988. Since then, the EU has undoubtedly made considerable progress, particularly with the Professional Qualifications Directive[87] of 2005 which consolidated over a dozen job-specific directives passed previously, as well as the adoption of a single Services Directive in 2006.[88] Today, it is relatively easy for professionals in the health industry, such as doctors or pharmacists, to work anywhere within the European Union. This also applies to people working in the traditional crafts sectors, such as carpenters or watchmakers. This is great, but not enough. Today, the system has too many inconsistencies and exceptions, lacking any logic. For a baker trained in Rome, it is great news that he can work in bakeries in Paris, Prague or Vienna without having to deal with any regulatory constraints. His qualifications acquired in Italy are automatically recognized in France, the Czech Republic, Austria as well as every other EU member state, despite the fact that their bread cultures are very different. Yet this is the beauty of the Services Directive: since there are no barriers, a baker can acquire the subtleties of bread-making in the different European regions with ease as long as he finds a master who trusts his shown ambition and offers him a job. Unfortunately, this is not the case for gardeners who have to first apply for recognition of their profession in the EU country they wish to work. Is the different treatment of bakers and gardeners really justified? Why do optometrists or opticians have to take compensatory training in order to test eyesight or fit contact lenses in an EU country different from where they received their basic training? Are the eyes and lenses of people in Finland, Poland and Portugal really all that different that we cannot trust the original diplomas acquired without conditions?

The list of professions that are not automatically recognized in each member state of the EU is astonishingly long, ranging from real estate agents to massage therapists, from private detectives to dance school owners. Even within the healthcare system, there are differences that seem impossible to explain: a general care nurse can relocate to any EU country and practice, as her qualifications are automatically recognized; yet those of a childcare nurse are not. A trained chemical laboratory technician from Spain can relocate to France without facing any regulatory hurdles, but a surgical assistant faces much greater challenges.

It is a very confusing system and all too often, such confusion leads to frustration and resignation. In a nutshell, it chokes any enthusiasm to move to another country within the EU. We believe that Europe cannot afford such negative sentiments if it wants to become a leading power in the twenty-first century and should therefore take initiatives to abandon silly and unnecessary hurdles. National politicians and the interest groups of the various professions frequently argue that safety and security make it necessary to keep the existing regulations and restrictions in countries in place. However, we do not believe that gap in quality between professional services in the different EU member states is big enough to justify the existing barriers. Moreover, we are convinced that consumers will soon find out which regions produce the best experts in a given profession or craft. In other words, let the market rule, not burdensome or unclear procedures.

We are glad that the European Commission has brought fresh impetus to the issue by releasing its Green Paper on Modernising the Professional Qualifications Directive in June 2011.[89] In the paper, the Commission underlined the need to better inform people willing or wishing to move from one member state to another about which authorities they have to contact regarding any issues relating to their professional work. 'The evaluation of the Directive, notably the public consultation in early 2011, has revealed this is a major problem for many stakeholders', says the Green Paper. 'In particular, respondents have signalled insufficient clarity on which authority is in charge of recognising their professional qualifications and which documents should be submitted. Insufficient information on what to submit, and to which authority, often defeats the objective of getting a quick decision by the host Member State.'

The Commission also suggests the introduction of a European Professional Card. Each authority allowed to issue such a card should feed the information written and stored on it (such as the name, personal details, the professional title and the diploma or certificate that led to it) into a European-wide information exchange system. This would allow 'a fast-track recognition process for the card holder', according to the Green Paper, which claims that 'a professional card would also offer benefits to service recipients, notably in terms of transparency. By presenting the card, professionals would offer a guarantee that they are competent to exercise in the profession.'[90]

We very much approve of such professional cards. While the Commission opts for a soft launch, stressing that it would not be mandatory, but gives mobile professionals only the 'possibility, but no obligation' to apply for it. Such a cautious approach might well be the best strategy for its introduction. Yet in the mid- to long-term, we see many benefits if they were issued generally. Just imagine if each apprentice or student in Europe were issued their card on their graduation. It could be the same size and shape as a credit card, with the name, photo and newly acquired professional title on it, possibly translated into some other European languages and ideally with the stars of the EU flag on it. A chip could be built in to the card, storing information about the holder's original certificate as well as, optionally, translations.

If such an initiative were carried out successfully, it could serve two purposes: first, it would provide EU citizens with a tangible piece of European identity, one they could always have in their wallets, similar to a driver's licence or bank card. Second, it would increase calls and demands (at a grassroots level) to harmonize professional titles within the EU, so that there is a European-wide understanding about which qualifications lie behind them.

A European Green Technology Agency

Europeans are the most environmentally conscious people in the world. While many Americans still think they can consume unlimited natural resources and Asians are often too preoccupied by issues of economic growth, most Europeans have long understood that we have to treat our environment and the planet differently than we have done so far – for our own benefit. Such awareness is particularly important in the transformation of our energy supply.

Generating sufficient energy at reasonable prices is vital for the well-being of Europe's economy. Yet achieving this has become an increasingly tricky business. 'Two thirds of our existing energy supply comes from countries which, in many respects, do not share our understanding of society and law. Such dependency can quickly leave us susceptible to blackmail', said the EU's Commissioner for Energy, Günther Oettinger.[91] He is right.

When Russia was in dispute with the Ukraine and cut off gas deliveries to them,[92] the supply through the pipelines to the EU came to a halt too. Since it was winter, some European households were chillingly reminded of the danger of any overdependence on one country. Brussels was powerful in its reaction to the dispute, but the national governments of EU member states and (nationally dominated) utilities regularly undermine a concerted effort when it comes to securing Europe's natural gas demand.

When it comes to oil it seems that the world, including Europe, has grown used to the fact that prices are dominated by a cartel (OPEC), which as it happens has its headquarters in a city of the European Union, Vienna. Oil prices are also heavily dependent on regional conflicts in the Middle East and the strategies of oil-rich countries, often ruled by despotic and erratic leaders. For Europeans, the best way to deal with them would be to form a phalanx and show absolute unity in standing up to these cartels. Yet again, national politicians and formerly state-owned or affiliated oil companies regularly shy away from such a close European line.

The biggest division, however, is evident when we look at Europe's differing stances on atomic energy. The shock waves from Fukushima led Germany to speed up its timetable to exit nuclear power, while it made France stand firm to its commitment that reactors would play a major part in the country's energy generation. Britain seems to have become more cautious in approving the construction of new plants. Many Italians saw the catastrophe in Japan as a confirmation that they were right to shut down their atomic plants after Chernobyl in 1986. Many Austrians experienced the same feeling of affirmation given the fact that they never let their one existing nuclear plant even start to operate. By contrast, the Prime Ministers of the Czech Republic and Poland felt compelled to publicly declare it impossible to eliminate nuclear energy in the near future, despite Poland not yet even having a nuclear plant. In their attempt to avoid any over dependence on gas deliveries from Russia, the former Eastern bloc countries Hungary and Slovakia are also rather open to nuclear energy as an alternative source.

It is not only Central Europe where we can observe huge ruptures in policies and public moods within the European Union. The Nordic countries are far from portraying their typical Scandinavian unity when it comes to this issue, with Sweden having reversed its decision to exit nuclear power not too long ago, while 'non-nuclear' Denmark has not even mentioned atomic power plants as an option in its newest energy policy plan. Regulating an issue as sensitive and wide-ranging as atomic energy on a national level is nonsensical. If an accident occurs in one of the 59 reactors in France, it is quite likely that other EU member states will be affected too: radiation does not recognize borders. From a political point of view, however, it seems that the topic has become too emotional and too heated to become anything like a common European strategy. We cannot change this fact, but we should learn from it on our way from fossil fuels and nuclear plants to renewable energy sources.

Most Europeans hope that the continent's long-term future energy production will no longer be dominated by coal-burning power stations, gas turbines and reactors, but by wind parks, solar panels, hydro power, biomass and ocean waves. They welcome the EU's set target that 20 per cent of the energy produced in Europe by 2020 should originate from renewable resources. Almost every EU member state is doing a great deal to manage and encourage this transformation, introducing new legislation and allocating billions in subsidies for renewable energy. The seeds of these national initiatives that were planted in the last few years have bloomed in some areas and quite a number of European companies have managed to become global leaders in their respective fields of renewable energy. However, there is a high risk that they will lose their competitive advantage soon. Both China and the United States are catching up quickly with their own initiatives.[93] With their market size and geographical landscape, they have an automatic advantage against each single European country and will soon overtake them – unless the EU member states quickly link arms and bundle their transformational efforts.

We think the best way to do this is by creating a European Agency for Green Technology. Such an agency should receive the mandate to co-ordinate the various activities in terms of increasing our energy and material efficiency, renewable energies and recycling. In short, it should develop a sustainable energy concept for Europe. A collective effort by a powerful new agency with a solid budget could put an end to the current piecemeal approach to green technology in Europe, where subsidies are often more driven by national considerations than business logic – such as the installation of solar panels in countries which do not exactly make it into the hall of fame in terms of sunny days. The massive dependency on geographical and climate conditions in the realm of renewable energies also explains why we deem it necessary to elevate the transformational activities to a European level. Only with a continent-wide view is it possible to foster the emergence of leading projects and for clusters of expertise and manufacturing strategically placed. In terms of an energy policy for the twentieth century, Europe has to quickly start to disregard national boundaries.

This requires a massive shift in mentality for national governments. After all, securing sufficient and affordable electricity and heating for households and businesses has been regarded as a matter of utmost national importance since the invention of the light bulb and radiators. Guarding these resources for the benefit of the electorate is seen by most governments as a pivotal task for the state. This is quite understandable, but once you scratch the surface you will soon discover that Europe's energy supply has long stopped being just a national affair. As soon as the European countries started to link their national power grids, it enabled electric current the chance to flow as strongly and as far as the lines allow. At the Leipzig-based European Energy Exchange, most registered traders who are in charge of securing sufficient energy supply for their companies or customers hardly care from which region the power originates that they are about to purchase. What is on their mind, first and foremost, is the price.

In an environment dominated by renewable energies, letting power travel over long distances becomes even more vital. Wind turbines are most efficiently deployed in shallow and windy offshore stretches, so it is quite obvious that the Dutch coastal lines have much to offer in this respect. However, since the amount of electricity generated there cannot be controlled or run on a set schedule but is instead predominantly determined by the moods of nature, an off-shore wind park often works most efficiently when it is linked to a power station with a reservoir where energy production can be stored. Such a plant can release the power of the reservoir's water pressure whenever it is necessary to generate electricity.

Within the boundaries of the Netherlands, it is unlikely that they will find a site that is suitable for such a power storage plant, because the country is notoriously flat, lacking the landscape for a plant based on a big altitude gap between the water reservoir and the turbines. In mountainous regions like the ones you find in parts of Sweden or Austria, however, the landscape for a storage plant is perfect. Consequently, the Dutch offshore wind park should be linked to a Swedish or Austrian reservoir to get the maximum benefit.

This example illustrates why a European approach is particularly important when it comes to renewable energies. Today, the European Commission appears to be rather on the sidelines. After it supported regional and urban energy management with the SAVE and SAVE II programmes in the 1990s, it set up the Intelligent Energy–Europe programme in 2004, with the aim of creating a network of local energy agencies.[94] The programme also provides financial aid to several dozen projects annually, yet with a total of €58m in 2010, the amount is tiny in comparison to the funding available in some European countries on a national level. This is why we recommend that the bulk of the billions currently allocated by the EU member states themselves ought to be transferred to the newly created European energy agency. This would give the agency enough muscle to speed up harmonization and the transition to wind, solar, hydro and biomass energy supply. The agency should not only be responsible for energy production based on renewable resources but also for a European-wide upgrading of the power grid, as the grid plays a cardinal part on the path to a fossil- and nuclear-free Europe. Estimates suggest that we need 45,000 kilometres of extra line capacity to enable, and intelligently distribute, renewable energy in Europe.[95] The sheer magnitude of this project would give the agency enough leverage to make sure that each EU member state will benefit from the agency's programmes and that there will be sufficient projects that energy and construction companies with different expertise can tap into.

We are well aware how difficult it will be to convince national governments to pool their funds for subsidies and let a European agency co-ordinate or even control the badly needed renewal of the grid infrastructure. It cuts deep into EU members' sovereignty. Moreover, farsighted national politicians know exactly what is at stake: renewable energy as a business will soon play a massive role in our economies. Those who master them will create an enormous numbers of jobs and wealth. Scientists estimate that the quickly developing sector for green technology will create 2.8 million new jobs by 2020 in Europe alone.[96] Every economy in the world wants a piece of this cake.

However, since green tech is based on a mix of engine building, plant engineering and highly sophisticated technical services, it fits perfectly into Europe's culture of skilled craftsmanship. Farsighted politicians all over the EU should also acknowledge this and unite to turn our continent into a unified global leader for green technology.

Towards a European Economic and Finance Ministry

Until 2008, it looked as if the European Monetary Union could look back on the first decade of its existence as a huge success story. What started with the birth of the European Central Bank as guardian of a single monetary policy in 1999 and became tangible three years later with the introduction of euro coins and notes on January 1, 2002 led to impressive stability and solidity in the first few years. Consumers benefited from extremely low inflation, invariably lower than in previous times with their national currencies. Companies enjoyed the cost advantages brought by the elimination of currency fluctuations, causing a new stimulus for cross-country trade within the eurozone. Between 1999 and 2007, it did not seem to matter that the structure behind the monetary union and the euro was incomplete and imperfect. Breaking the rules of the stability pact had little to no consequences on bond markets. As we all know, the global financial crises triggered by the collapse of Lehman Brothers changed the situation massively.

Many euro countries exhausted their budget in order to rescue banks and other financial institutions. At the same time, they faced shrinking GDPs, leading to reduced tax incomes. These two factors, combined with a profoundly shaken financial community fearing further debt defaults, culminated in a situation where some European states could no longer raise money at reasonable rates. Interest rates for their bonds were catapulted sky-high. When Greece faced bankruptcy for the first time in early 2010, it became evident that the European Monetary Union lacked the necessary rules to deal with the situation. The hope that the self-regulating power of the bond markets would never allow a country to expand its debt to unacceptable levels did not materialize. Action was needed.

Contrary to the constant string of bad headlines in the media, we believe that the many parties involved in Europe's currency and debt crisis did quite a good job – at least until we finished writing this book in 2012. In hindsight, it is always easy to claim that the first steps taken to rescue Greece, Ireland and Portugal could have come at a lower price or that the eurozone could have reacted with more speed or with more determination before Italy and Spain slipped into the sovereign debt crisis. In reality, the mix of political capital and monetary instruments that needed to be applied and approved by so many different players made it extremely difficult to achieve any consensus in due time – particularly since the cost, in terms of political capital, has been very high. In some European countries, people have been strongly hit by cost-cutting measures and mass unemployment. In others, there is a widespread fear or anger that their taxes will be used in an unacceptable fashion to pay the bailout bills.

Considering what is at stake, it is impressive how many national politicians have been willing to use their political capital to start painful reforms or agree to solidarity measures. We are also glad that, so far, all the players involved have acted responsibly enough to avoid insurmountable rifts between them, however tough the negotiations and however nationalistic the sentiments sparked by the media in the various member states. But once again, it is in Britain where these observations do not apply. Britain's determination to ask others, particularly the eurozone members, to act while they remain unwilling to participate in any solutions that require concessions culminated in David Cameron's decision in December 2011 to veto a new fiscal pact at the ungodly hour of 2.30am. It was meant to secure exemptions for the UK against freshly proposed financial market regulations enforced by the EU. Yet the tactic backfired and ended in isolation. Britain's euro sceptics might have celebrated the instance, but any person in favour of the European idea must have seen it as a poignant moment.

By 2012, the EU and the eurozone members had already taken some decisive steps to sooth the lingering sovereign debt crisis without managing to solve it. Reading about the EFSF[97] or ESM[98] might appear tedious and technical, yet the framework of these bailout funds was essential in terms of a more coherent and co-ordinated budget policy that is more resistant towards a financial crisis. The same applies to the fiscal pact, an intergovernmental agreement aimed at securing fiscal discipline among the EU member states by providing Brussels with stronger surveillance powers and setting automatic sanctions for misbehaving states.

There are other measures that have been taken or discussed during the crisis, many of them heavily disputed.[99] However, criticizing Europe's crisis management as an ineffective patchwork approach is equally easy, since picking out the steps that turned out to be counter productive could only be done in retrospect. What is crucial now, though, is taking firm measures to fix the flaws of the monetary union forever. In other words: we need to take initiatives to heal the euro's defects. We do not know how much time is left to complete this massive job, but we advocate that politicians and central bankers act soon. Otherwise, they might end up being haunted by the global financial community over and over again.

What is required? First, we have to deal with the root of the problem – budget consolidation. As is the case with consumers and companies, the credit-worthiness of countries depends on the amount of debt relative to its earnings. Some eurozone countries are in a very sound condition in this respect. The total debt of Estonia is below 10 per cent of its annual output, the GDP. The bigger euro countries, such as France, Spain or Germany had a ratio between 70 and 85 per cent in the first years after the sovereign crisis broke out, but were treated rather differently on the bond markets during this time. This is due to their different current growth levels, as well as contrasting predictions of how their national economies will develop in the future. The debts of Greece and Italy have exceeded 100 per cent for quite some time. This is huge, but the USA also has a debt-GDP ratio beyond 100 per cent and Japan more than twice as much. Both countries, however, find it much easier to raise money than the two Southern European members of the eurozone.

What can we learn from this observation? In fact, the lesson is simple: scale brings an enormous advantage when it comes to financial issues.

Bigger economies are regarded as more robust and stable and, thus, find it easier to successfully issue bonds with low interest. This is a clear indication that the members of the eurozone ought to converge their debt-raising policy and issue euro bonds.

Looking at their current domestic affairs, it will be relatively easy to get the Southern and Eastern European members of the eurozone to agree to such a proposal. Yet it will be very, very difficult to bring the ones in Central Europe to join the team. This, above all, applies to Germany. Europe's largest economy fears that taking such a step would make its own debt funding more expensive in the future and lead to a so-called 'transfer union'.

Whether this will happen or not very much depends on the framework established with the introduction of euro bonds. Therefore, it might be advisable for the German Chancellor to take a similarly positive public stand on euro bonds, as did the long-term Chairman of the 'Euro Group', Luxembourg's Prime Minister Jean-Claude Juncker. Yet such a stand should be linked to equally bold proposals:

- rigorous control of the Growth and Stability Pact;
- a European-wide banking union;
- an insolvency code for European states;
- a European Rating Agency.

A newly formed European Economic and Finance Ministry should become the executive guardian of the stability and growth pact, with the power to put a halt to any subsidies that a member state can receive once it is in breach of the debt ceilings stipulated in the pact. At the moment, of course, this would mean that punishments would have to be started immediately – with Germany, France and Belgium among the first to be punished, as all three have exceeded the limit of 60 per cent of the GDP debt-ratio for more than three consecutive years. The way to overcome this issue is by setting a transformation period: euro-zone members should be allowed until 2020 to meet the targets of the stability pact again.

As banks and their various machinations have not only triggered the European sovereign debt crisis but could remain a liability in terms of their balance sheets and risk-taking actions, it is important that a strong regulatory body controls them. Moving this task away from national bodies towards a European agency seems the most effective way in this respect. The supervision should comprise the right to close banks or force them to restructure as well as setting up and adminis-trating a savings and deposit insurance.

The existing European Rescue Fund should receive the mandate to allocate stimulus packages in times of economic downturns and, thus, assist countries to return to growth. Such assistance would counterbal-ance the regularly brought forward argument that the European stability pact is too rigid. Solid growth is one of the best ingredients to consolidate a country's economy. Yet this can only occur when it leads to sufficient tax revenues. In the past, European countries have all too often lowered taxes to bring in new businesses and investments. Such 'tax lowering competitions' under the roof of the European Union should be brought to an end.

For example, as long as Ireland defends its extremely low corporate tax, as if it were the Holy Grail, it cannot expect a huge amount of soli-darity from other members of the eurozone, which have lost out in the race to attract new enterprises because of this. In this respect, the big question is: does Europe want to continue giving multinational compa-nies opportunities to go on tax discount shopping trips and allow them to pit one EU member against the other, or is it prepared to take the control from them? We recommend that Europe's regions should stop their internal tax competitions and present themselves as a solid block with harmonized tax corridors. The European countries should also have enough self-confidence not to fear countries or regions from elsewhere playing the tax card too heavily. After all, Europe has more than enough to offer on other areas than tax, ranging from the size of its market to the skills of its people and social harmony. For us, it is clear: the praise for diversity within Europe ought not to include national tax levels. The idea of introducing certain taxes on a European-wide level, such as a financial transaction tax proposed by the European Commission, appears like a welcome step towards more tax harmonization – which, one day, might lead to a European Finance Ministry.

At this point, you might ask yourself whether we have reached the sphere of wishful thinking, far removed from political reality. Isn't it obvious that the national governments would never agree to a European super ministry with serious executive powers on topics such as finance and the economy? No, it isn't. Many national politicians know exactly that the EU needs to be equipped with tax authority and to have the chance to expand its co-ordinating mandate on a fiscal and economic level. Otherwise, Europe cannot continue to grow together. Admittedly, the initiatives proposed here would be gigantic steps rather than Europe's hitherto step-by-step approach. Yet the members of the European Union have proven in the past that they can accept such ventures, even if it means ceding large parts of their national sovereignty. They showed this early on in the European project when they equipped civil servants at the Commission in Brussels with a direct and unrestricted mandate to raid the offices of any company located on European soil whenever they sensed a violation of competition law. In the same vein, the EU member states similarly abolished border controls between their national frontiers. And some of them took a third massive step when they gave up their national currencies in favour of the euro. In other words, it does not seem completely implausible that the EU can take another step of such magnitude – with the creation of a European Economic Ministry.

In fact, we believe that a large part of the EU's population already longs for a unified approach in terms of economic and fiscal policy. Ordinary people increasingly sense that the masters of the financial markets are playing a cat and mouse game with elected governments. They have started to lose trust in politicians' ability to counter their power, and a powerful European ministry could be the answer to such concerns, assuming that the framework is right.

First, it should have the power to 'green-light' each euro bond tranche. If a country wants to benefit from lower interest rates by holding fellow euro members liable it needs to ask for clearance. Furthermore, it should introduce a set of rules that outline for bondholders (and everybody else, really) what happens in the future if an EU member state were to overstretch its domestic economy in an irreversible way. Right now we do not have any such rules. In the future, an EU state should be able to file for creditor protection – in a similar fashion to a company that is no longer able to service its debt and looks for respite to prepare for a fresh start. The scenario would go as follows: a state in dire straits calls on the European Economics Ministry for institutional protection over a certain period. Given that the ministry (or, alternatively, a branch of the European Court) regards the application as justified, it would then appoint a trusted administrator with the mandate to call for a creditor meeting and renegotiate payback conditions between bondholders and state representatives.

Some readers might find it odd that we suggest a unified insolvency protection for EU member states as a new European initiative. They might also deem it impossible to execute in an orderly way. Greece is no General Motors, you might argue. Well, from a creditor's point of view, it actually is. Obviously, a state that asks for creditor protection gives up the bulk of its sovereignty, strongly reducing the power of democratically elected representatives. Yet if you look at what has happened in Greece, you might agree that the manoeuvring space for the Greek parliament and government has become extremely slim. Most decisions are forced upon them.

Equipping EU member states with the option to file for a regulated period of creditor protection would bring much clarity regarding what will happen in case a country can no longer completely meet its debt obligations. Or, to put it in another way: it would take away a lot of insecurity. And if there is one thing markets and investors hate, it is insecurity. Once they see a blank, they always 'price in' a kind of doomsday scenario – which explains why, at some point, it became more expensive for Greece to raise money than for some of the poorest countries in the Third World.

In this context, it is perhaps important to clarify the precise terminology we are using. Regardless of semantic similarities with private insolvency law, in the case of nation states we are talking solely about returning countries to a position of solvency. Christoph Paulus, Professor of Law at Berlin's Humboldt University, rightly points out that there is neither liquidation nor an insolvency administrator who distributes residual assets to the creditor community.[100] The only issue at stake is enabling a country to return to normal functioning. Thorough analysis of the debt situation would be followed by the introduction of a distinction between two relevant scenarios:

- If a nation were only temporarily insolvent, the ESF, equipped with a new and expanded mandate for this matter, would bridge the liquidity gap. Private creditors could therefore be encouraged to keep hold of their receivables.
- If a country were permanently insolvent, it would have to negotiate a comprehensive restructuring plan with private creditors, possibly drawing on liquidity assistance from the ESM.

157

To simplify these restructuring processes, new government bonds issued in the eurozone would contain an identical contractual clause, known as collective-action clause. The clause would allow debts to be rescheduled, interest rates to be reduced and maturities to be extended, even against the will of a minority of the creditors.

Could this kind of project foster excitement and enthusiasm in Europe? Well, maybe. If we were to do it right and communicate it properly, two things would become clear. First, we would be able to reassure people that we can keep the euro under control. Second, we could adopt a lead role in the international community, setting a benchmark and laying the cornerstone for a new international financial architecture. In other words: Europe will lead the way.

Another domain where we need leadership is an initiative to set up a new lighthouse that can act as a beacon against the obscure machinations of the major rating agencies. S&P, Moody's and Fitch played a decisive role in the dealings that led to the biggest economic crisis since the 1930s. If they hadn't put their seal on a series of sub-prime papers, the trade with bad mortgages would have never flourished to such a disastrous magnitude. Today, nobody would seriously dispute that the rating agencies were clearly overly generous with their ratings in those days. There is also a reason for their generosity: they were paid by the architects of the securities. Now we ask you: how much credibility would you grant a triple-A rating on a washing machine when the product-testing agency that issued the rating was paid by the producer of the washing machine? Not a lot, we presume. Obviously, the two parties could keep their business connection in the dark. Yet once it turned out that the washing machines were seriously flawed and exploded, causing massive damage and injury, the ensuing investigation would reveal the dubious business model of the product-testing agency; it would most likely put the agency out of business. After all, it would have lost its major asset: its credibility.

In normal market circumstances, the same should have happened to S&P, Moody's and Fitch. It did not. Instead, the three agencies came out of the crisis with ever more power, dictating the 'price tags' countries have to pay to raise money in a fashion never seen before. This is frightening – and dangerous. The oligarchy of the three US-based agencies needs to be broken – by the creation of a European Rating Agency.

Roland Berger Strategy Consultants has started an initiative to persuade European governments and companies to form a consortium with the mission of setting up such an agency. Markus Krall has left his position as Senior Partner and Global Head of Risk Management of the consultancy to execute the idea. To make sure that from the outset it can establish itself as a serious counterweight to the big American players, the newly formed agency needs many experienced analytical talents and a structure that guarantees its independence. Both will not come cheap. About €100m will be necessary to launch the project. To us, however, there is only one way to make sure that the new agency is truly independent in its analyses: it should neither be paid by the players who issue securities nor by the ones who (plan to) buy them. One way to guarantee this is by securing enough funding to let the agency operate as a trust.

Some heads of governments of EU member states have already publicly endorsed the establishment of such a European rating agency. This is not a time to dither, but a time to take responsibility. One more thing: in case you are wondering to what extent a European Economic Ministry and a European Rating Agency need to be 'institutionalized' and to which country, if any, it should be 'attached', we are fairly open about this, since Europe's flexibility in this respect has hitherto turned out to be beneficial when it comes to turning initiatives into reality. To us, it is not outside the realm of the political reality to set up a European Economic Ministry as a new institution. Yet we believe that it could also emerge on a more informal level, such as a spin-off of the already existing group of finance ministers of the eurozone. In any case, it will certainly need to work closely with the European Central Bank. The same applies to a European rating agency.

Ultimately, what is important to us when it comes to new European initiatives on the economic and fiscal level is fixing the problems we currently experience with the euro. As we have established earlier on, Europe's common currency has so far turned out to be both a fantastic boon for the European identity as well as an inherent danger for the European project. The reason for this is that certain elements and eventualities were not thought through, nor have they been solved by deep consensus. It is high time we solidify the foundation of the euro and the European Monetary Union.

A new prestigious competition for the best European start-ups

One area where Europe clearly lags behind the United States is in its ability to put start-ups in the international spotlight. The two companies that have changed our day-to-day lives most in the last decade, Google and Facebook, both have their headquarters in Silicon Valley.

It is not a coincidence that they ended up in close proximity to other majors in the IT industry, such as Apple, Oracle, Hewlett-Packard and Intel, as well as some of the highest calibre venture firms in the world, such as Sequoia Capital or Kleiner Perkins Caufield & Byers (KPCB). To young entrepreneurs all over the world, 'Bay Area' made up of San Francisco and the Silicon Valley is the undisputed powerhouse that can turn business ideas into breakthrough companies with global appeal. This is no coincidence; neither is it a result of sheer market forces. Instead, the region's development into a technology hub was heavily bolstered by infrastructure and contracts provided by state-affiliated entities like NASA and the US Defense Department after the Second World War. The roots of Silicon Valley actually reach back to the first decade of the twentieth century when the US Navy set up a major research centre focused on radio and military technology. Later on, Stanford University also played a major part in drawing talent to the region.

Many European countries have also tried to establish such clusters with research sites and industrial parks, hoping that subsidies and incentives will allow them to prosper and let incubators breed sufficient start-ups with high potential and the ability to create many jobs. However, since these efforts were never co-ordinated on a European level, their impact remained limited. As a result, politicians and businessmen alike had to stay on the sidelines and watch how some of their biggest talents left for California to have their entrepreneurial spirits either awakened or further developed. Take Andreas Bechtolsheim, a Bavarian who became a co-founder of Sun Microsystems on the other side of the Atlantic and later was one of the early investors in Google. Or Frankfurt-born Peter Thiel, who was instrumental in the creation of the online money transfer system PayPal and who then turned into one of the most influential investors. He even sits on the board of Facebook. Yet it is not only influential members of the 'old guard' of the Valley who have European origins.

Many start-ups currently set up in this area have roots in EU member states. Czech-born and educated Roman Stanek is one such example. He is a serial entrepreneur who moved to the Bay Area years ago and has recently drawn much attention (and money) with his new start-up GoodData,[101] a cloud-based provider of business analytics. Another example is Frenchman Eric Setton who acquired his technological skills at the École Polytechnique in Paris, yet ended up as Chief Technology Officer of Palo Alto-based Tango,[102] a start-up that offers

161

free video calls on smart phones and tablet computers and is thus heralded as the next Skype. Speaking of Skype, we should note that there are indeed outstanding entrepreneurs, engineers and investors from Europe, as the world's most popular Internet telephone service was founded by a Swede (Niklas Zennström) and a Dane (Janus Friis), programmed in Estonia (the majority of the development team still works from there) and funded by a Luxembourg-based venture capital firm (Mangrove Partners).

Skype might be the most prominent example of a recent start-up with global appeal coming from Europe, yet it is certainly not the only one. The world's most widely used open source database, MySQL, was developed in Scandinavia. Today, it is used by some of the most frequently visited websites, such as YouTube, Google, Facebook and Wikipedia. The most popular online music websites, Last.fm and Spotify, were created in the United Kingdom and Sweden, respectively, and the biggest sharing platform for music, SoundCloud, is based in Berlin and run by Alexander Ljung, who was born in the UK and raised in Sweden.

All this illustrates that Europe neither lacks the technological talent nor the business acumen to develop start-ups with massive economies of scale and scope. The issue is rather that the majority of outstanding European founders see only two ways to bring their start-up to international prominence: they either feel compelled to take up residence in Silicon Valley, or sell out to a major US player. It is widely known that Skype was sold to eBay and then passed on to Microsoft. MySQL was acquired by Sun and ended up at Oracle. Last.fm became part of the American media company CBS. Now, in general there is nothing wrong with a successful sale, or 'exit', as venture capitalists call it. In fact, it is the beauty of a globalized economy that you do not have to look at passports in order to find out who can buy or sell an enterprise. There is also nothing objectionable about the fact that Europeans might prefer to move to the States. However, the problem is that in the high-tech start-up scene, the transatlantic exchange seems to be a one-way system. If Europe wants to manifest a leadership role in the global economy of the twenty-first century, it should do something to change that. But how?

Some might argue that the EU has to pick a single region and bundle all its efforts to establish and promote this region into Europe's prime hub for technology start-ups. In theory, this sounds like a good idea. Considering the political realities and the funding structure of the European Union, though, it should become quickly evident that this is not feasible for the time being.

In the very early days of working on a business idea and setting up a company, this is not even a big disadvantage, as many start-ups in Europe can find sufficient support on a national, regional or local level – in what is known as the 'seed phase'. Such support can include a range of incentives from local business plan competitions with prize money of a few thousand euros, specially designated offices and a research infrastructure that can be used for free or very little money, to grants or loans in the hundred-thousand and million euro range.

The lack of a European hub with a very high concentration of talent and money, as we find it in the Bay Area in the US, starts to turn into a problem once a start-up enters the next phase and wants to quickly expand. In this period, founders usually look for a large number of skilled people they can hire quickly as well as large amounts of capital. This applies particularly to groundbreaking business ideas, which sometimes need funding in the seven- or eight-figure sum range and employ dozens of engineers or researchers before they earn a single cent. Google, for example, didn't even have a revenue model in its first years of existence.

It is in these cases where Europe currently cannot compete with the US, as becomes evident by the statistics. In 2011, US-based venture capital firms injected a total of $28.4bn into start-up businesses.[103] The firms with the biggest wads of cash in their pockets are traditionally located around San Francisco. And since there is an old saying that the stars of the US venture capital scene insist on having the founders they fund within a 100-mile-radius from their office, one can presume that the bulk of the billions spent ended up somewhere in the Bay Area. In comparison, European-based venture capital firms have only invested $4.4bn,[104] not even a sixth of their American counterparts. As a result, just over 1,000 European companies received financial backing from them in 2011, while more than 3,600 start-ups based in the US managed to raise money during that year.[105]

Should that lead us to the conclusion that the European Union ought to raise its budget and beef up European venture capital funds by billions to match the financial muscle of their US counterparts? No. The EU's European Investment Fund (EIF) has already done a great deal in this respect. It has invested in pretty much all the venture capital firms based in Europe, with commitments totalling €3bn and the provision of a new funding source for business angels with the launch of the European Angels Fund (EAF) in March 2012. Quite often, the EIF has been the first and largest investor in their funds, thus laying the foundation for their very existence. Today's disparity between the venture capital scene in the US and Europe has not so much to do with public or even private money coming from the domestic front, but with the funds' ability to attract investors from elsewhere. A large proportion of the billions spent by venture capital firms in the Valley stems from China, the Middle East or other regions of the world. They are attracted by the idea of being a player in the game when the next Google or Facebook is being discovered, hoping for massive returns on their investment in such a case. They will be impressed when US venture fund managers take them on a 'grand tour' through the Valley, passing by the headquarters of the biggest pedigree names in the IT world, showing them the newest technologies and setting up meetings with the 'hottest' start-ups.

In contrast, these international investors with deep pockets will either look with scepticism at the European start-up scene (despite the fact that the average return of investment has surpassed US venture funds lately) or won't even have it on their radar. In short, Europe's best founders are not regarded as a vibrant community and, hence, lack sufficient visibility. This is not just a problem for attracting money; it is also an issue for the young European entrepreneurs themselves.

'On a national level, I know exactly what is going on in the start-up scene, which companies are hot and which business angels are particularly savvy. What I miss is the mingling on a pan-European level', said Friedrich Schwandt in conversation with the authors. Schwandt is founder of Hamburg-based statistics and ranking portal Statista, which recently rolled out its service to the United States. He and other top founders in Europe tend to leave their national boundaries quickly. Neither France, nor the UK or Germany is big enough for them. Yet due to the lack of a vibrant and coherent start-up community on a European level, they often regard it to be easier to move to the United States than expand within the European Union.

We believe an effective way to elevate the visibility of the EU's start-up scene and open new ways for founders to network and set benchmarks on a cross-border level is by launching a prestigious competition for the European start-ups with the most potential. The best way of starting this would be if several of the major European venture capital firms (such as London-based Balderton, Index and DFJ Esprit, Paris-based Sofinova and Partech, or Munich-based Earlybird and Target) came together and formed a consortium. Each firm could pay a few hundred thousand euros into the consortium, a reasonable amount for these fund operators. Ideally, the total amount raised would then be matched by the European Investment Fund or the European Commission. This would lead to sufficient funding to set up a back office to manage and organize the competition, including a glamorous awards ceremony and

165

substantial prize money for the winners. Through their substantial networks, the venture capital firms could encourage start-ups to take part in the competition or nominate them. The heads of the best-known entrepreneurial centres and university professors teaching entrepreneurship in Europe could also get involved, as nominators and evaluators of participants. In order to gain enough traction in the public sphere, highly reputed media partners should be brought in, such as *The Financial Times* or the *Economist*, which have the added advantage of publishing in English but have a global readership. This, of course, does not mean that business media outlets publishing in other languages, such as *Les Echos* in France, *Il Sole 24 Ore* in Italy, *Expansion* in Spain or *FT Deutschland* in Germany have to be excluded. Instead, they could complement each other in setting up a pan-European campaign, calling for applications for the competition. Later, they could feature the finalists, report on the festival and awards ceremony. After that, they should report regularly on the developments of the winners until the next round of the competition starts.[106] Knowing how engaging and inspiring clever founders with groundbreaking ideas can be, we believe that it could even be possible to engage some of the most outstanding European entrepreneurs to get involved in such a competition. With the right partners and guests, there is no doubt that such a pan-European start-up competition would become a must for ambitious start-up business founders all over the EU and turn a massive spotlight on the winners. Once it is established, the awards ceremony could be expanded into a multi-day event, giving founders, business angels and institutional investors several platforms to establish and groom contacts and instil a European start-up community feeling. In this respect, the competition would turn into a cross between the 'Oscars' and the Cannes Film Festival, if you forgive us the rather immodest comparison.

By the way: we are well aware that the US-based technology business magazine *Red Herring* already calls for the nomination of the best

European start-ups each year and awards the top 100 after a conference.[107] We appreciate this initiative. However, we feel that the *Red Herring* is organized by an American media company. Awarding the equivalent to the 'Oscars' in the European start-up scene, however, should be a European project.

Europe's new benchmark for intellectual capacity: the Nobel Prize Initiative

In the first decade of the twenty-first century, Europe's top companies have done a tremendous job in expanding their competitive edge in the global arena. They built upon the continent's industrial heritage and combined it with a modernized form of skilled craftsmanship, no longer based on protective structures but on innovative research. Europe's political leaders were not exactly as successful. In 2000, they agreed on three milestones to turn the European Union into the 'most competitive and dynamic knowledge-driven economy by 2010': promoting entrepreneurship, raising the employment rate to 70 per cent and raising R&D spending to at least three per cent of GDP. When it became clear that the EU would not reach these milestones, it simply decided to set them again in a slightly modified form, to be reached a decade later – by 2020.

In order to reach the target this time, we believe that it is particularly necessary to increase funding for first-class education and top-level research. Fearing to be seen to be fostering merely the elite, in the past European politicians have been rather reluctant to support its outstanding talent in a disproportionate way. They preferred broad programmes. We understand and appreciate the social component of such an approach. Yet we believe that it is of utmost importance in our

167

globalized society that Europe can let enough beacons of research and education shine to attract the best of the best in their fields from all over the planet. Since our world has transformed from industrial to intellectual capitalism, managing and increasing knowledge is of paramount importance. 'The overall objective is to cultivate innovation,' said Leif Edvinsson, Professor of Intellectual Capital at the University of Lund in Sweden, who is regarded as the world's first 'Chief Knowledge Officer'[108] when he was hired by Swedish insurance company Skandia in 1991. In his book *National Intellectual Capital: A Comparison of 40 Countries*,[109] Edvinsson and Carol Yeh-Yun Lin illustrate the connection between GDP and growth with intellectual capital.

Building up knowledge, of course, starts in school. The Nordic countries have spent a great deal of time and money on improving teaching methods and testing new ways of learning and with great success. We should try to expand such efforts in the European Union as a whole. Looking at universities, we have to admit that the US still has a massive lead over Europe when it comes to attracting the world's best minds to their world-renowned universities. On the East Coast, Harvard and the Massachusetts Institute of Technology (MIT) turned the area around Boston into the prime research hub, with many more universities and laboratories springing up. On the West Coast, Stanford University has played a major part in drawing talent to the region and shaping Silicon Valley. Today, more than a quarter of all American innovations stem from these two regions.

This should show Europeans how important cluster building is. It is one of the best ways towards 'knowledge navigation', as coined by Edvinsson. Europe, of course, has some positive results to show with its own knowledge clusters – on the research side. The Geneva-based European Organization for Nuclear Research, CERN, was set up in the 1950s to operate the largest particle accelerator in the world. As it turned out, the stimulating environment of the site led to many more impressive operations and inventions. In fact, the proposal for the World Wide Web was filed there. Inventing the Web as a kind of 'by-product' is amazing, by any standards.

This shows us just how important research projects with a highly ambitious mission can become for a region. Europe's decision to build its own global navigation satellite system, Galileo,[110] is regularly criticized for its cost. In our opinion, it was the right move and has already brought Europe a number of benefits, which can be seen in the aeronautical industry, for example. In fact, we recommend that Europe start more flagship research projects – projects that try to turn long-held visions of mankind into reality.

Launching new initiatives in education and research is vital for Europe if it is to not lose the war for talent that they are fighting against the States and Asia too. China is already massively expanding the infrastructure and funding of its universities and R&D centres, to make sure that they will reach clearly defined strategic targets.[111] Other countries in the Far East do the same.

How can we find out if Europe is successful on this front? We suggest taking the Nobel Prize as the benchmark. By 2020, Europe should be able to count more laureates each year than any other region, 20 per cent more than the US. Of course, this would be a symbolic benchmark, but its target is clear and easy to communicate. How well the Nobel Prize works as an index for the strength of an economy can be illustrated with an analysis of the performance of the US over the decades. Until 1949, only 41 winners came from America. It took five decades to reach this number, but less than 15 years to double it. In the 1980s, 47 US researchers and authors were awarded the prize. Between 2000 and 2010, this figure had catapulted and 73 of the winners during this period were US passports holders.[112]

Europe is still in the lead in the history of the Nobel Prize, but this is largely due to the fact that the 'old continent' has remained the best performer in the categories of literature and peace. Currently, in chemistry, physics and medicine, the number of laureates coming from the US and the EU is balanced, with Europe benefiting from the advantages built up before the Second World War. In economic sciences, however, the United States clearly dominates – with 43 winners from the US but only 16 from Europe, with half of these being British.

In the future, the Nobel Prize winners will no longer be divided between research institutions on either side of the Atlantic, as was the case, by and large, until the 1960s. Instead, the number of winners coming from other continents will increase significantly. This means that Europe will not only compete with the US in the annual race for Nobel Prizes, but they will also butt up against other regions and states, most notably China and India. Looking at the time, energy and money these two countries currently invest in education and research, we had better be prepared for future races against them.

Europe Direct – bringing the EU's achievements and ambitions closer to the people

We are certain that there are many more initiatives Europe could take. When a wholesaler of fruit and vegetables based in Munich told us that the vast majority of citrus fruits, tomatoes, cucumbers, olives and other products from Portugal, Spain, Italy, Greece and other EU member states in Southern Europe are transported by truck to Central and Northern Europe, we wondered why. 'It would take far too long to transport them by train', he replied. We took a look at the statistics and found that road transport had increased in almost every EU member states relative to rail transport in the last 10 years (excluding Austria, Sweden and the Baltic countries). It is now about four times as high as

the volume transported by rail. In fact, the percentage of goods transported by rail in Europe is much lower than it is in the United States.
For a continent that is proud of both its railway tradition as well as its
environmental consciousness, this ought not to be the case. It seemed
like another field in which we should start an initiative. Yet we found
out quickly that the European Commission had looked into this issue
years ago and proposed many measures to improve interoperability of
the national rail systems in terms of rolling stock, tracks and signalling.
In fact, it created its own unit to work on these issues: the European
Railway Agency was set up in 2004 and started in full operation in mid-
2006. Is it still too early to see the fruits the agency's efforts have borne?

The fact that we, two very passionate Europeans with a broad interest
spectrum, did not know anything about this issue made us wonder
whether the topic had been communicated poorly. And this brought us
to a much wider issue: the challenge of telling and selling the accomplishments of European integration. Explaining to Europe's citizens
where and how the European Union has improved their lives has turned
out to be one of the most difficult tasks of the European project. In
fact, it is the most difficult task of all. On panels and discussions, pro-
Europeans often refer to statistics in this respect. They come up with
figures showing GDP growth or illustrating that the euro brought even
more price stability than the Deutschemark, so much cherished by sen-
timental Germans. On a macro-economic level, these figures might well
prove the power of the European Union as a wealth creator. The problem is: for 'ordinary' people, they do not mean a great deal. Instead,
there is a tendency to withdraw to pseudo-sentimental feelings and
claim that things were so much better in the past – before the introduction of the common market, before the euro, before the 'dictates' of
Brussels. This tendency, of course, is encouraged by euro-bashing populists who tend to be quite savvy in bringing up examples of how
decadent and absurd the EU is. All too frequently, passionate

171

Europeans have too little on offer to counter these populist criticisms in a way that is easily understood by everyone. What is needed is to break down Europe's macro-economic achievements into memorable storytelling: examples of 'real' people who have benefited from the European Union in a clear and undisputable way.

We need to be able to hear the stories of real people like an engineer from Spain who could not find a job at home and moved to Germany to work for an engine builder whose head of personnel was desperately looking for new talent. Or the story of a young Belgian businessman taking over the struggling family enterprise, and seizing the moment when the export barriers to other EU member states fell and set up a subsidiary in Italy that soon started to blossom.

Do such stories exist? Well, we should stop asking ourselves if they do and start looking for them. One thing is for sure: the persuasiveness of such testimonials is enormous – and such stories can be very inspiring. Take a real case – the case of Claudia and Siegfried Zeller. Born and raised in small villages in Upper Austria, they moved to Southern France in 2007 when Siegfried was asked by his Austrian employer to run a subsidiary in Pau, a factory that produces and distributes plastic bottles. Claudia had studied law in Austria and decided to study French for a year when they moved. She was subsequently offered a job in France. In 2010, Siegfried was given the chance to run another production unit of his Austrian employer in Rastatt, Germany. Since Rastatt is very close to the French border, the young couple decided to look for a house in Alsace and settled in Seltz. Now they belong to the group of daily cross-border commuters, with the difference that none of the two countries they cross is their country of origin. In 2011, they had a baby – a truly pan-European offspring. Without the European Union, such a career and family path would have been very difficult, if not impossible.

We need more such stories with 'real' people – and we must tell them authoritatively, covering every aspect. Too often in the past, the

European authorities have reported their success stories without any real personal touch. Take the example of a special edition of the European Commission's *Single Market News* celebrating the 15th anniversary of the EU's single market. The 2007 edition is laden with figures and statistics, but it lacks the kind of stories that citizens relate to. The abolishment of the old customs barriers for goods is mentioned, it 'did away with 60 million tax forms per year', and almost appears as if the authors took it for granted that everybody would see this as a success story. Sure, it indicates that a lot of paperwork was eliminated. But who profited from it and in what way? Was it really impossible to find the owner of a small export-oriented enterprise and get him to reveal how much money he saved or how much it spurred exports, maybe allowing him to hire an additional employee?

One of the most personal stories in the magazine is written by MEP Malcolm Harbour, who candidly outlines his professional transformation from a guy working in the car industry to a representative in the European Parliament. In his piece,[113] he mentions how the 'cost and waste incurred' by different technical rules in Europe made a strong impression on him. He refers to the old French regulation that required cars sold in France to have yellow head lamps and asks, 'What were the special characteristics of French roads that made this unusual legal demand so jealously guarded?' We do not doubt for a second that getting rid of this rule as part of European integration helps Europe's car manufactures save money and, hopefully, lets them put their freed energy into something more productive than planning and accounting for a 'special' French head-light model. Yet we should not forget the romantics out there who fondly remember the 'glory days' when the headlights that illuminated the streets of France shone yellow instead of white. To counter such romanticism effectively, we need, for example, the personal story of a representative of a French car brand outside France who remembers how much easier his job became after this rule

173

came to an end and how many more Peugeots or Renaults he sold as a consequence.

Such stories could contribute to the idea that Europe's citizens discover opportunities or advantages for themselves in the harmonized single market, instead of regarding the development as threatening.

The European authorities have already made efforts to bring the EU closer to its citizens. The European Commission has started the Your Europe portal to give 'individuals and businesses practical information on their rights and opportunities in the EU'. Yet on closer inspection we find that it is not very customer- and, thus, citizen-friendly. Why is this portal only hosted on the impossible to remember URL http://ec.europa. eu/youreurope and not on www.youreurope.org? Why does the starting page only show shadowy illustrations of a family and business people instead of photos of 'real' people, which would convey much more warmth and emotion. And did anyone ever check how many young people who wanted to work in a different EU member state give up in despair when they came to the 'regulated professions database' on the site? However, we also detected elements on the portal which we thought were very well done. Under the section 'Qualifications for Employment', we were immediately drawn to a picture of a young woman with the caption 'This could be you'. Below the picture there is more information introducing Katarina from Slovakia. She is a pharmacist who would like to work in Austria. She apparently faced the problem that the Austrian authorities had asked her for translations of all documents accompanying her applications, and this was to be done by a certified Austrian translator. The passage did not spell out the further implications of the problem – and rightly so, because they are obvious: translating all her certificates costs time and money. The heading 'Solution', explains says that Katarina did not have to provide such translations, stating: 'The authorities aren't allowed to require certified translations of qualifications for doctors, general nurses, midwives, vets, dental surgeons, pharmacists or architects.'

We think that this website is very well done. It explains an issue and an opportunity in an easy to understand way. The 'official' Europe needs more of this type of communication.

Of course, we do not know whether Katarina really exists. And we presume it would be very difficult for a civil servant based in Brussels and responsible for this section of the site to find such a person. This is why we suggest a 'Europe Direct' initiative with the aim of setting up a direct link between the European Union's officials and its citizens. Such an initiative could start with tours made by EU representatives or civil servants through the many towns and villages of the union. They should ask the respective community administrations to give them specific examples of inhabitants who benefited or suffered in a specific way by European integration. They should stand on market places and engage people passing by in conversations. In those cases where Members of the European Parliament already have concrete examples of this kind from their constituencies, they should be encouraged to report them – to a special task force responsible for setting up Europe Direct.

Once a sufficient number of stories and examples are accumulated, they should form the basis of a testimonial campaign. New media, including social media, could play a pivotal role in such a campaign, as they provide the best way to gain direct reactions and, ideally, many other positive examples. On top of that, the European Union's vision for its future has to be much better communicated. The targets and growth strategy outlined in *Europe 2020*[114] is both inspiring for its citizens and anticipates the global challenges that lie ahead – yet the way they have been communicated is dull and technical. No wonder they haven't resonated among the people of Europe.

To be fair, communicating the numerous topics in an appealing and easily accessible style is a challenge. One way to overcome the challenge is to split the overall strategy into three different building blocks:

- **Sustainable Europe** – a role model for a resource-efficient and responsible growth.
- **Social Europe** – a healthy environment for social security and individual opportunities.
- **Open Europe** – the path for a free, tolerant and democratic society.

Each of these building blocks reflects specific European values and principles. Sustainable Europe entails the message that Europe is well aware that the 'carbon economy' is coming to an end, much more so than the United States or Asia. Europe neither denies nor ignores the fact that massive capacity shortages and climate issues are related to a global economy built on fossil fuels. It has seriously considered the massive implications these problems entail, since pretty much every major industrial product introduced in the twentieth century depended on oil or gas – not only cars and other means of transport, but also textiles, drugs, food, plastic products, to name but a few. Europe is keen to face these challenges head on and without leaving the growth path: with renewable energy, smart grids and ways of construction that ultimately turn ever building into an energy generator and storage facility. Sustainable Europe is also prepared to take action against financial markets going wild, as many of the meandering investment products have turned into beasts which bring no benefits but much harm to the real economy.

Social Europe fights for truly open labour markets and against youth unemployment. Excellent education, equal opportunities, tolerance and solidarity, as well as reforms and better co-ordination of social security systems and health care are the tools to win the fight against unemployment. Open Europe is the avid advocate for the protection of minorities and a bulwark for religious and cultural tolerance. It will not tolerate anti-democratic tendencies among its members or threats to curb the freedom or independence of the justice system.

Splitting the EU's strategy and vision into three different strands of communication allows for clearer messages, tailored for different audiences and events. Of course, the task of making them 'catchy' remains, as even these building blocks will only penetrate the hearts of the European citizens when they follow the rules of storytelling – stories that comprise 'real' people and real projects able to spark people's imaginations.

We are convinced that European integration has already brought major benefits to millions upon millions of European households. We are also confident that it is the best foundation for the generations to come. However, in order to fully awaken a truly European spirit on a broad level, we have to start turning macro-economic logic into messages that inspire and enthuse its citizens. Once we succeed on this front, we can rest assured that Europe will live up to its potential – and become a leading player in the global orchestra of the twenty-first century.

Conclusion

The title of our book suggests that Europe has a potential that has been neither fully recognized nor used. The best way to bring such hidden potential forward is to come up with a solid explanation of where the strong elements lie (i.e. the analysis, appealing to logic) as well as what could be achieved with them (i.e. the vision, appealing to emotions).

We firmly believe that the 'old continent' can turn into a new united European powerhouse if the right steps are taken. The first step, of course, is to convince others. This is never an easy task. Just think of the scene in the movie *Lawrence of Arabia* when Peter O'Toole as Lawrence arrives at the Howeitat tribe after he has crossed the hitherto thought to be impassable Nefud Desert. In the tent of the powerful leader of the Arabian Howeitat tribe, Auda abu Tayi, he tries to persuade him to join forces with him and the Harith, also an Arabian tribe, and fight against the Turkish occupiers in the port city of Aqaba, on the Arabian Peninsula. When Lawrence mentions that this is meant to be a mission 'for the Arabs', Auda abu Tayi (played magnificently by Anthony Quinn) cynically replies, 'The Howeitat, Ageyil, Ruala, Beni Sahkr, these I know. I have even heard of the Harith. But the Arabs? What tribe is that?'

The tribal leader refused to acknowledge the big picture, because he simply did not see the benefits for himself. He finally joined forces with Lawrence, but his motivation had less to do with a unifying mission than with self-interest, pride and gold. If the leaders of the European nations in the twenty-first century act in the same fashion, we will have to walk on a stony path to turn our vision into reality. On the other hand, we accept and even welcome a thorough questioning of the European project, as constantly testing means and motivations is the only way to avoid a grand vision turning into wretched illusion. To illustrate the danger of not doing so, we have a joke for you: Stalin, Khrushchev and Brezhnev are travelling together by train when the train suddenly stops. After a while, it still hasn't moved. Stalin shouts, 'Give the engine driver a good whipping!' His order is carried out, but the train doesn't get going. So Khrushchev then shouts, 'Rehabilitate the engine driver!' That, too, is done, but the train still fails to move. Finally Brezhnev announces, 'Dear friends, let us simply assume that the train is running.'

We do not want to assume or pretend that the European project is currently running very well. It is not. Yet the ongoing political bickering and public warnings of a break-up do not necessarily have to end up in a doomsday scenario. Instead, they might lead the European countries to move even closer to each other, for the benefit of all. Given the prevailing sentiment of the European Union as a 'talking shop' run by over-bloated bureaucrats and a 'fight club' for politicians driven by national interest, it is currently quite easy to be sceptical about any positive predictions for Europe, particularly in the years after the sovereign debt crisis had befallen the 'old continent'. From this crisis it has become painfully obvious that the euro was not built on solid foundations – one of the rare occasions when the European Union has ignored the path of deep and thorough consensus building.

On a superficial level one can put forward many reasons to argue against the emergence of a European identity and a unified Europe: the many different languages, traditions, cultures, political evolutions, social models and historical experiences, to name but a few. None of these objections are wrong, of course, yet they are irrelevant since Europe has the right foundations to build upon. The main purpose of this book was to show that there are indeed such foundations, first and foremost, on an economic level and on a political level too. This brings us back to the analytical parts of our book.

Europe's culture of skilled craftsmanship exists in a great variety of different intensities in the EU member states, but it is a phenomenon that is not restricted to single countries such as Germany or regions such as the Nordic states. It is a common denominator, which distinguishes our continent and is a very important criterion for our economic future. The top position of European countries in the rankings of the Global Competitiveness Report, published by the World Economic Forum, and their continuous improvement during the first decade of the twenty-first century are clear indications that we are heading in the right direction. It also shows that our region has the right ingredients to take a leadership role in the global economy of this century – this time not with a British, French, German, Italian or Spanish economy leading the pack, as was the case in the centuries before, but with one unified European economy.

Our ability to maintain and transform our industrial legacy into a new era will turn out to be of vital importance for our future. This is to our particular benefit in the field of green technology, an area that will massively transform the way we live and work, from the construction of buildings to new methods of generating, storing and dispersing energy. It is an area of industry, which above all, will create millions of new jobs. This is particularly encouraging for young Europeans who currently suffer from high unemployment rates and some must feel as if they belong to a generation with no future.

But there is a future for young Europeans and it will be a prosperous and fulfilling one, too, as long as Europe continues to cultivate its culture of craftsmanship and uses it to build a green economy based on renewable energies. The strong focus on sustainable growth in its targets for 2020 shows that the European Union has fully grasped what is at stake. No other region has better understood that the days of the carbon economy are numbered – an economy which has dominated the whole of the twentieth century and which has brought us not only material wealth and a plethora of new products – from cars and processed foods to plastic and synthetic textiles – but also wars, natural disasters and climate change.

So far, there is still much neglect around the globe about the dawn of the carbon economy, especially in the United States, but also in the emerging economies. 'The European Union is virtually alone among the governments of the world in asking the big questions about our future viability as a species on earth', states the American economist, activist and political advisor Jeremy Rifkin in his book *The Third Industrial Revolution*.[115]

If Europe sticks to its path, it will be able to rise to the occasion when fossil fuels are no longer affordable, both economically and environmentally. From then on, it will serve as a role model for many other regions in the world, including the US and China.

As Europe never fully converted to a US-style trading culture, it did not subscribe to the rules of stock markets, hedge funds and financial products as unconditionally as America. This might sound like an odd thing to claim, given the massive troubles the eurozone has experienced in the last two years. Admittedly, many European banks have fallen for the temptations of financial speculation, and many European states have indulged in a debt load that suddenly could no longer be met without colossal budget cutbacks or outside help. Nonetheless, there is still a difference between causing the excesses of the financial markets and falling victim to them.

For the time being, some continental European countries seem to be the only ones that are serious about curbing and cutting back these excesses, starting with their bans on short selling, to the suggestion of a financial transaction tax. We are aware that Europe is still far from succeeding on this front and that fixing this issue needs a globally concerted effort. However, the fact that the EU has a healthier social structure than America's or Asia's enables our continent to be more determined to put a halt to dubious financial products. A culture of skilled craftsmanship is particularly allergic to financial machinations that threaten or even harm the health of the real economy.

Europe's culture of consensus is its second asset to distinguish our continent. In order to successfully navigate through the complexities of a globalized economy, one has to have the ability to fully absorb the positions of both partners and people on the other side of the table, including their backgrounds and ways of thinking. Many European business people and political leaders have learned to deal with diversity in a productive way. They have had to. Irrespective of how exhausting or even frustrating consensus seeking sometimes is, Europeans understand that it is still the best way to go. They have internalized that it is almost always better to sit down than to walk away. They know that compromise is about reaching out, sharing – not taking away. To most Europeans, negotiations are not a round of poker but a game of chess that, among good players, often takes time and ends in a position where there are no losers. The higher the degree of sophistication, the more satisfying such a process can be – and the deeper the respect for the counterparts.

The history of the European Union has shown that such a consensual approach does not lead to inertia but brings about very sustainable results. Yes, there have been occasions when the European project has made a few bad moves. Nonetheless, in the long term, it has moved forward and maintained a positive direction – three steps forward, one step back perhaps – but not the reverse. It is particularly encouraging that Europe's culture of consensus has not been confined to the political arena, but it can also be seen in the way successful European companies are run. The European leadership style is based on respect and trust for colleagues, not hire and fire. The notion that you need some sort of superman at the top of a company who can centrally execute a strategy and quickly turn his own vision into reality might be typical for the US, but certainly not for Europe. At the height of the finance bubble, European companies were often criticized for their collaborative management and their accounting based on the principles of prudence. Today, we know how important these things are in order to stay competitive. The European way of management is something we can be proud of. It might turn into an export model. Before we get too proud, however, we should not forget that Europe has a long way to go to fully reach its potential. Our culture of skilled craftsmanship and consensus are valuable cornerstones for the construction of a European house, but they are – as cornerstones tend to be – a hard sell. This means that European leaders have to continue their building efforts, so we can soon reveal the good foundations and solid walls. Our suggestions for new initiatives are meant as guidance in this respect.

To us, the most important thing is to bring the European project closer to its citizens. As long as millions of our continent's inhabitants regard the EU merely as a distant, technical and bureaucratic affair, we will not succeed in building a unified Europe. We should no longer try to 'sell' the achievements of the European Union with statistical data that often means nothing to ordinary people. The opposite is true: these statistics are increasingly met with scepticism, as they are regularly spoilt by anecdotal 'counter-evidence' too-cleverly presented by so-called populists.

Unfortunately, the media plays a big role in amplifying the empty calls of such populists and euro-sceptics. Yet instead of waiting until the mass media changes its ways of reporting, we had better roll up our sleeves and learn to translate complicated macro-economic achievements into stories that touch the hearts of people. This does not mean that Europe should go in for populist propaganda. It means that we have to better master the art of storytelling. In fact, if you have a story to tell, we would be very glad if you would share it with us and send us an email to info@europeshiddenpotenital.com. The same, of course, applies to any other feedback.

If this book has contributed just a few memorable episodes in this respect, we have achieved what we hoped for. One thing is certain: while each of our arguments has to withstand all types of critical questioning, the outcome of our message is not just a rational affair to us but an emotional one, too. We really cherish the European way – and hope that it will lead to a prosperous future.

Notes

1 *The Economist*, July 21, 2012; http://www.economist.com/node/21559387

2 'Eurotrashed', *New York Times*, January 16, 2011; http://www.nytimes.com/2011/01/16/magazine/16Europe-t.html?pagewanted=all

3 'The death of the European dream', *Financial Times*, May 17, 2010; http://www.ft.com/intl/cms/s/0/f7997862-61e2-11df-998c-00144feab49a.html#axzz207U7Ho76

4 'L'union monétaire au bord de la crise de nerfs', *Le Monde*, November 19, 2010; http://www.lemonde.fr/idees/article/2010/11/18/l-union-monetaire-au-bord-de-la-crise-de-nerfs_1441792_3232.html

5 'Europa brennt', *Der Spiegel*, December 6, 2010; http://www.spiegel.de/spiegel/print/d-75476908.html

6 Roland Berger Strategy Consultants. *Europa führt!*, trs: Europe Leads! (Cologne: Bruno Media, 2011). The book was part of a series called 're:think CEO'.

7 He said this during a meeting with a delegation of European Finance Ministers in 1971 in Washington, D.C.; http://en.wikipedia.org/wiki/John_Connally

8 Take the role of IKB, a Düsseldorf-based bank whose main activity is lending to SMEs, buying certificates of a mortgage-backed collateralized debt obligation (CDO) called Abacus (Abacus 2007-AC1, to be precise). It was created by Goldman Sachs and 'structured', i.e. composed of a hierarchy of bonds. IKB bought notes for $150m which, despite their triple-A rating, were nearly worthless within a few months at the end of 2007. It was the only case where the Securities and Exchange Commission (SEC) started an investigation against Goldman Sachs (http://www.sec.gov/news/press/2010/2010-59.htm). The SEC accused Goldman of having been well aware that the underlying mortgages in Abacus were of poor quality and had therefore double-crossed its investors, since it knew that the hedge fund manager John Paulson bet against Abacus by 'shortening' it. The case was settled in July 2010 with Goldman paying a $550m fine and allowing the bank to declare that it had done nothing wrong.

9 'The banker the credit crisis couldn't touch', *Independent*, July 27, 2008.

10 The tax was introduced as a 'one-off' measure in December 2009 by the then governing Labour Party and brought about £3bn in revenues. The

subsequent coalition between the Conservatives and Liberal Democrats has not made it permanent by mid-2012, but the topic is a regular in the political discussion.

[11] News about legislation being worked on in this respect was first reported in January 2012. See, for example: http://www.dailymail.co.uk/news/article-2083684/Greedy-bankers-face-prison-Chancellor-prepares-new-law-target-reckless-bosses.html

[12] At that time, Sweden held the rotating presidency of the EU.

[13] 'EU unites behind call for bank bonus cap', *Financial Times*, September 2, 2009; http://www.ft.com/intl/cms/s/0/bb763cc8-97a1-11de-a927-00144feabdc0.html

[14] Most of the heads of US 'mortgage banks', such as New Century, Ameriquest, Golden West Financial or Countrywide were not held accountable for their management after their institutions collapsed. In the few cases where this happened, such as with Kerry Killinger of Washington Mutual (who was sued by the Federal Deposit Insurance Corporation, a government agency, for taking excessive risks for purposes of short-term personal enrichment), the settlement ($64m instead of the claimed $900m) was almost completely covered by insurance and did not require Killinger to admit any guilt. The CEOs of failed US banks which played a decisive role in the securitization of mortgages, such as Lehman's Richard Fuld or Stan O'Neal of Merrill Lynch also never had to deal with prosecutions. While these facts may well suggest their innocence in a legal context or indicate the difficulties of subsuming the activities of financial institutions under specific offences, critics argue that it was also challenging to overcome legal technicalities when it came to holding key people to account during the New Economy bubble or the collapse of Enron. However, in those cases many prominent figures were prosecuted and jailed.

[15] The US Treasury Department appointed lawyer Ken Feinberg in June 2009 to look into executive pay at companies that had received 'exceptional assistance' from the government during and after the financial crises. While his report states that the major banks benefiting from governmental bailouts – a total of 17 including Bank of America and Wells Fargo – had paid a total of $1.6bn in 'inappropriate' compensation, he did very little to reclaim any of that money, sparking criticism by the Congressional Oversight Panel.

[16] 'In my view, derivatives are financial weapons of mass destruction, carrying dangers that, while now latent, are potentially lethal', Berkshire Hathaway, Annual Report 2002.

17 Ferguson, Charles, *Predator Nation* (New York: Crown, 2012).

18 Rappaport, Alfred, Creating Shareholder Value: A Guide for Managers and Investors, (New York: The Free Press, 1999).

19 'Welch condemns share price focus', *Financial Times*, March 12, 2009; http://www.ft.com/intl/cms/s/0/294ff1f2-0f27-11de-ba10-0000779fd2ac.html

20 The Global Leadership and Organizational Behaviour Effectiveness Research Project (GLOBE) was founded in 1993 as a group of international social scientists and management scholars who study cross-cultural leadership. For details: http://en.wikipedia.org/wiki/Global_Leadership_and_Organizational_Behavior_Effectiveness_Research_Project

21 The investment sum was announced in January 2012 for the full year. The majority of the investments were taken by Samsung Electronics, the biggest subsidiary of the group.

22 China Association of Automobile Manufacturers; http://www.caam.org.cn/AutomotivesStatistics/20120113/1505067050.html

23 Roland Berger Strategy Consultants, *Trend Compendium 2030*, 2nd ed (Roland Berger: Munich, 2011); http://www.rolandberger.com/expertise/trend_compendium_2030/.

24 IMF: World Economic Outlook 4/2012.

25 http://europa.eu/about-eu/facts-figures/living/index_en.htm

26 Even the EU's citizens tend to believe that Europe is not advancing fast enough. In the regular polls conducted as part of the Eurobarometer surveys, there tends to be a gap between the perceived and desired speed of the European Community and European unification. You can find more details on these results at the interactive search system (http://ec.europa.eu/public_opinion/cf/step1.cfm) under the questions 'Eurodynamometer – current speed' and 'Eurodynanometer – desired speed'.

27 For example, compare the geographical revenue spread of these companies.

28 Best Global Brands 2011: http://www.interbrand.com/de/best-global-brands/best-global-brands-2008/best-global-brands-2011.aspx

29 http://www.interbrand.com/de/best-global-brands/best-global-brands-methodology/Overview.aspx

30 http://reports.weforum.org/global-competitiveness-2011-2012

31 http://reports.weforum.org/global-competitiveness-2011-2012

32 http://discover-elbphilharmonie-hamburg.com/en/

33 http://www.hamburg-fotos-bilder.de/2010/05/elbphilharmonie-hamburg.html

34 http://www.sunglass.it

35 Among them Factiva, LexisNexis and G+J Pressedatenbank.

36 'Murano's fragile future' (*Muranos zerbrechliche Zukunft*), *Die Welt am Sonntag*, November 8, 2009; http://www.welt.de/welt_print/wirtschaft/ article5125454/Muranos-zerbrechliche-Zukunft.html

37 For details, look at their website under the section, 'brands': http://www. formiaglass.it

38 http://www.luxottica.com/en/

39 http://www.safilo.com/

40 'Un pays sans industries est un pays sans avenir', Jean-Marc Ayrault, July 3, 2012, L'Assemblée National, Paris.

41 http://www.miba.com

42 http://www.gamesacorp.com

43 http://www.itpgroup.co.uk

44 http://www.pandasecurity.com

45 http://www.vision-box.com

46 http://www.surfaceslab.com/home/

47 You can find the figures in the *Bundesanzeiger*, Germany's register where limited companies have to publish their annual figures. Website: www. bundesanzeiger.de, company name: Horst Brandstätter Holding GmbH. See also the press release on Playmobil's website: http://www.playmobil.de/on/ demandware.store/Sites-GB-Site/en_GB/Link-Page?cid=FACTS2011

48 http://files.shareholder.com/downloads/ MAT/1982708023x0x555821/3C654248-30D8-4A8D-A8FC- 53A89560A3C3/2011_Mattel_Annual_Report.pdf, page 25

49 The issue became public on August 1, 2007 when Mattel-owned Fisher-Price announced that it would recall 83 types of toys produced in China, totalling almost a million units, due to lead paint contamination. During the course of the summer, Mattel had to announce more recalls and ended up recalling over 20 million units: (See, for example: 'Scandal and Suicide in China: A Dark Side of Toys', *New York Times*, August 23, 2007; http://www.nytimes. com/2007/08/23/business/worldbusiness/23suicide.html?_ r=1&pagewanted=all)

50 Eckert made this comment on October 25, 2007, when he announced a 'three-point check system' which, among other things, would require every vendor, contractor and paint storage facility to be tested before the manufacturing process begins. Read, for example: 'Mattel chief lays out plan for toy testing', *MSNBC*, October 24, 2007; http://www.msnbc.msn.com/id/21462674/ns/business-consumer_news/t/mattel-chief-lays-out-plan-toy-testing/#.T_wEn-3N2y0

51 During an interview with *Der Spiegel* on December 12, 2009; the English version of the interview can be found under: http://www.spiegel.de/international/business/interview-with-us-economic-recovery-advisory-board-chair-paul-volcker-america-must-reassert-stability-and-leadership-a-666757.html

52 http://www.think-act.com/en/book/green-growth-green-profit.html

53 Q-Cells and Solar Millennium in Europe as well as Solyndra and Uni Solar/Energy Conversion Devices in the US all filed for insolvency between mid-2011 and mid-2012.

54 'U.S. Imposes Anti-Dumping Duties on Chinese Solar Imports', May 17, 2012, *Bloomberg*; http://www.bloomberg.com/news/2012-05-17/u-s-imposes-anti-dumping-duties-for-chinese-solar-imports.html

55 Spanish companies, with Gameza being the biggest one, have managed to gain very strong positions in wind energy, while German and Austrian green technology enterprises prosper by the fact that both countries want to become renewable energy economies. While Germany's 'mainstream' solar panel producers have suffered a great deal through Chinese competition, more specialized technology providers, such as SMA Solar, and project developers, such as Wirsol or IBC Solar, still prosper.

56 Based on United Nations Data, the share of manufacturing in the GDP declined from 24.3 per cent in 1970 to 12.8 per cent in 2010 in the US.

57 http://www.bbc.co.uk/news/science-environment-15756113

58 January 5, 2012

59 Indications for this claim range from the UK's veto to the so-called 'fiscal compact' in December 2011, to announcements to 'audit' Brussels' competences, wishes to renegotiate the terms of EU membership as well as an increasing political desire for an in-out referendum.

60 Saint-Simon, Henri (1814), *De la réorganisation de la société européenne,* trs: On the re-organisation of European society (BiblioBazar, 2008).

61 In 1871.

62 There is actually a fourth official language, Rhaeto-Romanic.

63 http://ec.europa.eu/public_opinion/archives/eb/eb75/eb75_anx_full_fr.pdf

64 'Ukip's Nigel Farage tells Van Rompuy: You have the charisma of a damp rag', story and video, *The Guardian*, February 25, 2010; http://www.guardian.co.uk/world/2010/feb/25/nigel-farage-herman-van-rompuy-damp-rag

65 'Van Rompuy yet to establish himself as a dynamic political force', *Irish Times*, March 2, 2010; http://www.irishtimes.com/newspaper/world/2010/0302/1224265432742.html

66 During these years, the question was part of the bi-annually conducted Eurobarometer polls. For more details, check the database of the European Union's public opinion site; http://ec.europa.eu/public_opinion/archives/eb_arch_en.htm

67 Various executives of both Daimler and Chrysler stated this problem as the main reason why the merger ultimately failed, when asked by the authors in off-the-record conversations. Asked why, they mentioned that engineers in Germany simply did not see the benefits of sharing their knowledge with their US counterparts, because they thought that an exchange would be too one-sided. It then turned out that efforts to 'force' more co-operation, did not work, at least not in a wide range of areas. The problem of a lack of co-operation on this level can also sometimes be found in media stories. A broad overview of many issues surrounding the trans-atlantic merger can be read in a long feature published by the German magazine *Der Spiegel* ('Die Drei-Welten-AG', *Der Spiegel*, 24 February, 2012; http://www.spiegel.de/spiegel/print/d-18578729.html). Interestingly, the second attempt at a transatlantic 'automobile wedding' – this time it was Chrysler and Fiat who were getting 'married'– seems to portray a swapping of roles: now, it is more the managers in the US and Canada who increasingly regard the Italian plants as a 'drag' – CEO Sergio Marchionne has been quite outspoken about this. However, this time the core of the problem has less to do with the lack of engineering qualities in Italy but with too rigid employment laws and union agreements and a model, marketing and distribution policy which has focused too long on Italy and Europe instead of spreading to other parts of the world.

68 'The Five Minds of a Manager', *Harvard Business Review*, November 2003; http://hbr.org/2003/11/the-five-minds-of-a-manager/ar/1

69 http://www.handelsblatt.com/unternehmen/mittelstand/bosch-boss-

fehrenbach-fuer-den-titel-weltmarktfuehrer-koennen-sie-sich-nichts-kaufen-seite-3/3573824-3.html

70 http://www.bertelsmann.com/bertelsmann_corp/wms41/customers/bmir/pdf/PressRelease2009_engl.pdf

71 http://www.serco.com

72 http://www.mulliez-flory.fr/vetement-professionnel/groupe-mulliez.aspx

73 http://www.gamesacorp.com/en/gamesaen/

74 *The New York Times Magazine*, September 13, 1970.

75 The company terminated its contracts with Moody's and Standard & Poor's in October 2010 and has not been rated by an agency since then. Despite the lack of a rating, it still managed to place bonds worth a three-digit million figure by mid-2012.

76 Porsche gained this 'title' in 1998, five years after Wiedeking took the helm. The company delivered the highest profit margins year on year, not just until the end of Wiedeking's reign as CEO in 2009 but until the time this book was published. As an example for the reports in 2012, see: http://www.handelsblatt.com/unternehmen/industrie/sportwagenhersteller-der-profitabelste-autobauer-der-welt-heisst-porsche/6320746.html

77 'Deutsche Börse May Drop Porsche From MDAX Index, Luxury-Car Maker Refuses To Report Quarterly Results', June 5, 2001, *The Wall Street Journal* Europe.

78 The study on long-term growth rates are conducted every year; the latest publication is explained here: http://www.schwab.com/public/schwab/resource_center/expert_insight/investing_strategies/portfolio_planning/qa_estimating_long_term_market_returns.html

79 Louis L. Goldberg and Justine Lee. *Board Leadership Structure*; http://www.conference-board.org/retrievefile.cfm?filename=DN-011-10.pdf&type=subsite

80 Eurobarometer, February 2001. The data is also mentioned on page 12 of the 'Final Report of the High Level Task Force on Skills and Mobility', published on December 14, 2001.

81 Krueger, Alan B., 'From Bismarck to Maastricht: The March to European Union and the Labour Compact', *Labour Economics*, 7, (2000), 117—134; http://elmu.umm.ac.id/file.php/1/jurnal/L/Labour%2520Economics/Vol7.Issue2.Mar2000/193.pdf

82 'The Erasmus programme – studying in Europe and more', information on the Erasmus programme is provided by the European Commission; http://ec.europa.eu/education/lifelong-learning-programme/doc80_en.htm

83 Parey, Matthias and Fabian Waldinger, 'Studying Abroad and the Effect on International Labour Market Mobility: Evidence from the Introduction of ERASMUS', Discussion Paper No. 3430, (Institute for the Study of Labor, 2008); http://ftp.iza.org/dp3430.pdf

84 'Mobility in Europe', analysis of the 2005 Eurobarometer survey on geographical and labour market mobility; http://www.eurofound.europa.eu/pubdocs/2006/59/en/1/ef0659en.pdf

85 'Youth on the move', analytical report, Eurobarometer 319b, The Gallup Organization, fieldwork done in January 2011, published in May 2011; http://ec.europa.eu/public_opinion/flash/fl_319b_en.pdf

86 See the regulated professions database; http://ec.europa.eu/internal_market/qualifications/regprof/index.cfm?fuseaction=regProf.index&lang=de. In August 2012, the exact number was 4,809.

87 Directive 2005/36/EC. The directive on the recognition of professional qualifications was approved on September 7, 2005 by the European Parliament and Council; http://eur-lex.europa.eu/LexUriServ/LexUriServ.do?uri=OJ:L:2005:255:0022:0142:en:PDF

88 Directive 206/123/EC. The directive was approved on December 12, 2006 by the European Parliament and Council; http://eur-lex.europa.eu/LexUriServ/LexUriServ.do?uri=OJ:L:2006:376:0036:0068:EN:PDF

89 'Modernising the Professional Qualifications Directive', European Commission Green Paper, published on June 22, 2011; http://eur-lex.europa.eu/LexUriServ/LexUriServ.do?uri=COM:2011:0367:FIN:en:PDF

90 Ibid. This quote is from section 2.1, page 4 of the Green Paper.

91 Input – Burkhard Schwenker

92 This was the case in January 2009, after serious disputes between the Ukrainian gas company Naftogaz Ukrainy and Russian gas supplier Gazprom could not be solved. In fact, there have been numerous disputes between the two companies since 2005.

93 For details, check, for example, the China Greentech Initiative (http://www.china-greentech.com/re) or the SunShot Initiative of the US Department of Energy (http://www1.eere.energy.gov/solar/sunshot/index.html).

94   For details, see the European Commission's website, Intelligent Energy Europe; http://ec.europa.eu/energy/intelligent/

95   See, for example, the report of Deutsche Bank Research on Smart Grids, published on July 21, 2011; http://www.dbresearch.com/PROD/DBR_INTERNET_EN-PROD/PROD0000000000275988.pdf

96   http://www.renewableenergyjobs.com/content/eu-20-renewable-energy-target-can-deliver-2-8-million-jobs

97   The EFSF (European Financial Stability Facility) is a Luxembourg-based fund owned by the eurozone members with a lending capacity of up to €440bn, backed by guarantee commitments of the Euro Area Member States of €780bn. The fund's mission is to bail out eurozone member states with serious economic difficulties. The decision to start such a vehicle was made at an EU summit in May 2010.

98   The creation of the European Stability Mechanism (ESM) was signed in February 2012 as a fund to replace the European Financial Stability Facility (EFSF) and the European Financial Stabilisation Mechanism (EFSM). In mid-2012, it was ratified by 14 of the 17 eurozone member states, but has not yet been ratified by Germany, Italy and Estonia. Since both Germany and Italy will contribute a large stake of the capital requirement for the ESM, the fund could not be enforced by August 2012.

99   One example is the demand to expand the mandate of the EFSF or ESM, respectively, to bail out not just struggling countries but also their financial institutions, aimed at breaking the vicious circle of EU member states getting heavily indebted by rescuing their banks and then not being able to finance themselves any more, as was the case with Ireland and Spain. The idea was controversially discussed at the EU summit in June 2012. It was finally agreed that such direct aid should become possible, but only when a strong European-wide controlling body for Europe's banks is set up.

100   'Wir brauchen ein Insolvenzgericht für Staaten', trs: 'We need a Bankruptcy Court for countries', interview with Christoph Paulus (Professor of Law at Humboldt University, Berlin), *Deutschlandradio Wissen*, January 16, 2012; http://wissen.dradio.de/staatspleiten-wir-brauchen-ein-insolvenzgericht-fuer-staaten.33.de.html?dram:article_id=14501

101   http://www.gooddata.com/about

102   http://www.tango.me/about-us/

103   According to the MoneyTree Report by PricewaterhouseCoopers and the National Venture Capital Association (NVCA), based on data from Thomson

Reuters; http://www.pwc.com/us/en/press-releases/2012/annual-venture-investment-dollars.jhtml

104 According to Dow Jones Venture Source; http://www.dowjones.com/pressroom/releases/2012/01302012-Q4EUVC-0007.asp

105 Ibid.

106 The model is based on an existing start-up initiative called enable2start (www.enable2start.de) which was founded by one of the authors of this book.

107 http://www.redherring.com/top-100/

108 http://www.csaspeakers.com/our-speakers/profile/leif_edvinsson

109 Yeh-Yun Lin, Carol and Leif Edvinsson, *National Intellectual Capital: A Comparison of 40 Countries* (London: Springer, 2010).

110 http://www.esa.int/esaNA/galileo.html.

111 To find out more, check 'Outline of China's National Plan for Medium and Long-term Education Reform and Development (2010-2020)', July 2010, Beijing; https://www.aei.gov.au/news/newsarchive/2010/documents/china_education_reform_pdf

112 http://en.wikipedia.org/wiki/List_of_Nobel_laureates_by_country

113 'From Common Market to Single Market – 40 years as a Single Market Campaigner', Malcolm Harbour MEP; http://ec.europa.eu/internal_market/smn/smn47/docs/mep_harbour_en.pdf

114 http://ec.europa.eu/europe2020/index_en.htm

115 Rifkin, Jeremy, *The Third Industrial Revolution* (Basingstoke: Palgrave Macmillan, 2011).

Index

Index